Christian Eschatology
and the Physical Universe

Christian Eschatology and the Physical Universe

David Wilkinson

t&t clark

Published by T&T Clark International
A Continuum Imprint
The Tower Building, 11 York Road, London SE1 7NX
80 Maiden Lane, Suite 704, New York, NY 10038

www.continuumbooks.com

British Library Cataloguing-in-Publication Data
A catalogue record for this book is available from the British Library

ISBN: 978-0-567-04545-4 (Hardback)
       978-0-567-04546-1 (Paperback)

Typeset by Fakenham Photosetting Ltd
Printed and bound in Great Britain by CPI Antony Rowe Ltd, Chippenham, Wiltshire

For the students and staff of St John's College

Contents

Preface

Does matter really matter? It would be easy to argue that Christian faith seems to look forward only to the existence of a disembodied soul after death in a non physical spiritual heaven. Certainly there are some strands of Christian fundamentalism whose prophecies, embodied in such popular best-sellers as the *Left Behind* series whose view of the future opposes any sense of care for the environment or in extreme forms loses any sense of responsibility for this world at all.

Yet such a separation between the spiritual and the material is deeply embedded across a wide spectrum of western Christian theologies and pastoral practices. As N. T. Wright has recently shown it is behind 'saving souls', many hymns and funeral liturgies, and is held by a number of contemporary theologians (Wright 2007: 20–41). However, such a separation sees the physicality of the world as trivial or indeed evil. The flesh, the body and the world become something to be destroyed rather than valued.

Theology is not the only area of human knowledge to explore the future. In the last decade, the end of the physical Universe[1] has become a hot topic in science. Cosmologists have used a new wave of astronomical discoveries from the Hubble Space Telescope, supernova explosions and the microwave background radiation to talk about the fate of the Universe with a confidence missing only a few years ago. Such predictions going billions of years into the future may be dismissed easily in terms of their implications for living in the present or for our views of God's relationship with the Universe. But they raise a fundamental question, that is, does the matter and space-time of this Universe matter to God?

The last few decades have shown a rich avenue of thought concerning creation. The discoveries of Big Bang cosmology and the rise of six day creationism have prompted Christian theology to re-assess its models of God as Creator, the nature of the creation narratives and the whole dialogue of science and religion (Wilkinson 2001; Gingerich 2006). Environmental pollution has forced theology to rediscover themes of care and stewardship and the importance of the natural world. Might the same be true if we look at the long term future of the Universe? Is God's ultimate plan to fry the Universe to total annihilation or to stand idly by as it freezes in a heat death of billions of years?

My concern is therefore to explore the science and religion dialogue as it explores the future of the Universe. As both an astrophysicist and a Christian

---

[1] While there are different conventions, in this work the particular Universe we inhabit will be capitalized, while reference to other possible universes will use the lowercase 'u'. Following this convention the Earth and Sun will also be capitalized. Quotations from authors may use a different convention.

theologian this has been of interest to me over a number of years and is one of the questions always raised at talks that I give on science and theology.

Yet this is not simply a question for science and religion. From the *Matrix* movies of the Warchowski brothers to the best selling *Left Behind* series we see a fascination with the future of the physical world, raising questions of the value of the material world and hope of redemption. It is here that Christian theology has much to say, but in recent years has lost its confidence, in stark contrast to the claims of science. Yet I am convinced that Christian orthodoxy need not be worried by the future which science paints. Indeed, it has a unique voice which takes the questions and futility of the scientific picture to a place of hope for the physical Universe.

This work shares with Wright's *Surprised by Hope* a passion for the importance and centrality of bodily resurrection to Christian hope, but wants to push further for what this means for the physical Universe. What begins to emerge is a re-discovery of one of the central biblical narratives, that of new creation.

It is a pleasure to acknowledge discussions with Professors David Brown, Ann Loades, Sir John Polkinghorne, Trevor Hart, Sir Arnold Wolfendale, FRS, Carlos Frenck FRS and Bishop Tom Wright. Indeed David Brown was a generous supervisor while an earlier version was being prepared for submission as a PhD thesis. This work was supported by St John's College, Durham University. I am grateful to the former Principal, David Day, who opened up this opportunity, and to staff and students who have and continue to be outstanding colleagues.

This piece of work however would not have been possible without the love, support and grace of my family, Alison, Adam and Hannah. I owe them a great debt of gratitude.

Chapter 1

Visions of the End

1.1 The end of the world in science and pop culture

Predictions of the end of planet Earth are both terrifying and popular leading many scientific authors to feel that they must speculate about the future (Ward and Brownlee 2004). Stephen Hawking, one of the best known cosmologists of our time, concludes that 'by 2600 the world's population will be standing shoulder to shoulder, and the electricity use will make the Earth glow red hot' (Hawking 2001: 158). He argues that human DNA will increase in its complexity rapidly and that this needs to happen in order to live in complex world and to keep ahead of electronic systems. It is a somewhat disappointing and unsubstantiated argument but it is interesting that Hawking feels the need to address such issues.

The British Astronomer Royal, Professor Martin Rees, Lord Rees of Ludlow, has also picked up on this fascination with the future. He speculates on the many risks presented by the future including lethal engineered viruses, rogue nanotechnology, experiments eroding the atoms of the Earth or tearing the fabric of space-time, in addition to environmental damage and concludes that the odds 'are no better than fifty-fifty that our present civilisation on Earth will survive to the end of the present century' (Rees 2003: 8). In the face of such pessimism, he sees the future of human beings as giving hope for the future of the cosmos itself. The development of science coupled with human ingenuity means a spread of human intelligence across the Universe making us less vulnerable to being wiped out by one major event.

Popular culture certainly seems to feel the need to address such issues. Hollywood films such as *Deep Impact* and *Armageddon* concern comets heading for the Earth threatening 'an extinction level event'. Tidal waves destroy New York, humanity takes to deep caves to survive and astronauts are dispatched on a last ditch attempt to avert disaster. A similar cataclysmic future is also seen in *2012*, a movie which was supported by a clever internet campaign predicting the end of the world. In addition, the *Terminator* films of James Cameron and the Warchowski brothers' *The Matrix* gaze forward to a nightmare scenario where the world has been taken over by machines with developed artificial intelligence. Each of these movies bring science into dialogue with the place of and threat to human beings in the future (Benjamin 1998; Seay and Garrett 2003; Walliss and Newport 2009; Geraci 2010). Such 'eschatological fictions' and a future apocalypse, argues Kermode, give pattern to historical time, by providing a beginning and an end and therefore meaning (Kermode 1967: 35).

Paralleling this move in fictional writing about the future of the world, we are also beginning to see a similar move in the context of scientific discoveries about the future of the Universe. This has been particularly the case since 1998 when the question of the end of the Universe itself has grown in its public profile. When two groups of astronomers published data on the future of the Universe the influential journal *Science* named it the science breakthrough of 1998. Such was the unexpected nature of the data that it sent the scientific community into near panic, with the accompanying array of articles and media programmes. While the science has been fascinating, it is the questions of meaning that it poses that have captured the imagination of many people. In the midst of this, we encounter a central theological question. Can the claim of a Universe created and sustained by God give meaning to this understanding of historical and future time?

1.2 Eschatology working overtime

Popular definitions of eschatology speak of that branch of theology that is concerned with such final things as death and judgment, heaven and hell and the end of the world itself. Christian eschatology is much broader than such a definition, exploring the relationship between the future and the present. This gives it a complexity in its usage, for example it is claimed New Testament scholars use at least ten different meanings of the word 'eschatology' (Wright 1996; Caird 1997; Walls 2008).

In this way it is fair to say that, in von Balthasar's famous dictum, eschatology has recently been working overtime since its office was shut down in the nineteenth century (von Balthasar 1960: 276). Indeed Hebblethwaite is right to characterise theology in the twentieth century as dominated by eschatological thinking (Hebblethwaite 1984: 131–98).

'Eschatology' as a term first appeared in 1677 in Abraham Calov's Systema locorum Theologicorum (Sauter 1988: 499). Yet prior to the last century, in Barth's equally famous statement, Protestant theology had relegated eschatology to a perfectly harmless chapter at the conclusion of Christian dogmatics (Barth 1933: 500). Its rediscovery came from biblical scholars such as Weiss and Schweitzer who looked again at the New Testament understanding of the Kingdom of God and saw the eschatological dimension of the gospel. Much debate then followed over the relationship of the present and future elements of the Kingdom and whether the New Testament speaks of a visible return of Jesus to inaugurate the definitive Kingdom (Schwöbel 2000: 217–41).

In the light of this debate it is usual to distinguish three main positions. A futurist eschatology, where the Kingdom is not present in any way in the present, has few contemporary adherents among biblical scholars. The second position, realized eschatology, was proposed by C. H. Dodd who suggested that the Kingdom was already present in the person and acts of Jesus. Such a view was restated recently by Tanner as an option which would negate the need for dialogue between science and theology on the issue of the end of the Universe (Tanner 2000: 222–237). Yet as Jeremias pointed out, such a position does not do justice to the future element within the New Testament (Jeremias 1972: 230), or indeed we may add the Christian doctrines of judgment, death, heaven and hell. He preferred a third model of eschatology that is in the process of realization or as others have named it 'inaugurated eschatology' (Witherington III 2002: 52–65). However, the meaning of this for the physical Universe has rarely been articulated or indeed considered.

Alongside this movement in biblical studies, eschatology has become of key importance in systematic theology. In this, Jürgen Moltmann has held a central place in modern eschatological thought (Moltmann 1967, 1996). Moltmann responded to the earlier work of Bloch who had suggested that all human culture is moved by a passionate hope for the future that transcends all alienation of the present (Bloch 1986). Drawing on the biblical idea of revolutionary apocalyptic hope, he saw within it a vigorous social critique and prophetic vision of social transformation. He provided a secular vision of hope, reflecting Marxist ideology and the optimism of the 1960s. Thus, 'history was pregnant with the future', that is possibilities for the future were already inherent in present. Moltmann agreed with the importance of hope, but argued that such hope could only be grounded in the promises of the God of creation and resurrection. Hope was based on the transforming work of God in contrast to secular ideas of social transformation:

> 'The Christian hope is directed towards a novum ultimum, towards a new creation of all things by the God of the resurrection of Jesus Christ. It thereby opens a future outlook that embraces all things, including also death, and into this it can and must also take the limited hopes of a renewal of life, stimulating them, relativising them, giving them direction.' (Moltmann 1967: 17)

Therefore, theology needed to rediscover the corporate Christian conception of hope, as a central motivating factor in the life and thought of the individual and the church. Moltmann was suggesting that the theological task was 'hope seeking understanding'. This passionate plea for the importance of eschatology succeeded in a reorientation of the theological landscape. Yet, does a discussion of the future of 'all things' include an engagement of these theological themes with the future of the physical Universe? As we shall see while theologians have worked overtime on hope in the context of the personal, political and communal, there has been little concern for the material beyond planet Earth.

1.3 Left behind or burnt up? The new fundamentalism

'Apocalyptic is the mother of all Christian theology,' wrote Käsemann (Käsemann 1960: 100) and this is nowhere as true as it is within US fundamentalism. Fundamentalism in its Western Christian incarnation comes from a series of twelve books published between 1910 and 1915 called 'The Fundamentals', edited by A. C. Dixon. They attacked liberal Christianity and insisted on what became six fundamental tenets of belief which were the inerrancy of Scripture, the virgin birth, substitutionary atonement, bodily resurrection, authenticity of biblical miracles and pre-millennialism (Melling 1999). Such pre-millennialism was given popular form in an international best seller *The Late Great Planet Earth* (Lindsay 1970). Since then millennial speculations have become 'America's favourite pastime' (Wojcik 1997: 6) or the 'doom-boom' (Jewett 1984: 9–22), as apocalyptic best-sellers and movies have grown in popularity.

In 1995, Tim LaHaye and Jerry Jenkins wrote the first novel in what came to be known as the *Left Behind* series (LaHaye and Jenkins 1995). This first book of a projected twelve began with a rapture of believers, that is, Christians are taken off to heaven by an invisible return of Jesus. There then follows a seven-year tribulation period while unbelievers remain on Earth to be subjected to countless horrors at the hands of the antichrist, before the final return of Christ and his triumph in Armageddon. The popularity of this series should not be underestimated. It is a publishing phenomenon, having sold over 40 million copies worldwide, been translated into over 20 languages, and is a regular feature of the New York Times Bestseller List. It has spawned a children's series of books, movies, games and even calendars.

Why has such an apocalyptic future become so popular? The constituent theology can be traced back to the 19th century (Kyle 1998; DeMar 2001; Riddlebarger 2003) and is based on an interpretative framework which combines the claim of biblical literalism with the writer's special insights of prophetic interpretation, numerology, paranoia and a belief in the chosen nature of the USA to do God's will. It picks up on the folk Christianity of American society and exploits people's fascination with the future. It provides an interesting contrast to Fukuyama's proposal that consumer capitalism and western liberalism had spawned a new beginning in global history (Fukuyama 1992). Indeed pre-millennialists see Fukuyama and all those who speak of a new world order as a threat because such a future can be produced without the intervention of Christ.

It is important to take this movement seriously, and to respond to its underlying theology. LaHaye's theological explanation of the series (LaHaye 1999; LaHaye and Jenkins 1999; Hitchcock 2004) majors on two biblical passages, 1 Thessalonians 4.13–18 and 1 Corinthians 15.51–57, to justify the premillennial rapture. In both passages the physical resurrection of believers is interpreted as disappearance to heaven in the rapture. This is coupled with a sense that this world is beyond redemption, for only when Jesus comes again will it be put right. Therefore there is no point in trying to reform it, and for those left behind the challenge is to save your own souls. The key theological move here is to replace resurrection with rapture. A neglect of the physicality of the resurrection of Jesus leads to no physicality in the image of the general resurrection of believers and a lack of value for the physical creation.

In discussing what happens at the end of the seven year period of tribulation, LaHaye bases his view on Revelation 21. His picture is primarily of the destruction of the heaven and earth, although it has certain nuances. He sees 2 Peter 3.4–14 as pointing to destruction with fire, 'producing a refurbished earth to begin the Millennium', and Revelation 21.1 referring to a total destruction of the earth and its atmosphere but not the Universe or the dwelling of God. The new heaven and new earth will be physical although LaHaye is unclear in terms of what this will mean (LaHaye 1999, 355).

We see in all of this some key questions. First, apocalyptic imagery in the Bible is used to give hope for the far future. Within a strict position of biblical inerrancy, the different apocalyptic pictures are used to interpret each other. Thus Revelation is filled out with ideas from 1 Thessalonians, in a way that leads to an eschatology that borrows from a wide range of biblical authors but is foreign to all of them (Hill 2002a: 203). We are left with the question of whether such passages can be used in this way and is it what they really mean? Second, questions of continuity and discontinuity between this creation and the next in terms of judgement, destruction, recreation and human life are central to pictures of the future. Third, how does a theological view of the future control how people live their lives now? For the *Left Behind* authors it seems that as the future is determined there is no point to pursue peace negotiations and indeed that nuclear war is inevitable.

This phenomenon can be easily underestimated. It may not be theological mainstream, but the theological mainstream must engage with it not least to help the large number of evangelical Christians to better understand the nature of creation and new creation (Frykholm 2004; Price 2007). In addition, its presence and influence within certain political circles in the most powerful nation on the Earth may effect political decisions such as the neglect of environmental responsibility (Guyatt 2007). A Time/CNN poll in 2003 found that 59 per cent of Americans believe that the events in Revelation are going to come true, which demonstrates the importance of the task of public theology that needs to be done.

1.4 The future in the dialogue of science and religion

If systematic theology has largely left untouched the end of the Universe, then it would be expected that it would be a central subject for those involved in the dialogue between science and religion. Interest in this dialogue has grown phenomenally in academic courses, conferences and publications drawing in both scientists and theologians.

Much of this dialogue has been focused on the methodologies of science and theology and has concentrated on issues such as origins, the nature of human beings and God's action the world. However, up until the late 1990s the end of the Universe was largely neglected in an arena where it should have felt at home. Since 2000 there have been a few pieces of work which have addressed these questions (Benz 2000; Ellis 2002), including the Center of Theological Inquiry Eschatology Project at Princeton (Polkinghorne and Welker 2000; Polkinghorne 2002b).

However, this is simply the beginning of work in this area. None of these publications engage at depth with the biblical data so valued by the devotees of the *Left Behind* series. Neither do they reflect any real engagement with the discoveries of an accelerating Universe. Both ask for further work in this area and this is what this book attempts to do. Taking the scientific developments and the biblical data seriously moves the conversation on into the area of systematic theology. The eschatology of the physical Universe is too important to be left simply to the science/religion dialogue alone or to fundamentalist fiction. Of course it is difficult to keep up with a rapidly changing scientific arena. Indeed, at the interface of science and religion, some theologians fall into disrepute because their science is decades out of date. Such a work as this risks this same trap, yet it will also highlight how some systematic theologians are not just out of date but not even in the same century.

If we are going to take seriously the end of the Universe, the dialogue of science and religion will be important in showing how other issues have been addressed fruitfully. In a series of books, McGrath has explored the methodological parallels between science and theology. In his 'scientific theology' he uses common themes of the scientific enterprise to illustrate the related challenges faced by theology (McGrath 2001–3). Exploring nature, reality and theory, he argues that both science and theology are best understood in terms of critical realism (Peacocke 1990: 343; Barbour 2000: 113; Russell 2002b: 276). Such a critical realist of both science and theology is important if there is going to be any meaningful dialogue as it pledges both science and theology to explore a common reality even if they do so in differing ways. As Polkinghorne rightly notes:

'If science were not giving us verisimilitudinous knowledge of the nature of the physical world, its prognostications about the future would lose their force and the sharpness of the challenge they present to theology would be blunted. If theology were not concerned with a verisimilitudinous understanding of the nature of a faithful Creator, its attempt to speak of eschatological matters would amount to no more than the disguised exercise of a technique of consolation for the uncertainties of the present.' (Polkinghorne 2002b: xix)

Therefore we will take the insights of both science and theology about the end of the Universe with seriousness. As both explore a common reality it will be fruitful and necessary to bring them into dialogue with each other, a dialogue that has been sadly lacking despite the fascination with the future, the rediscovery of eschatology and the growth of interest in science and religion.

Chapter 2

Ending in Futility: The Future Pessimism of Science

If science was optimistic with its ability to shape the world at the turn of the century in 1900, then one hundred years later such optimism has been tempered with much pessimism about the future. While science stills holds out the promise of salvation to many, pessimism can be seen in environmental catastrophe, comet impact, the end of the Sun and the end of the Universe itself. Examining each of these aspects will lay some of the scientific groundwork and illustrate a range of theological engagement.

2.1 Environmental catastrophe

The use of global resources, such as food in the face of growing population, defor-estation and the overuse of fossil fuels, has received a great deal of interest in recent years with the growth of environmental concern. Coupled with issues of global pollution such as the dumping of waste, global warming and the destruction of the ozone layer, the situation is extremely serious. The Scientific Assessment Group of the Intergovernmental Panel on Climate Change concluded that if the current situation of the emission of greenhouse gases continues then models predict an average increase in temperature for the Earth of between 1.5 and 6 degrees in the next century (Houghton 2001; Houghton 2004). The implications of this for sea-level changes, eco-systems, population movement and world economic health are severe (Monbiot 2006). The Stern Review published by the UK government in 2006 concluded that all countries will be affected, although poorer countries will suffer earliest and most, even though they have contributed least to the causes of climate change. While it is possible through dramatically reducing the emission of greenhouses gases to stabilize the effect, it is no longer possible to prevent the climate change that will take place over the next two to three decades[1].

It is an area that Christian theology has taken increasingly seriously. In a much quoted paper, the historian Lyn White argued that our ability to harness natural resources was marred by the deep rooted assumption that:

'we are superior to nature, contemptuous of it, willing to use it for our slightest whim ... We shall continue to have a worsening ecological crisis

[1] http://www.hm-treasury.gov.uk/independent_reviews/stern_review_economics_climate_change/stern_review_report.cfm

7

until we reject the Christian axiom that nature has no reason for existence but to serve man … Both our present science and our present technology are so tinctured with orthodox Christian arrogance towards nature that no solution for our ecological crisis can be expected from them alone.' (White 1967: 1203)

Thus, in his view Christianity bears 'a huge burden of guilt' for the environmental crisis. Yet Christian theology has responded to his call for a 'refocused Christianity' able to put ecology centre stage (Berry 2003; Northcott 2007; McFague 2008; Horrell 2010). It has re-examined its doctrine of creation and the relationship between salvation and creation. While, as we shall suggest, this has sometimes lacked a strong emphasis on new creation, such a re-examination is an encouragement to do a similar thing with the end of the Universe. In particular we might re-state White's challenge of whether Christian theology believes that 'the Universe has no reason for existence but to serve man'.

2.2 Comet or asteroid impact

The Earth is not only under threat from the human abuse of the environment but also because of the possibility of collision with either a comet or an asteroid. There is substantial evidence for a comet impact leading to the dinosaur extinction of 65 million years ago (Billoski 1987: 75–76). A rock some 6 miles wide left the Chicxulub crater off Mexico's Yucatan Penninsula. Some think this led to climate and vegetation changes but more recent work suggests the entry of the rock into the Earth's atmosphere generated a 'heat pulse' raising the temperature suddenly and fatally (Robertson et al. 2004: 760–768). More controversial is whether this mechanism could be responsible for the apparent cyclicity in mass extinctions and sea-level changes in Earth history. Such mass extinctions happen roughly every 30 million years and such a cyclicity of cometary impacts has been ascribed to the gravitational perturbation of the Oort comet cloud by an interstellar gas cloud, close star or unseen planet. However we have shown that it is unlikely that all such extinctions are caused by cometary impacts, as such a possibility would only occur every 250 million years on average (Bailey, Wilkinson, and Wolfendale 1987: 863–885; Wolfendale and Wilkinson 1989: 231–239). It therefore seems that other mechanisms such as enhanced volcanic activity may be responsible.

Yet not only comets could be a threat. Some 2000 asteroids have orbits which cross the orbit of the Earth, and therefore potentially could cause catastrophic environmental conditions for human beings. Asteroids are smaller but can be equally deadly. The impact of the 21 fragments of comet Shoemaker-Levy on Jupiter in 1994 demonstrated the possibility and indeed seriousness of such impacts. Scars existed in the Jovian atmosphere for more than a year (Barnes-Svarney 1996: 125–127). The impact of an asteroid only 100m wide would lead to tidal waves or an explosion which would destroy a large city depending on whether it impacted on sea or land. Smaller asteroids not leading to extinction events may be expected every 0.3 million years, while larger ones capable of mass extinction every 100 million years.

Such a serious possibility has recently led to serious political discussion on how the Earth may be protected (Belton 2003) and the NASA Spaceguard Survey, an exhaustive mapping of the bodies and their orbits in the solar system[2]. The changing of orbits of those bodies with a possibility of Earth impact could then be considered, either through nuclear explosions or through a 'space tug' attached to the asteroid (Schweickart et al. 2003: 34–41). It would seem likely that some human beings would therefore survive this threat, although a major disaster cannot be ruled out.

The challenge of this to Christian theology is a reminder of the fragility of the Earth environment for the development of life. If God is seen to be in the creative process of evolution, then the wastefulness of such a process shown in mass extinctions needs to be taken seriously. Further there is a reminder that human beings are not isolated from the rest of creation in their future. These are theological questions which we will need to return to. In addition, there is an interesting question as to our need to minimize risk. A programme to save the Earth from a major impact would cost over $1 billion over 10 years. But how does that risk compare to those who could be saved from premature death through an investment in primary healthcare in the developing nations? There are serious ethical questions here concerning those with technology, money and power alongside theological questions of how we cope with risk in the future. Do we want to be so in control of the future through technology that we feel we can be 'risk-free'? What does that say about our view of this life and indeed human power over creation?

2.3 The death of the Sun

Whether or not a comet hits, we know for certain that in 5 billion years, the Earth will be uninhabitable. The Sun will come to the end of its available hydrogen fuel and will begin to swell up, its outer layers swallowing up Mercury, Venus and the Earth. It will then lose its outer layers and the centre will become a white dwarf, an object of high density about the size of the Earth. Without the heat and light of the Sun none of the remaining planets will be habitable.

At this point, it is envisaged that human beings will have moved away from the Earth to colonize the Galaxy, finding new stars and inhabitable planets. It may be worth noting in passing that this may not be as easy as it sounds. Although there has been significant success in observing the existence of planets around other stars and there are some claims that Earth-like planets may be common (Mayor and Frei 2003), there are good arguments for believing that the Earth may be unique in its environment (Lissauer 1999: C11–C14). However, human beings seem capable in the future of living on vast space stations or even engineering planetary atmospheres for their own benefit. Indeed, serious scientific work has already been done on the warming of the surface temperature of Mars in order to make it habitable (Zubrin and Wagner 1997; McKay 2000: 45–58). Rees sees the importance of this 'terraforming' as giving the human race

---

[2] http://impact.arc.nasa.gov/reports/spaceguard/index.html

a safeguard against possible disasters affecting the Earth (Rees 2003: 170). Yet if new worlds were settled, another danger lies 5 billion years ahead. Galaxies have a local movement imposed on the general expansion of the Universe and one of our nearest neighbours, the Andromeda spiral galaxy, will crash into us. This would raise the problem of travelling to a safer world even more difficult due to the vast distances of millions of light years between galaxies.

Theologically the death of the Sun heightens the challenges already described. It is an important reminder that God's purposes cannot be tied to the Earth for eternity. Further, the movement to other planets raises interesting ethical questions. First, is the question of who would move? Past experience would suggest that it would be the rich who move to the new unspoilt worlds leaving the poor behind in the degraded world. Second, questions of the ethics of environmentally changing other worlds have provoked some debate. What gives human beings the right to take over new worlds, particularly if there is some life-form however primitive already there. The answer to such questions goes beyond any utilitarian ethic to considerations of creation, the stewardship of human beings, sin and the corporate nature of human beings. The early chapters of Genesis may be a good overture not just to our place on this planet but as guidelines for colonising other 'gardens of edens'! The sense of God as Creator of the whole Universe gives a bigger perspective to questions of the use of natural resources. The understanding of the sinfulness of human beings cautions us to some of the dangers ahead. From a purely humanistic view Rees comments that 'individuals will make mistakes, and there will be a risk of malign actions by embittered loners and dissident groups' (Rees 2003: 4). The corporate nature of human beings raises questions concerning power relationships in the expansion of human civilisation beyond the Earth. These are issues well recognised by the writers of science fiction and perhaps now it is the time for theologians to begin to take them with more seriousness. While our main focus in this book will be the longer term future for the Universe we shall see these questions return in our discussion. In particular, can human science and technology deliver us from the pessimism of the future?

2.4 The 'Doomsday Argument'

While very few philosophers and theologians have taken seriously the dangers of the future, one of the exceptions is the philosopher John Leslie (Leslie 1998). However, Leslie is not concerned too much with theological issues as with assessing the so-called 'Doomsday Argument' developed independently by physicists Brandon Carter and Richard Gott (Carter 1983: 347; Gott 1993: 315–319).

The foundation of this is the application of a kind of Copernican principle to our position in time. The Copernican principle became powerful in reminding us that we did not have a special location in the Universe. In a similar way Carter argued that we should not assume that we were living at a special time in the history of humanity. We would not expect our species to be alive in the first billionth of the human race that in the future was going to spread through its entire galaxy. This suggests that humans will not survive for much longer, for if we did then we would be living at an extraordinarily early epoch in human history.

Leslie defends it strongly, but it depends on a number of questionable assumptions (Bostrom 2002). First, what leads us to expect that being alive at an extraordinarily early epoch is unlikely? Such an assumption is reminiscent of part of the motivation of the Steady State model of the Universe proposed by Bondi, Hoyle and Gold in the 1960s. Their motivation was to avoid ours being a special time, as well as other factors including the influence of atheism (Kragh 1996). If there was a beginning to the Universe then by implication, not all times would be the same. Their 'Perfect Cosmological Principle' stated that the laws and properties of the Universe should appear the same to all observers at all times. They accepted that the Universe was expanding, but argued that this phenomenon could be better understood in a 'steady state' model of the Universe, where there was no beginning but matter was continuously being created throughout space. This new matter added to the Universe at the very small rate of one hydrogen atom per cubic centimetre every 10,000 years, keeps the density of the Universe constant as it expands. Yet observation proved them wrong. There was a beginning to the Universe and therefore our observation of the Universe did change with time. There is no reason to believe that we should be living at non-special time in the history of human beings.

Second, the argument assumes the prior probability of the human race spreading through the galaxy. Yet one can raise the question of what is the status of the future in all of this? Davies defends the argument by appealing to Einstein's view that the future is 'already there' (Davies 1995: 258–264). However, this imposes on Einstein a philosophy of determinism that does not flow naturally. Indeed as we shall in Chapter 6 the nature of the future, both scientifically and theologically, is rather more subtle than that.

Third, how do we define humanity? Should we include other intelligent beings in different parts of the Universe or indeed intelligent machines that might come after us? If these possibilities are allowed then there is no clear way of using the logic of the argument and indeed the argument collapses.

For these reasons I suggest that the argument cannot show that the human race has a doomsday in the near future. Yet Leslie is right that the argument:

> 'acts very strongly only as a way of reducing confidence in a long future for humankind: confidence that such a future "is as good as determined" …
> The most it could do would be to refute the view that its spreading across the galaxy was virtually certain.' (Leslie 2000: 122)

The theological questions raised here are interesting. The first is the place and significance of human beings both on the Earth and in the Universe, and the nature of the future. The second is the need for Christian theology to interact with such questions. If the Universe is understood as creation where human beings have a special though non-exclusive place within it, and if God has purposes for the end then the argument does not make sense. That is, the Doomsday argument may only apply if there is no structure of creation and eschatology applied not just to human beings but also to the Universe as a whole. The challenge for theology is therefore clear to provide such a structure.

2.5 The end of the Universe

The end of the Universe in scientific terms is both simple and very difficult to predict. The simplicity is that Einstein's theory of general relativity gives equations that tell us how any universe containing matter and radiation will change with time under the influence of gravity. The important discovery of Hubble in 1929 that the redshift of other galaxies was indicating the expansion of the Universe, therefore posed the question of what will happen in the future.

Two decades ago, the Universe was believed to be slowing down in its expansion and cosmologists saw two possible futures (Islam 1983: 114). The first was that it could reach a point where the force of gravity acts to reverse the expansion of the Big Bang, collapsing the Universe back to a Big Crunch. In such a scenario, a maximum size will be reached in not less than another 20 billion years (the current age of the Universe is 13.7 billion years). As the Universe shrinks, the galaxies will merge, the sky as seen from any surviving planet will become as bright as the surface of the Sun, stars will explode, and protons and neutrons will be reduced back to a quark soup before the Universe either disappears in a quantum fluctuation or reaches a state of infinite density known as a singularity.

There was then some speculation on whether the Universe would 'bounce' into a new Big Bang. The process of expansion and contraction then could go on indefinitely, although there was some debate as to the kinds of Universe that would be produced (Jaki 1977: 233–51; Barrow and Dabrowski 1995: 850–62). Davies suggests that such an oscillating Universe is attractive to Eastern religion, in which cycles of creation and destruction figure prominently, as well as to those who have a deep seated uneasiness with the linear view of time that predates Western scientific thought (Davies 2002: 45).

However, a second scenario was also on offer. Some argued that there might not be enough matter in the Universe to make it collapse. If this was the case, the Universe expands forever becoming more and more a cold life-less place full of dead stars, a so-called heat death.

For a number of years, cosmologists struggled to decide between these two possibilities. The key was thought to be how much matter there was in the Universe, and this was difficult because gravitational studies of the local movements of galaxies indicated a large amount of unseen matter, that is dark matter. This is a form of matter that did not emit light and its nature was unknown. However, since 1998 cosmology has undergone a massive revolution, with unexpected consequences for the end of the Universe. Two groups were at the forefront of this research. The Supernova Cosmology Project of Saul Perlmutter and the High-Z Supernovae Search which was headed by Brian Schmidt and Adam Riess (Riess et al. 1998: 1009; Riess et al. 2001: 49–71; Perlmutter 2003: 53–60).

To see how the Universe is expanding one must look at distant objects that emitted light much earlier in the Universe's history. If one knows the intrinsic brightness of these objects, then a comparison of their intrinsic brightness and their brightness as measured from Earth gives their distance. This 'standard candle' method then allows the comparison of their redshifts (which gives their recession velocity) and distances in order to see how the Universe was expanding in the past compared to now.

Both groups used supernovae explosions as these standard candles. In particular, Type Ia Supernovae, which are the explosions of white dwarfs onto which matter has fallen from a companion star, can be used as standard candles over cosmological distances, as for a few days they shine nearly as brightly as a whole galaxy. Now Type Ia Supernovae are not all exactly the same brightness. However, by studying the way the supernovae brighten and fade this uncertainty can be reduced so that distances can be known to within an error of 7 per cent which is equal to the best of astronomical distance indicators. These explosions are quite rare and they fade very quickly. So techniques were developed to survey a million galaxies in a typical night's observing and from that find more than 10 supernovae.

The results indicated that far from the Universe slowing down, the expansion of the Universe was actually speeding up. This sent a shock wave through the scientific community in terms of how to interpret this conclusion. One possibility is that the data is misleading. For example, for some reason supernovae may be fainter in the past, and therefore look further away. That seems unlikely but remains a possibility. Or perhaps the predictions of General Relativity, on which the expanding Universe is based, are wrong. This would be unexpected because of the success of General Relativity in so many other areas. If both of these options are rejected, then one is forced to the conclusion that some unknown type of material or force throughout the Universe is accelerating its rate of expansion, the so called 'dark energy' (Calder and Lahav 2008: 13). It is this final conclusion to which most scientists have been drawn (Knop et al. 2003: 192–137; Kirshner 2004).

In fact such an interpretation has been confirmed by more recent results from the Wilkinson Microwave Anisotropy Probe (WMAP). Combining data from this satellite which has looked at temperature variations and polarisation variations across the microwave background radiation with other diverse cosmic measurements such as the large-scale distribution of galaxies clustering, Lyman-alpha cloud clustering and the supernovae results has led to some extraordinary conclusions (Peiris et al. 2003: 213). First, the Universe is 13.7 billion years old (with a margin of error of close to 1 per cent), and the Hubble constant $H_o = 71$ km/sec/Mpc (with a margin of error of about 5 per cent). Second, the Universe will expand forever. Third, the Universe is composed of 4 per cent atoms, 23 per cent cold dark matter, and 73 per cent dark energy.

This new force therefore controls the expansion of the Universe even though it has no discernible effect on scales less than a billion light years, that is, we do not see its effects in our local stars and galaxies. The dark energy has the totally unexpected feature that it does not attract like gravity but repels. Due to this repulsion force the Universe is accelerating in its rate of expansion. What is this dark energy? Einstein in applying general relativity to the Universe had suggested a cosmic repulsion, represented by his introduction of a 'cosmological constant' into the equations, in order to achieve a static rather than contracting Universe. He rejected such a suggestion as his 'biggest blunder' yet physicists have returned to it.

Some have suggested that the vacuum itself can exert a force for it is a seething mass of particles and anti-particles. However, it has proved difficult for fundamental quantum theory to reproduce the observed amplitude of dark energy. Current predictions overestimate it by more than a hundred orders of magnitude. The further difficulty of this vacuum energy is that it is completely inert, maintaining the same density for all time. This means that the cosmological constant would have to be fine-tuned at the beginning of the Universe. This is an example of an anthropic balance, that is, something in the law and circumstance of the Universe that is 'just right' for the existence of life. Some cosmologists such as Rees and Weinberg pursue an anthropic explanation for this fine-tuning, involving the concept of many universes and the fact that our existence selects for us this particular Universe (Rees 2000).

Alternative suggestions include that the dark energy is some kind of scalar field, rather like the scalar field which propels cosmic inflation early in the Universe's history. Some have suggested a new idea known as quintessence, which refers to a dynamical quantum field that gravitationally repels. The advantage of quintessence over the vacuum energy is that quintessence may interact with matter and evolve with time, so might naturally adjust itself to reach the present day value without the need for fine-tuning. The further advantage to cosmologists is that quintessence compared to the vacuum energy, may undergo all kinds of complex evolution. Theorists however are only speculating at this point. Some suggest that quintessence springs from the other dimensions required by string theory.

The language used by cosmologists in all of this is interesting. The Universe is commonly termed to be in the region of 'eternal expansion'. Further, those who suggest quintessence do so not only for scientific reasons. Ostriker and Steinhardt write:

> 'As acceleration takes hold over the next tens of billions of years, the matter and energy in the universe will become more and more diluted and space will stretch too rapidly to enable new structures to form. Living things will find the cosmos increasingly hostile. If the acceleration is caused by vacuum energy, then the cosmic story is complete: the planets, stars and galaxies we see today are the pinnacle of cosmic evolution. But if the acceleration is caused by quintessence, the ending has yet to be written. The universe might accelerate forever, or the quintessence could decay into new form of matter and radiation, repopulating the universe ... the universe had once been alive and then died, only to be a given a second chance.' (Ostriker and Steinhardt 2001)

It is interesting that they are looking for some hope in this cosmic picture. As we shall see they are not alone in such speculation.

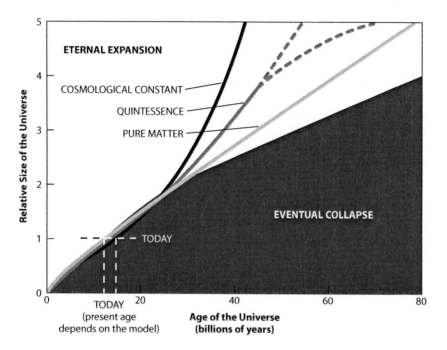

Figure 1: The future of the Universe. No longer do we believe that the Universe is in the region of 'eventual collapse' but the observations indicate one of the models of 'eternal expansion'. (Taken from *Scientific American*, Jan 2001).

Of course, there may be a completely different form of explanation. That is that General Relativity is wrong on large cosmological scales. Thus the 'dark energy' would simply be the discrepancy between relativity and a more complex theory of gravity. A further alternative is that we currently in our equations of cosmic expansion approximate the Universe as homogenous. However, the Universe does have significant clumpiness, and Wiltshire has suggested that this can induce the illusion of accelerating expansion (Wiltshire 2007: 1101).

More precise measurements of supernovae over longer distances may be able to separate quintessence from the vacuum energy, and indeed differences in the acceleration rate produce small differences in the microwave background radiation. The initial results from WMAP suggest that the dark energy may be more like a cosmological constant than quintessence. However, a number of current surveys may be able to distinguish these different explanations through observations of discrepancies between the expansion history of the Universe and the rate of growth of cosmic structure within that overall expansion (Blake 2008: 19–24).

So what will be the future of such a Universe? When the Universe is 10^{12} years old, stars cease to form, as there is no hydrogen left. At this stage all massive stars have now turned into neutron stars and black holes. At 10^{14} years, small stars become white dwarfs. The Universe becomes a cold and uninteresting place composed of dead stars and black holes. According to some theories of particle physics, protons themselves should decay at 10^{31} years. All that would be left would be some weakly interacting particles and a low-level energy background (Adams and Laughlin 1997: 337–72). In fact there may be an even more pessimistic future for the Universe. If the Universe came from 'nothing' could an ever-expanding Universe with an infinite future go back to nothing? With an infinite time to wait eventually any process with a finite probability of happening will happen (Barrow 2002: 23).

2.6 The future of life in the future of the Universe

In one sense this scientific work does not affect the overall message, for whether in a Big Crunch or wasting away, the Universe will not be a place of increasing fruitfulness and creativity but a place where all life will end (Krauss and Starkman 1999: 58–65). Human life will not be able to continue, even if it survives the end of the Sun or the collision of galaxies. Now of course Barrow is correct when he comments that, 'universes that meet the necessary conditions for life are big and old, dark and cold' (Barrow 2002: 4.8). Without a future of futility the Universe would not have had the balances in law and circumstance necessary for intelligent life to develop. Here is an important insight that life brings with it death.

How have the scientific community responded to this? There are those who have said that at the end of the day it does not matter. So the words of Dawkins could sum the feelings of some who see that the Universe 'has precisely the properties we should expect if there is, at bottom, no design, no purpose, no evil and no good, nothing but blind, pitiless indifference' (Dawkins 1995: 133). Yet many cosmologists have not been content with this. They have attempted to find hope in different directions.

2.6.1 The endless fertility of bubble universes

Some have pointed to the possibility that this Universe may be one of many and therefore the demise of this Universe needs to be seen in the context of 'endless fertility' of new universes. The status of this speculation needs to be carefully examined. It is true that a multitude of universes has been proposed. As we saw, an early version was in the bounce of Big Crunch into a Big Bang. The present data however rule out such a possibility for the future. Then there has been the suggestion favoured by those who attempted to apply quantum theory to the origin of the Universe according to Everett's interpretation of quantum theory (Everett III 1957: 454–62). This says that whenever a measurement is made of the quantum world the universe fulfils all quantum possibilities forming a new universe with each possibility. This leads to literally billions and billions of independent universes all slightly different to each other.

Part of the motivation for speculation about other universes has been the attempt to explain the extraordinary balances in law and circumstances that make life possible, which goes under the umbrella term of the anthropic principle. Rees points out the apparent fine tuning of six numbers, including the ratio of the electric force/gravitational force and the number of spatial dimensions in the Universe, which determine the kind of Universe we inhabit. He shows very elegantly how if any of these numbers were slightly different to what they are, then no life would exist in the Universe. He also notes the contingency that the basic laws are intelligible and calls this 'remarkable'.

He then goes on to reject those who would say that this is just the way things are. These balances are so extraordinary that there must be a deeper story to their existence. However, Rees does not see God as the answer. He notes it as a possible explanation but then moves on without assessing it or arguing against it. His own answer is that the anthropic principle selects this Universe out of many. He views this as 'compellingly attractive' and 'a natural deduction from some (albeit speculative) theories' (Rees 2000: 150). It is a fascinating account. It demonstrates the fallacy of trying to prove God through the design argument because God is not the only answer for design. The anthropic principle and other universe theories are an alternative.

Yet what is the status of the 'speculative theories'? Leaving aside oscillating universes and Everett's speculations, the subject of other universes has become a popular topic in contemporary cosmology (Smolin 1997; Randall and Sundrum 1999: 4690). Work on black holes raised the possibility of gateways to other universes, as matter collapsing into a singularity at the centre of a black hole could be shunted sideways to create a new universe connected to us by a wormhole (Fahri and Guth 1987: 149). Even on a conservative estimate of the number of black holes this would mean our Universe was connected to billions of other universes. This possibility has been a major interest of Hawking in recent years. His work on the evaporation of black holes led to the basic question of what happens to the matter that fell into such black holes. The answer he suggests is that it goes off into baby universes (Hawking 1993).

More recently some inflationary models which solve certain problems with the early Universe predict lots of bubble universes as well as our own (Linde 1994: 32–39; Garriga and Vilenkin 2001: 043511). Yet are these speculations metaphysical or physical? The trouble with all these theories of many Universes is just how do you pass information from one universe to another in order to know that it is there? The question must be asked in what sense other universes exist if they have no observable consequences either practically or in principle (Rees 2002: 70). Russell argues that the bubble universes predicted by inflation are not metaphysical speculation, as they are a consequence of a physical theory (Russell 2002b: 278). Yet this is surely pushing the point too far. They are predicted only by some inflationary models and these models may turn out not to be the best models for the early Universe. Further these other universes still need to have observable consequences beyond their prediction from certain theories, no matter how successful those theories are.

The speculation about multi-universes is interesting and cautions against the re-emergence of the design argument based on anthropic balances. Yet in terms of hope for the future one cannot help but agree with Polkinghorne that they 'present a scene of occasional islands of meaningfulness erupting within an ocean of absurdity' (Polkinghorne 2002b: 65). Indeed Davies suggests that there may be the motive of wanting life to go on in that our descendents could decamp into a newborn universe via a wormhole or even create their own baby universe in the lab for future habitation (Davies 2002: 49). The hope is that life and mind might transcend actual universes.

2.6.2 *Dyson's life in all directions*

Alongside those who have argued that life is a cosmic necessity in terms of its appearance in the Universe (Davies 1998; de Duve 1995), there are those who want to argue that intelligent life will never die out. Freeman Dyson saw that a Universe ending in a Big Crunch would mean that life would come to an end. However, in an open Universe, he suggested that biological life would adapt first through genetic engineering to redesign organisms that could cope in such a Universe. He was struck by the ability that intelligent life has in manipulating the environment of the Earth. Extrapolating that forward he concluded that the combined resources of natural and artificial intelligences should be able to maintain some form of life in the Universe over the next trillion years (Dyson 1979: 449–50; Dyson 1988). Human consciousness would be transferred to new kinds of hardware that would be able to cope with the ultra low temperatures of a heat death Universe, including for example a complex dust cloud. Such a cloud could maintain itself for ever (needing to hibernate for long periods) and collect an endless amount of information. Thus he concluded, 'life and intelligence are potentially immortal'.

While we can note that such a picture of human consciousness decanted into a cold cloud of dust and hydrogen may not provide an attractive hope for many, more importantly Dyson's optimism has not been shared by many other scientists (Krauss and Starkman 2000: 22–31; Davis 1999: 15–27). His view is dependent on a number of controversial assumptions.

First, consciousness is simply defined as a type of complex physical structure. Indeed, Dyson works with a model of life based on computers and information processing. His calculations simply show whether some future life form might be able to store and metabolise energy indefinitely. This is a somewhat minimal definition of intelligent life. Even if a computer or dust cloud could mirror the complexity of the human brain, would this infer consciousness? Boden has suggested that in the absence of a body such clouds could not satisfy any self-organising principle of living unity (Boden 1999: 231–48; Boden 2002: 216). Further, work in situated robotics and indeed the philosophy of mind takes the physical interaction between body and the world to be essential to intelligence (Brooks 1991: 139–59; Clark 1997; Boden 2000: 115–43). Embodiment is central to both self and intelligence, through the self extending into our physical and cultural environment. It is unclear as to whether a dust cloud could give this kind of embodiment. More importantly could consciousness survive without any other consciousness to relate to? The aspect of life seen in relationships is extremely important. We will return to the importance of embodiment later within the context of Christian hope for the future.

Second, Dyson's scenario is dependent on the survival of matter. If as some theories of particle physics predict, the proton does decay there will come a point when the Universe will only consist of radiation, and the complex structures cannot be maintained (Dyson 2002: 141; Rees 2002: 78). Frautschi has also pointed out that on longer timescales the 'life-form' would find it difficult to maintain internal structure due to quantum mechanical effects (Frautschi 1982: 599). The effect of all of this is that there is a limit to Dyson's immortality.

Of course Dyson's picture is based on the picture of the Universe before the recent data that it was accelerating in its expansion. An accelerating Universe is even less conducive to Dyson's eschatology. As Rees points out Dyson's optimism was based on the belief that there seemed to be no limit to the scale of artefacts that could eventually be constructed (Rees 2002: 79). But with the recession between galaxies increasing in its acceleration, local effects will form island systems of galaxies with large separations leading to a limit as to how large any network can be. In such a situation Dyson himself acknowledges that life cannot survive forever and tries to use quintessence to avoid this consequence (Dyson 2002: 148).

Dyson's attempt to prolong life in all directions does not work. Yet it remains an interesting illustration of the scientific attempt to find hope in a pessimistic scientific picture.

2.6.3 Tipler's physics of immortality

Another attempt for scientific immortality has been pursued by Frank Tipler (Tipler 1994). Tipler has been one of the cosmologists at the forefront of thinking concerning the anthropic principle. Extending the anthropic principle into the future, he proposed with Barrow 'the Final Anthropic Principle':

> 'Intelligent information processing must come into existence in the Universe, and once it comes into existence it will never die out'. (Barrow and Tipler 1986: 23)

In a similar way to Dyson he speculates about what might be possible technologically in the next billions of years. He sees life as information processing and suggests that, although humans themselves might die, information processing would continue within computers. Indeed, our consciousness may be transferred to computers. As computers expand across space then information processing would increase. He argues that it is possible on such a model that a point will be reached when an infinite or maximum amount of information will have been processed, and 'life' has expanded everywhere in the Universe.

This 'Omega Point' contains all the information of the Universe and could change the nature of the Universe itself. This is a point outside the space-time of the Universe, which is the destination and haven of life when the Universe disappears. It is this point, 'the completion of all finite existence' which Tipler identifies with an omniscient, omnipotent and omnipresent God. This 'God' must exist as 'life must exist forever'. Life has achieved 'God-like' attributes. Immortality for Tipler is simply that there are an infinite number of thoughts before the end of the Universe. Such a picture is a long way from the Christian belief in resurrection and new life within a personal relationship with a Creator God.

This is an interesting exercise in speculation but is it any more than that? For Tipler the Omega Point theory is a model for an omnipresent, omniscient, evolving personal God, transcendent and immanent. It is a model that he argues is only dependent on key concepts from cosmology. Further he suggests that it leads to a future universal resurrection of the dead very similar to the one predicted in the Judaeo-Christian tradition, for the Omega Point has the capacity to provide this resurrection. This he believes gives hope for the future.

Once again this scenario is dependent on a number of assumptions. First, Tipler's speculations are dependent on the Universe being closed; in fact this is a particular prediction of his theory, which Tipler is proud to point out. In the early 1990s it seemed to be a good bet! However, as we have seen earlier in this chapter the present evidence is that the Universe is not closed, but it is increasing in its expansion rate. It will never collapse to a Big Crunch. The evidence for this is good and is a direct falsification of Tipler's god. Second, as with Dyson, can consciousness be so easily transferred to digital computers? Some have argued for the possibility as a way of achieving immortality, but it is highly problematic (Crevier 1993: 278; Kurzweil 1999; Moravec 1988). Third, even if through something like quintessence the far future of the Universe could be brought back to a Big Crunch, there seems little justification for believing that complex structures necessary for life could be maintained anywhere near the final state of Big Crunch, or indeed that we would have enough knowledge to predict how structures would behave (Ellis and Coule 1994: 738).

In addition there are a number of philosophical flaws with Tipler's position, as well as a number of errors of logic and consistency (Stoeger and Ellis 1995: 163). It involves endowing this geometrical construction, the Omega Point (which may or may not come into existence), with personal characteristics. Second, it involves seeing physics as the only discipline to answer all the fundamental questions of the Universe. Third, it involves unwarranted assumptions about the character and necessity of life in the Universe. All of these problems make Tipler's speculation very vulnerable. It again shows the attempt to give a scientific basis for hope. Even discounting all of the problems, what sort of immortality is achieved? It seems to be a desperate way of responding to the futility of the Universe and it fails completely in the light of an accelerating Universe.

2.6.4 What is the point of a lifeless Universe?

Carl Sagan coupled expertise in planetary research with a rare ability to communicate science at a popular level. Reflecting on death he wrote:

> 'I would love to believe that when I die I will live again, that some thinking, feeling, remembering part of me will continue ... The world is so exquisite with so much love and moral depth, that there is no reason to deceive ourselves with pretty stories for which there's little good evidence. Far better it seems to me, in our vulnerability, is to look death in the eye

and to be grateful every day for the brief but magnificent opportunity that life provides'. (Sagan 1997: 215)

One could say a similar thing about the Universe. It may be transitory and yet have value, allowing intelligent life to appear. However, what is fascinating about cosmological speculation on the end of the Universe is that few cosmologists are prepared to simply live for the here and now.

This end of Universe in the heat death of futility raises a great deal of pessimism within the scientific community. As we have seen the model of quintessence is pursued partly for the hope for the future that it offers. It may even be that Hoyle's model of a steady state universe without beginning which he advocated almost alone to his death may have been attractive not only because it dispensed with 'God at the beginning' but also gave an infinite hope for life in the future (Hoyle, Burbidge, and Narlikar 2000).

Bertrand Russell lamented:

'... the world which science presents for our belief is even more purposeless, more void of meaning ... all the labours of the ages, all the devotion, all the inspiration, all the noonday brightness of human genius, are destined to extinction ... and the whole temple of man's achievement must inevitably be buried beneath the debris of a universe in ruins.' (Russell 1957: 107)

The atheist Peter Atkins uses this 'naked purposelessness of nature' as another strand in his attack on religion (Atkins 1986: 98), while Paul Davies suggests that an 'almost empty universe growing steadily more cold and dark for all eternity is profoundly depressing' (Davies 2002: 48). A similar lament is voiced by Nobel Prize winner, Steven Weinberg:

'The more the universe seems comprehensible, the more it also seems pointless. But if there is no solace in the fruits of research, there is at least some consolation in the research itself ... The effort to understand the universe is one of the very few things that lifts human life above the level of farce, and gives it some of the grace of tragedy.' (Weinberg 1977: 144)

In a later book he comments on that widely quoted passage:

'I did not mean that science teaches us that the universe is pointless, but only that the universe itself suggests no point.' (Weinberg 1992: 255)

There may be defiance against the pessimism in the very fact that because we understand the end of Universe then this gives meaning. That is, meaning is to be found in the whole process whatever the end. There is something in that. But, as we have seen in Dyson and Tipler, there needs to be more than that. Indeed, Barrow points out that the pessimistic long range forecasts of the future of the Universe in the 19th century played an important role in the development of philosophies of progress (Barrow 2002a: 23).

The challenge for Christian theology is clear from this. What hope can be offered? In a Universe which points towards futility is there any deeper purpose or story which puts human life into perspective? Davies suggests:

'It is no coincidence that some Christian fundamentalists challenge the second law of thermodynamics, with its prediction of cosmic degeneration and decay. These fundamentalists reason that a universe that can undergo renewal and be sustained for eternity is more God-friendly than one that decays.' (Davies 2002: 46)

This is misleading and lacks any evidence. In fact as we have seen the majority of fundamentalists prefer discontinuity of a brand new creation replacing this old worthless creation. This is not done by challenging the second law of thermo-dynamics. Indeed most creationists use the second law of thermodynamics to challenge both Big Bang cosmology and evolution (Peacock 1989). Nevertheless, the broader point which Davies is attempting to make can be accepted. That is, the future of the Universe needs to be taken seriously by Christian theologians.

It is a challenge for systematic theology as it forces us to re-examine some of our doctrines of creation, new creation, hope and providence. It is to this that we now must turn.

Chapter 3

The Limited Universal Responses of the Theologians of Hope

Very few theologians have taken seriously the scenarios for the end of the Universe. It cannot be argued that this is because the scientific picture is very recent. The scenarios of heat death and Big Crunch have been with us in outline since the work of Einstein and Hubble in the 1920s. In fact, as early as the 1850s, Lord Kelvin and Helmholtz explored the implications of the 'running down' of the Universe predicted by the Second Law of Thermodynamics (Thomson 1852: 304–6; von Helmholtz 1961; Goldstein and Goldstein 1993). The popular books and talks of Eddington and Jeans in the 1930s concerning the heat death of the Universe provoked some responses from a few theologians of which the most detailed was a series of lectures in 1931–33 by William Inge (Inge 1934). In fact Inge saw heat death as challenging the materialist dream of human progress of the future as opposed to hope based in the Creator and sustainer of the Universe.

Since that time theological engagement has been shallow and sporadic. An interesting contemporary example is in the work of Keith Ward, whose theological engagement with other scientific insights into the Universe has been commendable. However on the end of the Universe he claims, 'It is within Christianity that the far-future universe has been an explicit topic of theological debate' (Ward 2002: 240). Yet in his paper discussing this, he only references Teilhard de Chardin, Lossky and Schweitzer from the Christian tradition and all before 1960. He then briefly refers to Colossians 1.15ff, Romans 8.19, 21 and 1 Thessalonians 4.13–18 which he interprets as saying that 'within one generation, perhaps … the physical Universe would be transformed into a material Paradise, in which there would be no more sun or sea, suffering or death' (Ward 2002: 242). These views belong to 'archaic' forms of thought. More important is:

> 'The goal of the universe, the reason for which it exists, is to have a community of conscious personal agents who live beyond decay and suffering in full awareness and love of God … From this point of view, exactly what happens in the future of the physical universe is irrelevant'. (Ward 2002: 244)

This is not untypical of the kind of engagement we will see in leading thinkers in the area of systematic theology. They exhibit universal claims that fall short of their ambition, a shallow interaction with the scriptural material referring to the future of the physical Universe and an overemphasis on the future of the person compared to the future of the Universe itself.

Part of the problem is that systematic theologians have not been in sufficient dialogue with either biblical theologians or with scientists. Indeed, it is an area where scientists and theologians show a large degree of mutual cynicism. Hardy writes: 'It is partly due to the widespread avoidance of direct engagement with creation and eschatology by theologians ... that scientists and those of a speculative turn of mind have turned to such wider issues' (Hardy 1997: 112, 122). Meanwhile, Tipler wants to 'rescue eschatology from the hands of theologians who with a few exceptions ... are quite ignorant of it' (Tipler 1994: xiii). Likewise, Dyson wants to 'hasten the arrival of the day when eschatology, the study of the end of the Universe, will be a respectable scientific discipline and not merely a branch of theology' (Dyson 1979: 447). Here are challenges from the scientific community for theology. What has been the response within the theological community?

3.1 A Universe of no value or interest

Mascall bemoaned the widespread misconception of the Christian community that 'Jesus Christ is of immense significance for human beings, but of no importance whatever to the rest of creation' (Mascall 1966: 163). Since that was written, much work has been done on the environment, both theologically and practically. Perhaps because of this, interest has been deflected away from other questions about the future. For example, Moltmann's *God in Creation* shows an environmental perspective but does not go further to discuss the physical Universe (Moltmann 1985).

Why is there such a lack of theological enthusiasm to deal seriously with the end of the Universe? First, gazing into the future is perceived to be very difficult and subject to a great deal of scientific uncertainty. The origin of the Universe is often presented as a solid scientific fact, and therefore theologians feel that they are on more solid ground. This may be illusory, as any models of the origin of the Universe share with predictions about its future the assumption that the laws of physics apply at any time in the Universe's history and the model is only as good as the evidence on which it is built. Of course, the evidence of the redshift of galaxies, the microwave background and the helium abundance in the Universe forms a strong basis for the Big Bang, allowing us to be more confident about the origin rather than the future. However, the future is not totally unknown, and we have already surveyed the increasing evidence for the futility of heat death.

The second reason is shared with theological work concerned with the origin of the Universe, that is, there is an inherent difficulty in discussing the beginning and end of the Universe from inside it. Can the beginning and end of the Universe be viewed as events in history open to scientific and theological exploration? This question should lead to a degree of humility, but does not mean that it is useless to engage with the beginning of the Universe. Indeed for the Christian theologian belief in the Universe as creation means that the beginning and end of the Universe are appropriate topics for theological work.

Third, theological work on the end of the Universe has suffered from the theological excess of former years. Predictions of the end of the world, hell and damnation preaching, and the absurdity of some theological speculation have given eschatology a bad name. Work on the origin of the Universe may seem safer, although the spectre of seven-day creationism is always in the background. Yet the existence of theological excess indicates the need for good theology in this area rather than silence. Theology needs to reclaim and explore the relationship between eschatology and the physical Universe.

Fourth, it is difficult to see initially how work on the end of the Universe has any practical value. Does it really matter whether the Universe will end in 100 billion years? Does it have anything to say to questions of justice or Christian lifestyle? The strength of the revival of interest in Christian eschatology has been in part due to the way that theologians such as Moltmann have earthed the future in the past and present, with a moral implication for human response. It is difficult to see how this may be the case concerning events which are predicted billions of years in the future. Connected with that is the simple yet not trivial fact of the length of times involved in the discussion, which are difficult to imagine from a human perspective. Yet such timescales are also true of the beginning of the Universe. This has not stopped theologians in a fruitful exploration of the relationship of creation to present day concerns, not least in a Christian affirmation of science itself.

The end of the story is as important as the beginning. Of course the beginning and ending of a story may just be part of the myth to express the here and now. Creation and Judgement are in one sense events not far off, in that they indicate to the human being that all life is gift. Nevertheless, Christian theology has traditionally wanted to say that they are more than that. That is in part in the way that they have been related to the whole of the created order not just human life. Conway Morris agrees and goes on to say that 'a universe without an eschatological dimension is a universe that is incomplete, if not crippled' (Conway Morris 2002: 161). Indeed, 100 billion years of the Universe's future pose similar challenges as the immensity of the 10^{22} stars. As Stephen Clark comments,

'Immensity, or the imagination of immensity, awakens in us a recognition of that Infinite which surrounds us and confronts us.' (Clark 2002: 193)

Fifth, a much more basic reason has been the nature of the relationship between science and religion. Some theologians would view scientific insights as irrelevant to systematic theology. Certain followers of Barth would want to build eschatology in isolation from the issues of Chapter 2. Certain fundamentalist theologians would want to speak of eschatology in conflict with the scientific insights based on Big Bang cosmology. Likewise a model of science that saw the predictions of the end of the Universe in the context of an idealist or instrumentalist view of science would not see any need to bring them into contact with Christian eschatology. However, these are views of the relationship of science and Christian theology that have little to commend them. In contrast if both science and Christian theology are characterised by critical realism, then the common reality that they are both committed to becomes the foundation for a common dialogue. On such a view scientific research will pose questions for serious dialogue with theology. Indeed, as we shall see, such critical realism is reinforced by reflections on the end of the Universe.

Sixth, one cannot escape from a simple observation that regardless of any theological position, systematic theologians are largely ignorant of contemporary science. Contemporary science of course moves at a rapid pace. In Western culture where science education is often divorced from those who follow study in humanities, ignorance of science amongst most theologians is one of the inevitable results. Yet it is not just ignorance of the facts. It is often an attitude that either feels threatened by science or unconvinced of what can be at times highly arrogant claims. While this situation may be understandable, the need exists to develop the dialogue wider than just those who have a special interest in the science/religion field. Considering the eschatology of the physical Universe might be one way of widening that dialogue.

Seventh, there has been a general trend in the last few decades of systematic theology to emphasise the goodness of creation. This has come from a number of sources. As we have seen a Christian response to environmental abuse has been to stress the goodness of God in creation. This has been necessary in responding to those Christian groups who have seen creation as simply a place where human beings need to be saved from for the future life. In addition, feminist theologians and others have stressed the goodness of the body against those Christian tradi- tions that have associated the body and sex with sin. In such a 'culture of the goodness of the physical' it is not easy to take seriously the futility of creation. It is somewhat odd in that theologians are prepared to think seriously about the physicality of the beginning rather than the end.

Eighth, we need to ask whether systematic theology has been controlled more by philosophical concerns rather than the biblical narratives or scientific insights. Certainly in questions of eternity being seen as atemporal or in the development of omniscience, theology seems to have looked more to its Greek rather than Hebrew foundations. We shall need to explore this question in more detail in the forthcoming chapters.

This lack of consideration of the end of the physical Universe is a serious problem for theology. However much we might want to stress the goodness of creation, we need to think seriously about the end. Its absence illustrates Feuerbach's dismissive characterization that 'the world has no value, no interest for Christians. The Christian thinks only of himself and the salvation of his soul.' (Feuerbach 1957: 287) Feuerbach linked this neglect of the natural world with neglect of human culture and the physicality of the body. The physical creation, the human body and the end of the Universe need to be all considered and integrated.

Yet this neglect of the end has not always been the case. In particular, John Wesley had a strong emphasis on God's saving purposes for the physical creation (Maddox 2004: 21–52). He was influenced by Hartley's *Paradise Restored* which explored exegetical arguments that the millennial period must include all of creation, not just humanity (Hartley 1764: 1–73) and Burnet's *Theory of the Earth* (Burnet 1684–90), which had pioneered the eighteenth century enterprise to marry the Bible's account of creation, the flood and the new heavens and new earth with modern science. Wesley seemed to be very impressed with Burnet's picture of the way God would restore the conditions of paradise back on the Earth (Wesley 1993: 22.213–4). Interestingly enough in the light of the Earth being swallowed up by the end of the Sun, as a premillennialist[1] Burnet saw the restored paradise as a temporary situation and speculated that the Earth might be changed into a sun or a fixed star!

Wesley would not follow Burnet on this. Instead he saw new creation as an action of God leading to a permanent change. He included in support of this Knight's *A Discourse on the Conflagration and Renovation of the World* (Knight 1736) in volume 20 of his own *Works* (1773), where Knight suggested that the power of God would reform and improve the heavens.

In his later years the new creation became one of the major themes of his preaching (Wesley 1988: 2.500–10). He saw continuity and discontinuity with this creation. The new creation was a physical place, but far better. One of the features of Wesley's view of new creation was that a range of animals would be present in this renewed creation. His 1781 sermon 'The General Deliverance' took Romans 8.19–22 as its text and he used it to speak of animal salvation (Wesley 1988: 2.437–50). Wesley followed this up two years later by publishing in the Arminian Magazine an extract from John Hildrop on animal salvation. Wesley pointed out that far from being a minor issue animal salvation was central to our confession of the goodness of God. For if God did not redeem all his creation then God had not truly overcome the work of Satan.

Wesley's emphasis on the physicality of new creation and his need to explore the question of animal salvation is motivated by a picture of the redemption of all creation. This picture of the redemption of all creation came from what he saw as a clear scriptural picture. It is interesting too that Wesley, although in what may be judged a rather naïve way, brought his biblical convictions into direct contact with the science of his day.

It is that theological insight that should motivate us to take the end of the physical Universe seriously. Indeed, there is a clear conviction among contemporary theologians that we must recover a deeper appreciation for the biblical affirmation of the cosmos, both as God's good creation and as the object of God's renewing work (Schwöbel 2000: 235–6). Theology must interact with the whole of creation if we want to think and speak of the God of creation.

Hardy has been one of the few contemporary systematic theologians who have attempted to address the question of the end of the Universe, desiring a combined account of creation and eschatology (Hardy 1996: 157). He suggests that such an account might proceed on:

1. Creation keeps the Universe from ending, but also brings it to an end.
2. Covenant is a way to view the dynamics of the created Universe with two aspects – obligatory and promissory.
3. These dynamics result from a radical gift/self promise on the part of God, in which God gives to the other (universe, world, humanity) varying capacities

[1] See Appendix A for a note on millennium theology.

for finitude, full possibilities of development, and redemption in the face of evil.

4. This action of God requires worship, and in this creation and eschatology return glory to God.

This is a helpful starting point but Hardy is somewhat disappointing in applying this to the scientific picture of the end of the Universe. Indeed, after pleading for integration of the current understanding of cosmology he does not interact with it at all. Hardy needs a number of bridges between theology and cosmology in order for the integration to proceed. Can we therefore take Wesley's big vision of new creation and Hardy's commitment to a combined account and see how that might work out in a way that takes both science and Christian eschatology seriously? It may be natural to look for help in this to those whose names are often mentioned with such an enterprise, that is, Moltmann and Pannenberg.

3.2 Moltmann's limited universal eschatology

Moltmann's emphasis on hope and his claim that eschatology must be universal, suggests a thorough engagement with the theme of the physical Universe.

Bauckham summarises Moltmann's eschatology as:

- Christological
- Integrative
- Redemptive
- Progressive
- Theocentric
- Contextual
- Political and Pastorally Sensitive

This summary, which has received Moltmann's own approval (Bauckham 1999), does sound all embracing. The resurrection of Jesus Christ from the dead is the starting point of Moltmann's eschatology. Hope is based on the future promised and entailed by the resurrection of the crucified Christ. In this, Christology and eschatology are in a mutually interpretive relationship. The history of Jesus can only be understood against the eschatological background and eschatology gets its character and content from the history of Jesus (Moltmann 1990: xiv). It is this fundamental link which distinguishes true Christian eschatology from utopian dreaming (Moltmann 1967: 17).

In particular, the resurrection of Jesus is the paradigm for the new creation of all things, by which he means 'animals, plants, stones and all cosmic life systems' (Moltmann 1990: 258). This is all encompassing language but does it include the Universe as a whole? To this we will need to return.

The resurrection as paradigm for the new creation is to be welcomed. It means that eschatology is based on something beyond the natural physical processes, that is, God's act of new creation provides the continuity of old and new in the renewal of creation (Moltmann 1996: 69). Further, the new creation is not a restoration to original perfection but a 'transformation in the transcendental conditions of the world itself' (Moltmann 1996: 272). For Moltmann, God does not destroy the world in order to re-create it, nor does some inherently eternal part of creation survive into new creation. The resurrection demonstrates the transformation of the whole, whether it be the body of an individual or the world. The nature of that transformation is from temporal creation to eternal creation just as the resurrection was the transformation of the mortal into the eternally living Christ. Indeed, Christ's solidarity with the dead and the transfigured form of all of his temporally lived life means that the whole of what has happened in the lives of all creatures and in the whole of the time of this transient creation, will be gathered up, healed and transfigured into eternal life and eternal time.

If redemption is restoration to the Garden of Eden, then why should human beings not fall again and be in need of another redemption? Moltmann avoids this age-old problem by arguing that the new creation exceeds restoration. It is redeemed from the imperfections of this creation, which he sees as transience and death, and is therefore secured against sin. Once again, we see the key role of eternal time in Moltmann's eschatology. When temporal time becomes eternal time, transience and death lose their power. Moltmann sees transience and death as intrinsic to the temporal character of creation, positively pointing forward to eternity and giving us a longing for eternity, while negatively making sin and death possible.

It is a strong model of redemption, not identifying it with the progress of human history to utopia, or to an end without fulfilment. We are not merely dominated by our history. Neither is that history unimportant in a form of eschatological escapism. That is surely the strength of Moltmann's position. Yet the weaknesses in Moltmann point us forward to some important questions.

3.2.1 An earth bound eschatology?

Moltmann argues that eschatology must be universal. That is, it must be all embracing, not separating soul from body, individual from community, human history from the whole of creation. Bauckham and other sympathetic commentators praise Moltmann for taking seriously the non human creation and not being dominated by anthropocentricity in eschatology. But is such praise merited?

The Coming of God does seem to have this non-anthropocentric eschatology. It deals with personal eschatology (eternal life), historical eschatology (the Kingdom of God), and cosmic eschatology (the new heaven and new earth). These aspects are integrated by seeing eschatology as centred in God who comes to indwell his whole creation. This universal eschatology seems to be important for two reasons. First is the doctrine of creation. The unity and consistency of God's relationship to creation requires that new creation be all encompassing, that is nothing will be lost, all will be restored (Moltmann 1996: 255, 269–270). Second, Moltmann stresses the interconnectedness of all things. Humans cannot be humans without body, or without community or without living in creation. Thus, 'there is no redemption for human beings without the redemption of nature' (Moltmann 1996: 260).

This sounds fine but the claim that this is a non-anthropocentric eschatology is simply unconvincing when the detail of Moltmann's argument is analysed. Moltmann continually confuses the term 'world' with 'creation' and 'cosmos', using them interchangeably. For example on new creation he writes:

'A mutual indwelling of the world in God and God in the world will come into being … Through their mutual indwellings, they remain unmingled and undivided, for God lives in creation in a God-like way, and the world lives in God in a world-like way.' (Moltmann 1996: 307)

His non-anthropocentricity stops at the edge of the Earth's atmosphere. He is right to point to the need of an integrative eschatology but his own horizon is limited. While he mentions 'cosmic life systems' there is no engagement with the question of the physical Universe. The physical Universe is part of God's creation and has to be included in his redemptive work. It is also intimately connected with human life on this planet. The stars of the Milky Way galaxy have provided the raw materials out of which intelligent life on the Earth has emerged. Further human life is dependent on the future conditions and evolution of the physical Universe. It must be included in the theological picture.

His earth bound eschatology is due in part to his inability to engage with the specifics of scientific discovery and in part by the need to be contextual. Bauckham argues that Moltmann's eschatology is an eschatology that has a clear historical and global context. In his response to this, Moltmann argues that this is quite natural, as he is always a pastor and politically involved. However, he seems to be blind to the full weight of Bauckham's point. In responding to the myth of human progress to utopia, and the threats of nuclear extinction, environmental pollution and poverty, Moltmann does produce an eschatology which is relevant and is a spur to action on these issues. However, it is easy to be trapped by the context or develop an eschatology that is dependent on certain selected aspects of the experience of the world.

Moltmann criticizes the myth of human progress as secularising select parts of the Christian eschatological tradition, for example believing that there is an end point to the historical process but without the intervention of God. Yet he risks a similar danger. With his emphasis on the Earth rather than the cosmos as a whole, his eschatology is dependent on that context, leading as we shall see to the importance of the millennium reign of Christ on the Earth as a transition to new creation.

3.2.2 A resurrection from transient time to eternal time?

While the resurrection surely indicates transformation, it is unclear whether it really points to the conclusions that Moltmann draws from it. He is unconvincing in suggesting that the transformation is characterized by the change from transient time to eternal time. It is here that lack of specific inter-action with the science is paralleled in the lack of specific engagement with the biblical texts concerning resurrection.

The gospel accounts of the resurrection appearances of Jesus speak of a strong relationship to historical time. Jesus spends a certain length of time with the disciples, he eats, he speaks, he develops relationships, and he teaches – all of which are time dependent. The key seems to be that Jesus is no longer bound by the constraints of time, in the sense of having to journey between different locations, and of course will not undergo the negative processes of the passing of time such as decay and death. Moltmann's argument would be more convincing in terms of time if based on the ascension rather than resurrection.

In addition, does the whole of time need to be gathered up, healed and trans-figured? At the level of persons, I am what I am now because of my past and because of my future possibilities. I bring those things naturally with me into any relationship. Within redemption of the person, my history is not a separate thing that needs redemption; it makes me who I am. While Ward may be correct in suggesting that memory needs to be transformed in new creation so that both suffering and joy can be seen in wider context (Ward 1998: 307), this does not need the whole of time to be gathered up in eternity. This would surely fall into the trap of a 'sterile totalization and a rigid unification' of time that leaves little room for temporality and subsequent change (Welker 1998: 317–28; Conradie 2002: 286).

In the same way the cosmos is as it is, because of its history. The processes of decay and death, far from being ready for redemption, have provided the novelty and complexity of the Universe today. For example if one star had not run through its time and ended with a supernova explosion, some of the atoms of carbon that make up the human body would not be here. Moltmann is overreaching in his attempt to be all embracing. As raised by Bauckham, in the all encompassing 'nothing is lost, all will be restored', what if God creates things for a temporary purpose? Will they all be restored? The problem is bigger than Bauckham seems to indicate. One could go further and ask will dinosaurs and bubonic plague be restored? Or does the star that created my carbon need to be restored, particularly when other stars are being created?

There are more problems of such a view of the transformation of time and space. Moltmann suggests that in the new creation all time and space will be present together:

> 'All times will return and – transformed and transfigured – will be taken up into the aeon of the new creation. In the eternal creation all the times which in God's creative resolve were fanned out will also be gathered together.' (Moltmann 1996: 294)

Does this mean that the new creation will be timeless? This may deny growth, personhood and relationship in new creation. Moltmann does not accept a timeless new creation, but he does seem to be very close to it. In a different context, Macquarrie pointed out:

'If everything is to return to an undifferentiated unity, then creation would have been pointless in the first place, and all the risk of creation, and its suffering and striving, would have been sheer waste.' (Macquarrie 1977: 360)

Bauckham makes a similar point in relation to Moltmann. In Moltmann's picture are time and space simply imperfections? Yet without them new creation could not be what it will be. Moltmann seems to be arguing against the limitations imposed by time and space but is the way to do this really effective? What is the point of giving this creation time, space and freedom if God is going to simply supersede them?

These problems are due in part to Moltmann's understanding of transience. It means more than temporal change. In fact, it seems to contain a sense of change that leads to decay. In order to guard against sin and decay is Moltmann going too far and reducing the importance of temporal change as a force for both good and evil?

Finally, the restoration of all things implies the universal salvation of all human beings. Moltmann is quite clear about this, believing that any talk of conditional immortality or hell is not consistent with logic or the Christian picture. Yet does this deny real human freedom and is there an adequate sense of justice in this picture? One cannot help but feel that such a view of the restoration of all things denies space, time, freedom, personhood, self giving love and growth which are fundamental to a Christian understanding of Creator and creation.

3.2.3 Can eschatology be too Christocentric?

Does such a Christological eschatology allow serious engagement with the doctrine of creation? *The Coming of God* claims that it develops Moltmann's earlier work, in particular his understanding of how creation is fulfilled or completed in the eschaton. Thus is *God in Creation* given an eschatological dimension in *The Coming of God*? To an extent the answer is yes but as we pointed out earlier his understandings are not of creation in a cosmic sense, but of creation in terms of the Earth motivated primarily by ecological concerns. This may be in part due to a limiting of the cosmic horizon by a Christology which stresses too much Earth centred incarnation.

The importance of a Trinitarian understanding is crucial here. Now of course Moltmann sees eschatology as a Trinitarian process, taking place within the changing relationships of the divine persons, completed when the Son hands over the kingdom to the Father (Moltmann 1981). A Trinitarian understanding is not excluded by his Christological eschatology but the danger of an over-emphasis on the resurrection may under-emphasize the work of the Spirit in new creation. It is this work of the Spirit in new creation which may give a much wider cosmic horizon.

Certainly, Moltmann's vision is at times very large. 'The Coming of God' is the 'eschatological goal of creation as a whole' (Moltmann 1996: 318). For Moltmann, it is the restriction of God's omnipresence that allows creation. In the new creation there will be the immediate presence of God and the new creation itself will be the dwelling of God. He will both rest from and rest in creation.

Hans Urs von Balthasar has argued for the consummation of the world in God (von Balthasar 1988). Seeing the inter-Trinitarian processes of creation being a gift from Father to Son and redemption as a gift given by Son to Father, the eschatological picture becomes the Son uniting all things in himself and thus drawing human beings and all creation into intimate relationship with Father. Moltmann however argues on the basis of Isaiah 6.3 that eschatology is about the glorification of God within creation. It is simply part of the process of the way God enters creation though Wisdom and Word, being present in the Shekinah in the history of Israel, and in incarnation and the indwelling of the Holy Spirit. Moltmann sees this as complementary to von Balthasar, seeing mutual indwelling of God in the new creation and the new creation in God. But is this a valid reading of Isaiah's 'glory' and 1 Corinthians 15? We will need to ask this key question of whether Moltmann and others are right to see a contrast between creation and new creation as a restriction and a universalising the presence of God. We might note at this stage that Isaiah 6.3 is not obviously an eschatological reference. The 'whole earth is full of his glory' in 'the year that King Uzziah died' (Is 6.1).

These kinds of questions expose the tendency of Moltmann's project of systematising to take over and impose theology upon the biblical texts. Eschatological thinking does need a robust dialogue between biblical studies and systematic theology.

3.2.4 *Does eschatology need the Millennium?*

For Moltmann, eschatology is a process which the resurrection has set going. Building on one of his favourite passages (1 Corinthians 15.22–28), he writes that it is a process which 'has its foundation in Christ, its dynamic in the Spirit, and its future in the bodily new creation of all things' (Moltmann 1990: 241).

It is this emphasis on process that raises the idea of Christ's millennial reign, as a kind of transitional kingdom between old creation and new creation. It is initially a surprise that Moltmann explores it with seriousness while for many theologians it has remained a topic simply for a few American evangelicals (Grenz 1992). Yet Moltmann argues that the present church needs to recover the hope for God's further transformation of this world that is fostered by eschatological millenarianism (Moltmann 1996: 131–202). Bauckham agrees that models of the millennium carry influential connotations for construing the present state of affairs but is rightly critical of Moltmann on two counts (Bauckham 1997: 263–77). The first is that Moltmann fails to distinguish adequately the range of major models. In particular, Moltmann equates future-oriented or eschatological millenniarism with premillennialism, failing to distinguish the postmillennial version. Thereby he ascribes to premillennialism a stimulus for present reform that is more typically found in postmillennial representatives (See Appendix A for the various models of the millennium). Second, and more importantly, Bauckham questions the need for the millennium as a distinct state. He argues that we would do better instead simply to reclaim the biblical model of God's new creation as the new creation of this world.

Inherent in the debate about the millennium is the attempt to see a bridge between this creation and new creation, while affirming the value of both. It is an attempt to handle the transformation of space and time. Bauckham is correct that Moltmann's introduction of millennium eschatology is unnecessary. In fact it limits further his eschatology. It illustrates Moltmann's Earth-centred eschatology for there seems little consideration of what this millennium reign may mean for the Universe (Moltmann 1996: 144).

3.2.5 An eschatological future for time?

Part of the motivation for Moltmann towards progressive eschatology is his view of time. Moltmann's rejects the criticism that his concept of eternal time is timelessness. It is not static, but imaged as cyclical time, unlike the irreversible time of the present creation. Moltmann is attempting to distance eschatology from an immanent historical process. This he sees as dependent on a number of cultural assumptions about time. First, that time is linear. Second, it is a continuous process and third that the flowing of absolute time does not change. On the basis of these assumptions the present loses significance as simply the transition from past to future and the future flows from past and present. Causality means that there is no openness to the future and continuity suggests a model of inevitable progress. This denial of openness and alternative possibilities is used to justify the continued dominance of the powerful.

Moltmann is right to question these assumptions, many of which are built on Newtonian physics. In the light of general relativity, quantum theory and chaos theory our present understanding of time is very different. If he had interacted with this in a serious way he may have seen that time is a little more complex and subtle, and indeed the natural world gives some support to his philosophical understanding of time. Moltmann suggests, in contrast to the popular assumptions, that there is a qualitative difference between past and future, easily seen in the potentiality of the future. In addition, time is complex, with history itself having multiple possibilities. Finally, the Sabbath illustrates that rather than flowing steadily, time can have interruptions in which time is treated differently.

It is out of this that he sees this time as characterized by transience, which is both good and bad – either bringing all things to nothing or allowing a future open to God. In contrast, eternal time involves temporal movement without entailing the loss of the before as one moves on into the after:

'In the aeonic cycles of time, creaturely life unremittingly regenerates itself from the omnipresent source of life, God. An analogy is provided by the regenerating cycles of nature, and the rhythms of the body which sustain life here. The purposeful time of history is fulfilled in the cyclical movements of life's eternal joy in the unceasing praise of the omnipresent God. The preferred images for eternal life are therefore dance and music,

as ways of describing what is as yet hardly imaginable in this impaired life.'
(Moltmann 1996: 295)

Bauckham once more is quick to see the possible flaw. Does such a view of time mean that nothing new can happen? Does this exclude any kind of novelty and as we have pointed out above does this mean there is no personal growth in eternity? How can novelty be maintained without old things passing away?

We must press this further. The analogies of cyclic time used by Moltmann are not helpful. The regenerating cycles of nature and the rhythms of the body do not sustain life without their interaction with linear time. As the cycles interact with linear time then novelty arises. The seasons are dependent on the history of the Sun and lead to the birth and death of many things in the natural world. The rhythms of the body are played out within the overarching development of birth and death. Much better analogies of cyclic time are stories of closed time loops beloved by science fiction writers. These time loops are hell rather than heaven because of the lack of novelty. It is extremely difficult to argue for novelty without some form of linear time and without other things passing away. Novelty in the Universe cannot be separated from the increase of entropy (disorder), which gives time a linear direction.

With all of these problems, would it not be better to reject any concept of time at all in terms of the new creation? In this case, theological speculation would simply have to acknowledge a discontinuity that stopped any further discussion. Moltmann is not prepared to do this, as he resists the transposition of eschatology into eternity, which characterizes the approach of Barth and Bultmann. Here, the timeless God is always present, providing a vertical dimension of eschatology at any point on the horizontal linear time of human history. Moltmann rightly sees that this devalues this creation and its created time. Equally, Moltmann resists transposition of eschatology into time. Eschatology cannot be limited by time, as it merely becomes a continuance of human progress. More recently Moltmann, perhaps in the light of the above criticisms, re-emphasises that apocalyptic divides time into two qualitatively different aeons, the time of a transitory world and the time of a future eternal world (Moltmann 2002: 259). His footnote justification for this is general and without page reference. Is he trying to justify it from scripture? But this in itself is unconvincing given the complexity of apocalyptic thought.

Instead of distinguishing between eternal time and transient time, which is Moltmann's third way, it may be better to develop a model concerning not the nature of time but how this creation is limited by space-time. Moltmann simply confuses the whole area. Again perhaps in response to criticism, and difficulty of translation, he later stresses that eternity means 'power over time' (Moltmann 2002: 259). This is much more helpful and in line with the model which I will develop later. Redemption of the future from the power of history can still be seen in this model. Space-time limits our possibilities, immersing us in a complex network of causality and openness. The effect of sin is further to limit those possibilities, closing us off from God's alternatives. The liberation from these limits demonstrated in the resurrection allows us to value space-time without being controlled by it. In fact, Volf echoes this importance of the interaction of sin with the limits of space-time when he argues in response to Moltmann that redemption is crucial because sin is a more fundamental obstacle to the creation of a new world than transience (Volf 1999: 251).

3.2.6 *Moltmann and the end of the Universe*

Moltmann's eschatology has much to say to the scientific pessimism described in the previous chapter. In response to the despair at the futility scenarios of the end of the Universe, Moltmann reminds the theologian of the importance of hope. It is this hope that gives new significance to the present. Such hope leads to action to care for the environment. In the other scenarios of despair, hope may be more about confidence in the promises of God rather than direct action.

Further Moltmann's stress on the importance of God transforming the creation is helpful in resisting two other approaches. The approach that sees God simply allowing the creation to progress to some kind of Utopia through evolution and human technology is denied by the future of the physical Universe. The opposite approach which sees eschatology having no link at all to this Universe, denies the value of the Universe as creation. Transformation gives a model where both continuity and discontinuity between creation and new creation can be held together.

Finally, Moltmann goes some way in showing the importance of non-anthropocentric eschatology. It does not go beyond political and ecological concerns but at least it is in the right direction. Eschatology must go beyond personal salvation and embrace the whole cosmos as creation. Moltmann's inability to do this is partly due to his political and ecological concerns, which in many ways are welcome. However, it is also due to his inability to take science seriously. Moltmann is aware of the problem, suggesting that 'without cosmology, eschatology must inevitably turn into a gnostic myth of redemption, as modern existentialism shows' (Moltmann 1996: 260). Yet, he fails to follow this through. His review of the interaction of eschatology and cosmology is a six-line mention of Teilhard de Chardin and Whitehead. He then comments:

> 'I do not propose to make the pointless attempt to develop a scientific eschatology, in order to either affirm or confute scientific ideas about the end of the world – the world's death through cold, or its collapse in the cosmic melting crucible – as religious creationism has tried to do with evolutionary theory and the notion of the Big Bang. Earlier ideas about the infinity of the universe are as far removed from theological eschatology as are modern ideas about the end of the universe. What I should like to do, however, is to work out the tangents, or points of access, for the dialogue of scientific theories, and hope that I may be successful where the concept of time and space are concerned.' (Moltmann 1996: 261)

This is unconvincing. There is a difference between a 'scientific' eschatology and holding cosmology and eschatology together. Indeed, not all attempts at dialogue with evolutionary theory and the Big Bang have been 'religious creationism'. I have suggested elsewhere that such dialogue has had important consequences for both science and theology (Wilkinson 1990: 95–116). Such a dialogue concerning the end of the Universe would be also fruitful.

Moltmann fails in establishing a dialogue. Even limiting the questions to time and space he fails to discuss in any detail general relativity (the link between time and space, our perceptions of time and space), quantum theory (reversibility of time, uncertainty in time measurement), chaos theory (irreversible time, openness in the future) and entropy (the arrow of time). Only 3 contemporary books get 'tangential' mentions and the brief paragraph on such issues is unclear and riddled with mistakes (Moltmann 1996: 286). It may show a lack of generosity to criticize a theologian for ignorance about science but if he is going to claim an integrative eschatology these issues cannot be avoided. He continues to bemoan the lack of dialogue on this subject between scientists and theologians (Moltmann, 2002: 259). He pleads for a new 'natural theology' in which scientific findings tell us something about God, and theological insights tell us something about nature (Moltmann 2000: 64–83). In this later work he does briefly touch on the expanding Universe, multiverses, other life on other worlds, and the open universe. Yet he is still unconvincing in clarity, details or references to scientific work. While trying to nuance his view of eternity he still argues for the 'unique return of everything' (Moltmann 2002: 261). Such lack of detailed engagement does not invite the scientists into the dialogue that he so badly wants.

These limitations stop Moltmann's eschatology being truly integrative or universal. Yet the questions he raises are worth further exploration. What is the role of time and space in this creation? Are they imperfections waiting for completion? Will there be time and space in the new creation and what will be their relationship to the time and space of this creation? Is there a way of holding together novelty and growth, with redemption of history and decay? There may be some help in thinking through the relationship of the limits of space-time with the doctrines of sin and redemption, while taking Moltmann's emphasis on the importance of the action of God in the resurrection as the paradigm of the new creation.

The responsibility of hope in the context of the cosmos is to see beyond the despair and futility of the scientific future. The Universe has new significance in light of God's promise about the future. Those who look at the beginning of the Universe find that science raises questions about purpose and design which have natural answers in the incarnation, which reveals the existence and nature of the Creator. Those who look at the end of the Universe find different questions of purpose, but they may also find answers in the resurrection which points forward in hope to the coming of God.

3.3 Pannenberg and the physics of immortality

The other theologian to claim to take these issues seriously is Wolfhart Pannenberg. In his questions to scientists he asked whether the end of the Universe could be reconciled with Christian theology (Pannenberg 1981:

65–77). This is not surprising given the nature of Pannenberg's theological work. He has explored the importance of reason, revelation, history, resurrection, anthropology and eschatology, leading to him being called 'the most comprehensive theologian in the 20th century' (Braaten and Clayton 1988: 9).

His systematic theology can be characterised as 'Reason for Hope' (Grenz 1990), with God's self disclosure, although lying at the end of history, being proleptically present in Jesus. Of particular relevance is Pannenberg's commitment that theology should be in the public arena rather than privatised and therefore the need to relate theology to other disciplines. Thus he wants theology to interact with science. In terms of the future, Pannenberg states that 'all reality is referred to the future and is experienced as eschatologically oriented' (Pannenberg 1971: 2.237). Thus God 'touches every present concretely as its future in the possibilities of its transformation' (Pannenberg 1971: 2.246). Further, Pannenberg wants to make an affirmation of the ontological primacy of the future itself as the actual locus of the fullness of the divine being, with this future not seen as a period of time separated from the present but intertwined or interwoven with the present.

From such a basis we would therefore expect that Pannenberg would be one of the key theologians in examining the implications of the future of the physical Universe for systematic theology. Similar to Moltmann we will be disappointed in such an expectation but we will see that his theological project raises important question for the future of the physical Universe which we will need to address.

3.3.1 Taking science seriously

On a number of occasions, Pannenberg specifically criticizes Barth's decision to refrain from any reference to scientific insights in the doctrine of creation in his preface to *Church Dogmatics* (Pannenberg 1993: 50–71). For Pannenberg, any doctrine of creation must interact with science. Peters likens much of contemporary theology and science as two communities playing with volleyball on either side of the net but not passing it over. He sees Pannenberg as one of the few prepared to play the real game (Pannenberg 1993: 12). Hefner agrees, seeing the strength of Pannenberg's position being that theology becomes a full partner with science in academic discussion (Hefner 1989: 135–151). Santmire suggests that he takes 'into account recent trends within the sciences but also engages those who work within the sciences on their own terms, all in the quest for a viable Christian theology of nature in our time' (Santmire 1996: 88–90).

These are bold claims. Pannenberg himself is quite explicit about the importance of science. Theology must be influenced by the insights of natural science or it will become irrelevant. At the same time, unless God is properly considered, a scientific theory cannot fully comprehend the world it seeks to explain, as it is creation. While seeing theology and science as needing one another, he goes further to think of theology as scientific as it adopts the same method, and deals in part with the same finite reality. He sees theology as the 'science of God' with each theological assertion having the logical structure of a hypothesis, which is subject to verification. Assertions are then tested by their implications. Thus, assertions about God can be tested by their implications for understanding the whole of finite reality, a wholeness that is implicitly anticipated in the ordinary experience of meaning. The idea of God becomes the hypothesis raised by Pannenberg to provide the most adequate explanation for the experience of meaning. Here Pannenberg's emphasis on the future is important. We anticipate the wholeness that will come in the eschatological future. Direct confirmation of the hypothesis is dependent on the actual coming but there is indirect confirmation in the increased intelligibility it offers to our experience of finite reality.

Pannenberg wants to forge a common ground, respecting the specific differences between science and theology yet allowing a dialogue. He attempts to set up such a dialogue in a number of theological questions to scientists.

3.3.2 *Theological questions to scientists*

In his paper 'Theological Questions to Scientists', Pannenberg sets out his starting point:

> 'If the God of the Bible is the creator of the universe, then it is not possible
> to understand fully or even appropriately the processes of nature without
> any reference to that God. If, on the contrary, nature can be appropriately
> understood without reference to the God of the Bible, then that God
> cannot be the creator of the universe'. (Pannenberg 1981: 65)

Pannenberg therefore poses a number of questions from theology to science. It is important to note each of these for they give an insight into both his theological agenda and his view of science:

• *Is it conceivable, in view of the importance of contingency in natural processes, to revise the principal of inertia or at least its interpretation?*

Pannenberg follows Blumenberg who suggested that the introduction of the principle of inertia (that is, the innate potential of persistence for any physical reality) replaced the dependence of the physical reality on God's activity of continuous creation. Pannenberg argues that this deprives God of his role in the conservation of nature. He links inertia with the Universe being self evident and self preserving, and thus wants to revise this concept in line with the Christian doctrine of creation.

• *Is the reality of nature to be understood as contingent, and are natural processes to be understood as irreversible?*

Here Pannenberg wants to raise the question of initial conditions within the scientific description of the Universe. He points out that the laws of physics describe regular patterns within the Universe but do not specify initial conditions.

The laws themselves have to exist in time but do they reflect the historical nature of reality? Pannenberg argues that the biblical reality is historical, and so the laws of physics must be seen in an historical perspective. Note that this does not mean how the laws have arisen in human culture, but the way the laws themselves represent the irreversible flow of time.

- *Is there any equivalent in modern biology of the biblical notion of the divine spirit as the origin of life that transcends the limits of the organism?*

Pannenberg argues that the biblical writings see the work of the spirit as relating specifically to life. Therefore within the evolutionary process and within human anthropology is there any reflection of transcendent reality?

- *Is there any positive relation conceivable of the concept of eternity to the spatio-temporal structure of the physical universe?*

This at core is the fundamental question of how does God relate to the Universe? Pannenberg argues that eternity cannot mean timelessness. The hope for resurrection means that salvation has to connect this creation with that which is to come.

- *Is the Christian affirmation of an immanent end of this world that in some way invades the present somehow reconcilable with scientific extrapolations of the continuing existence of the universe for at least several billions of years ahead?*

Pannenberg calls this question the 'most difficult'. He then goes on to state that it represents:

> 'obvious conflicts between a worldview based on modern science and the Christian faith ... To this question there are no easy solutions ... Perhaps one should, rather, accept a conflict in such an important issue, accept it as a challenge to the human mind to penetrate deeper still into the complexities of human experience and awareness. It does not seem unreasonable to expect that a detailed exploration of the issues involved in the question concerning time and eternity may lead one day to more satisfactory ways including biblical eschatology in an interpretation of the natural world that should take appropriate account of modern science'. (Pannenberg 1981: 76)

However, after noting the difficulty he proceeds no further. In contrast to his work on the other four questions in which he attempts to analyse the key biblical concepts and then offer them as a challenge or insight to the science, he remains silent on this issue. This is somewhat disappointing in the light of his forceful claims on the relationship of science and theology. Pannenberg and other theologians should be encouraged to continue to ask such questions. Pannenberg wants to transform the separation between science and theology into common dialogue, but two problems remain. The first is will any scientists listen to his questions and think it worth pursuing them? The second is whether Pannenberg's view of science is authentic enough to allow a dialogue to take place? To explore the nature of these problems, we need to redirect some questions back to Pannenberg.

3.3.3 Is the future deterministic in nature?

If God is the 'power of the future' then what is the nature of that power? Some have argued that this means that God is a God of total determinism, a 'kind of Calvinism set into temporal reverse gear' (Gilkey 1973: 53).

This has led Pannenberg into a number of dialogues with process theologians. He argues that 'the power of the future should not only create possibilities, but actualities as well ... [establishing] the complete dependence of everything real upon God' (Pannenberg and Ford 1977: 319–320). Polk has argued that Pannenberg's position needs to be seen in the light of the power of God as love giving freedom to his creation (Polk 1988: 162). Pannenberg himself does not want to follow the process position of Polk but goes some way to agreeing with him (Pannenberg 1988: 323). However, this does not convince Drees. He points out that Pannenberg moves from consideration of the totality of time to the primacy of the future as making the whole complete. This is in conflict with a physical understanding of time in which completeness would not derive from moving to the future but from a situation where all times were present. Further, Drees sees this as leading to determinism driven from the future (Drees 1997: 242). Others also point out the risk of determinism in Pannenberg's picture. The relationship between God and human beings is directed from the future in such a way as to put into question the possibility of human responsibility for history. This takes away relationship, trust and freedom (Sponheim 1977: 390–394; Stewart 2000: 158).

This risk of determinism is very real. Pannenberg seems stuck with a Newtonian world-view of science, and seems to ignore quantum theory or chaos, which suggest at the very least an undermining of determinism and perhaps an ontological openness to the future. Pannenberg must encompass within God as 'the power of the future' both the reality of the future and its uncertainty in the epistemological and ontological realms. If God is the power of the future, how does God relate to both the predictability and the uncertainty?

3.3.4 An adequate theology of nature?

Pannenberg wants to construct a 'theology of nature'. He prefers this term rather than 'creation' which speaks to many people simply about the beginning rather than God's continued sustaining of the creative process. Within this theologians must 'relate to the natural sciences as they actually exist' (Pannenberg 1988: 21). This is a clear statement of intent but does he come near to it?

Pannenberg continually stresses the importance of contingency in science and sees this as a natural link to theology. He suggests that the Israelite understanding of God was built on a reality characterized primarily by contingency, particularly in the Exodus. Even the regularities in nature observed in the Old Testament, which for us would be a reflection of the laws of physics, 'were conceived as dependent on the contingency of the divine will, not only in view of their origin but also in view of their continuance' (Pannenberg 1970: 36). Thus the world could have been different as its creation is a free act of God. In addition to creation, Pannenberg speaks of God's conservation, that is, creation is sustained by God and characterized by uniform laws and by the course of contingent events. Finally, creation will experience a transformation of evil into good, and this direction can be discerned in the event of the logos incarnate in Jesus and the eschatological Kingdom of God. The incarnation is a signpost pointing to the end.

Pannenberg is right that the laws of science need initial conditions, and is helpful in drawing a parallel with contingency in the biblical literature. He suggests that it is the physical laws which 'get the attention' while the laws themselves only work with the inclusion of initial conditions which are contingent. This resonates with the observation of the contingent nature of the anthropic balances in the physics of the Universe. Hawking's attempt to produce a quantum theory of gravity which would be a 'theory of everything' covering not only the expansion of the Universe but also its initial conditions may sound like a scientific attempt to do away with any contingency. In fact, Ward raises this issue as something that Pannenberg needs to interact with (Ward 1995: 343). Pannenberg seems ignorant of Hawking's work. However, as I have suggested elsewhere, even in Hawking's picture there are contingent elements such as the nature of quantum theory and the value of the physical constants (Wilkinson 2001). Pannenberg's emphasis on contingency is still valid and so he rightly sees that contingency is an important area of dialogue.

However, these insights are undermined by Pannenberg's limited understanding and confused handling of contemporary science. This may be excused for some theologians, but for Pannenberg has to be seen in the light of his insistence that science is so important. Russell pointed out that Pannenberg's theology of nature could have been supported by quoting the 2nd law of thermodynamics for the irreversibility of time and the anthropic principle for contingent conditions (Russell 1988: 23–43). Yet Pannenberg makes no specific reference to either. The 2nd law of thermodynamics was famously the illustration used by C. P. Snow to attack the 'two cultures' approach between science and the arts. He despaired of highly educated people who could not describe such a basic law of physics. Pannenberg fails this basic test.

As we have seen the anthropic principle points to the law and circumstance of the Universe being finely balanced to make possible life. It points to the contingency of the Universe in terms of its initial conditions. First noted in 1976 by Brandon Carter, it received a full and international exposure in 1986 in the best-selling The Anthropic Cosmological Principle (Barrow and Tipler 1986). Pannenberg's theology of nature paper written in 1988 makes no reference to the anthropic principle. Furthermore, his most recent example of science is the General Theory of Relativity of some seventy years earlier, and his most recent quote of a scientist is from 1974. In fact Pannenberg's actual engagement with cosmology undermines totally his claim that 'our task as theologians is to relate to the natural sciences as they actually exist'. In his only discussion of the Big Bang, he primarily relies on a book published in 1949 (von Weizsäcker 1949) which leads him to a confused view of the General Theory of Relativity, undue importance being given to 'Bondi's steady state model' (which was actually Hoyle, Gold and Bondi's model and by 1970 had severe problems) and complete ignorance of two of the most important developments of the 1960s which were singularity theorems and the microwave background radiation (Pannenberg 1970: 43).

As with the earlier criticism of Moltmann, some may think that such criticism is too strong. Indeed in later papers, Pannenberg responds to the criticism of Russell and others by engaging more with the anthropic principle and the arrow of time, although not in a fully convincing way. However, it is an important criticism in that it undermines Pannenberg's comprehensive claims for his theology and his attempt to dialogue with scientists. If theology is going to make a meaningful engagement with the scientific view of the origin or end of the Universe, it must relate to the natural sciences as they actually exist. As we have seen in Moltmann and other theologians, an eschatology divorced from such engagement does not do justice to the Christian doctrine of Creator and creation. Pannenberg unfortunately does not fulfil his own ambitions.

Pannenberg is more convincing on more general matters. His argument that metaphysical conceptions guide the development of science has much evidence for it and is a useful reminder of the interplay of science and theology. He sees science as a 'provisional version' (Pannenberg 1985: 20) of a description of the world, incomplete without interpretation. Eaves has challenged Pannenberg that science does not present provisional versions, but Pannenberg is surely right in seeing the need of a fuller description which includes both science and theology (Eaves 1989: 185–215).

3.3.5 How can we conceive of the Spirit being active in the natural world?

Pannenberg believes that science can help to shape our theological thinking. He suggests that the work of the Spirit can be described in terms of the force of a field, as an immaterial force causes physical changes. This is a bold suggestion which has serious implications for providence.

He argues that it is not a new idea. Newton saw gravitation as an expression of the immaterial activity of God (Jammer 1957; Koyré 1957: 163–164). This is correct although it must be added that Newton also saw God as intervening to move the planets back into their orbits. Pannenberg further suggests that Faraday saw body and mass as a concentration of force at particular points of the field. He quotes Berkson to argue that Faraday intended the concept of field to function not only as a correlate with physical bodies, but also as a final explanation of bodily phenomenon (Berkson 1974: 52). This reading of Faraday that exalts field over body, is pressing the point too far. Faraday saw both of equal importance.

However, Pannenberg sees the advantage of a field concept as giving priority to the whole over parts. Following Jammer he argues that the field concept in modern physics came from the Stoic doctrine of divine pneuma giving cohesiveness to the Universe (Jammer 1971–84: 2.923). This had an important impact on patristic theology of the divine spirit especially in creation. Pannenberg resurrects this idea to speak of the dynamic presence of the Spirit exerting force within the Universe rather like the gravitational field exerts force on planetary bodies.

Wicken attacks Pannenberg on the grounds that the field concept physicalizes the concept of God and that Pannenberg has reshaped the field concept completely out of its original context (Wicken 1988: 45–55). Some generalized physical theory may serve as meaningful metaphor for God's cosmic presence but we may need to be careful in pushing it too far. Pannenberg replies that the Spirit in the biblical tradition is not mind but force, comparable to the wind. He defends reshaping on the basis that it is deliberate and done in continuity with its conceptual history. That is, the concept of field emerged as a development of the Stoic doctrine of pneuma (spirit), which was related to the early Greek idea of pneuma as moved air, an idea which is rather close to the ancient Hebrew term for spirit (ruah). He also suggests that such a field concept 'sheds new light on current scientific problems' and mentions quantum theory and non-equilibrium thermodynamics. However, what does this mean? He does not go on to spell it out in any detail. The closest he gets is to say that the 'priority of future over present and past might create new possibilities of interpretation' (Pannenberg 1989: 256). Pannenberg may be referring to Wheeler's interpretation of quantum theory, which suggests that the world is brought into being by an observer, but it is not clear how these things are linked.

Pannenberg certainly believes that the field concept is helpful for theological reasons. In his view, it gives a better understanding for the idea of God as Spirit, breaking the association of spirit with mind and intellect from Origen onwards, avoiding excessive anthropomorphism in the conception of divine reality and reflecting the biblical view as the Spirit as breath or wind. Further, 'the finite realities of physical fields can be imagined as constituted by the presence of the divine spirit, as forms of its creative manifestations' (Pannenberg 1989: 258). Finally Pannenberg extends a similar concept to biology, suggesting that we appropriate the language of self organizing systems (exploiting the thermodynamic flow of energy degradation) for interpreting organic life as a creation of the Spirit of God.

This may sound quite attractive but has a number of problems. The model of a field has to be qualified in so many different ways that you wonder whether in the end there is any point using it at all. For example, the field description in physics has an energy density associated with it. What does this mean for God? Wicken's point of physicalizing God has some force to it. Further, if a field has a low energy density and gradual variation then the particle associated with it would be inconceivably lightweight and large, the size of a supercluster of galaxies. Again what does that mean for God? The field concept cannot be divorced from its corresponding particle description. Finally, a field can vary in strength from place to place. The problem with this is how the Spirit of God is affected by a Universe destined to expand for ever, where other universal fields decreases in strength in the future. This is not an appealing view for Christian eschatology! Pannenberg's problem is that he wants to push the field analogy for the work of the Spirit too far. It becomes at times more than an analogy, even to the extent of a physical description. The analogy itself however may have some useful insights and we will return to this later.

3.3.6 *Pannenberg's dialogue with Tipler*

Therefore there are a number of difficult questions for Pannenberg's desire to open up an authentic dialogue between scientists and theologians. However such a dialogue has been attempted with Tipler and acts as an interesting picture of specific engagement between science and theology on the future of the Universe.

Tipler responds to Pannenberg's fifth question to scientists first in an article given at a seminar on Pannenberg and then at greater length in a popular science book (Tipler 1989: 217–253; Tipler 1994: xiii). He speculates that the Omega Point theory is a model for an omnipresent, omniscient, evolving personal God, transcendent and immanent. He believes that it gives a physical foundation for Pannenberg's interpretation of eschatology, that is, how the future makes an imprint on the present. This is because the Omega Point itself brings the Universe into existence.

Pannenberg gives an enthusiastic response with some qualifications (Pannenberg 1989: 255–271; Pannenburg 1995: 309–14). He welcomes Tipler's scientific search, as on the basis of critical realism, they are exploring the same truth. Pannenberg does find coherence between the Big Bang and doctrine of creation and sees this as supporting rather than contradicting the theological assertion that the world was created. While McMullin finds Pannenberg's proposal for scientific and theological cosmology too strong (McMullin 1981: 50–52), Pannenberg finds in Tipler even greater support for Christian eschatology. He suggests that Christian affirmations from biblical exegesis, and thinking about God's relationship with the world begin to make sense in a new way in the perspective of Tipler's argument. This, he argues, gives confidence concerning the truth claims of traditional eschatological affirmations. Pannenberg is attracted by Tipler's speculations because of the role of the future. This mirrors Pannenberg's eschatological perspective, although he questions what it means to say that the Omega Point creates the Universe. Nevertheless, only in the eschaton is God fully known so Pannenberg agrees with Tipler that God is known in the future. Further, omnipotence can retrieve life and so the resurrection of the dead is possible.

However, Pannenberg raises a number of questions against Tipler's position. First, he does not agree with the necessity of the continuous existence of life in the Universe, which is stated by the strong and final anthropic principles. Pannenberg wants to keep the existence of life contingent in order to emphasise that both creation and new creation are the work of God. Second, Pannenberg notes the close link between humans and the rest of creation implied by the anthropic principles, but wants to focus the future in one human life, that is Jesus. Christian theology sees realized in him the intended destiny of the human creature (and thus the destiny of all created existence) in relation to God. Therefore, rather than continued existence being in vast universal computer systems, Pannenberg asks whether Tipler's model can be focused in just one person, Jesus? The resurrection demonstrates that Jesus has ongoing life and he is Lord of the future. So the Omega Point has already happened in the resurrection of Jesus rather than at the end of the Universe. Third, Pannenberg is doubtful whether Tipler's model can fully incorporate the Christian view of the eschatological overcoming of evil. Fourth, Pannenberg questions Tipler's use of the many universes interpretation of quantum theory, which would deny the contingency of this Universe. Finally, Pannenberg sees that Tipler's position cannot be classed as Christian because he is not convinced by the resurrection of Jesus.

This is an interesting dialogue illustrating a number of issues in eschatology and the future of the physical Universe. Pannenberg is to be commended for both stimulating and participating in the dialogue. However, his welcome of Tipler's model is too enthusiastic. As we saw in Chapter 2, Tipler's speculations are dependent on the Universe being closed and on a large number of other dubious assumptions. Pannenberg rightly wants to avoid the question of whether consciousness can be so easily transferred to digital computers by seeing Jesus as the continuance of existence. Yet this in itself raises difficult questions. Surely the biblical imagery of being 'in Christ' is very different to seeing the whole consciousness of humanity swallowed up in Christ. Where is the dynamic of relationship in this?

Pannenberg does not take seriously the other scientific and philosophical problems with Tipler's position. By welcoming Tipler's speculation as giving confidence to Christian affirmations about the future, he buys into all of this. His five qualifications then try to get him out of the situation but one wonders whether it is worth it in the first place. Leaving Tipler aside, Pannenberg could make the case of God's sovereign action in creation and new creation, the significance of the resurrection of Jesus and the tension between creation and new creation as a way to address the problem of evil as all important elements in responding to the future of the physical Universe.

3.3.7 The present status of Pannenberg's end of the Universe

Despite his comprehensive claims Pannenberg falls short of a rigorous engagement with both the history of science and contemporary cosmology. Further, he has difficulties in his key concepts of the Spirit as a force field and in determinism with respect to the power of the future. It is these limitations that marginalize Pannenberg in relation to the dialogue of science and the Christian faith. If Pannenberg is posing questions to scientists concerning the end of the Universe, then his understanding of science is not authentic enough to allow an extensive dialogue to take place. It is important to note, as we shall see in the next section, that the few scientist/theologians such as Polkinghorne and Russell, who have recently written on the end of the Universe have very little interaction with Pannenberg.

Pannenberg's theological agenda is bold and comprehensive. In such an agenda, criticism is easy. In fact Pannenberg has attracted much criticism in terms of the exclusion of reciprocity and mutual transformation in his theory of knowledge (Stewart 2000: 158), his blindness to his own context and subjectivity in stressing universality and objectivity (Placher 1992: 195; Walsh 1992: 306; Schüssler Fiorenza 1993: 239; Molnar 1995: 330), over reliance on rationalism (Grenz 1991: 272–85), lack of interaction with liberation theologians and feminist critiques (Fackre 1993: 304–6) and not taking postmodernism more seriously (LeRon Shults 1999). In addition, we have suggested that in terms of Peters' analogy, Pannenberg has wanted to pass the volleyball over the net of science and theology but sometimes his aim has been way off target. However, the attempt has much to commend it and some important lessons emerge for systematic work on the future of the Universe.

First, Pannenberg stresses the importance of the future for any doctrine of creation. As Haught comments:

'A biblically inspired vision of the future provides a suitable framework for both evolutionary science and the religious quest for meaning. The original source of all values does not reside primarily in the past, nor in the vertical timelessness of an eternal present, but in the rich realm of possibilities that we refer to faintly as future'. (Haught 1999: 220)

The beginning and the end must be held together.

Second, Pannenberg stresses the importance of science, and indeed the risk of bringing science into engagement with theology. Any natural theology or theology of nature runs this risk, and any attempt to bring systematic theology into real dialogue with the scientific picture of the end of the Universe may be both fruitful and frustrating.

Third, Pannenberg shows the importance of holding together continuity and discontinuity in thinking about the relationship of creation and new creation. His view of the resurrection of the dead is interesting:

'It is our present life as God sees it from his eternal present. Therefore, it will be completely different from the way we now experience it. Yet nothing happens in the resurrection of the dead except that which already constitutes eternal depth of time now and which is already present for God's eyes – for his creative view!' (Pannenberg 1970: 80)

This view has been criticized by Hick on the basis that there is no further development of character beyond death (Hick 1976: 225). In reply, Pannenberg argues that time and eternity must have some positive relationship (Pannenberg 1984: 119–39) at this positive relationship can be seen in the tension between continuity and discontinuity. Ward picks up on a tension within Pannenberg's theology, asking whether the eschatological fulfilment is beyond space-time. If this is the case then what is the relation of space-time to it, and how can there really be, as the final state of the Universe, a 'transfiguring presence of the eternal in the temporal'? (Ward 1995: 343) I suggest that this can be held together by seeing the new creation having time but not under the constraints of time. In order to encompass this Pannenberg needs to integrate new creation more fully into his scheme of God as the power of the future. Indeed this is one of the major failings of his scheme. The future is given perhaps too much power but its nature is not fully explored.

Finally, as might be expected from even a cursory reading of Pannenberg, we are left with the importance of resurrection. For Pannenberg the resurrection is the prolepsis of the eschatological revelation of the meaning of universal history. In bringing science and eschatology into real engagement we are beginning to see that the resurrection is key.

So, perhaps Pannenberg's supporters are too optimistic that Pannenberg shows that theology has something to contribute to science that will otherwise be wanting. Part of the reason for this is Pannenberg's limited experience of science. He demonstrates this limitation in specific knowledge of science and in terms of his feel for the scientific process. With the notable exception of Tipler he has therefore been limited in inviting many scientists to engage with him in dialogue.

3.4 The scientist-theologians

A significant part of the dialogue between science and theology has been the work of those of those who have been trained as professional scientists and have moved to theological work (Polkinghorne 1996b). One would expect that at least among these scientist theologians there would be a significant engagement with the issue of the end of the Universe. However, the engagement is mixed among the leading names in the field.

Barbour and Haught have very little to say about the end of the Universe (Barbour 2000: 113; Haught 1995). This is interesting not least because of their sympathy for process theology. One might expect that the predicted end of futility would pose major questions for process theology, and we will explore this in Chapter 8.

Peacocke is explicit in his view that such eschatological questions should be given little time:

'All speculation on detailed scenarios of this consummation, the theological exercise called "eschatology", surely constitutes a supreme example of attempting to formulate a theory underdetermined by the facts. As such, it seems to me a fruitless and unnecessary exercise'. (Peacocke 2001: 48)

It is interesting that he uses the same phrase 'underdetermined by the facts' concerning cosmological claims of the origin of the Universe. While Peacocke is judicious in assessing biological models, his view of both cosmology and eschatology is less than satisfactory. We get a clue as to why in his view there are few facts when he states:

'What is the cash value of talk about "a new heaven and a new earth"? The only propounded basis for this seems to me to be the imaginings of one late-first-century writer (in Revelation) and the belief that the material of Jesus' physical body was transformed to leave the empty tomb. I have already indicated that the latter is at least debatable and the former can scarcely be evidence. So what is left is belief in the character of God as love and that God has taken at least one human being who was fully open to the divine presence into the divine life – the resurrection and ascension of Jesus. Is not all the rest of Christian eschatology but empty speculation?' (Peacocke 2001: 135)

Peacocke severely underestimates the resources on offer. His dismissal of eschatology in relationship to the physical Universe can be traced to his lack of emphasis on a physical resurrection, a devaluing of biblical revelation as a possibility and therefore a lack of detailed engagement with the biblical accounts.

In its place Peacocke at times comes close to Teilhard de Chardin in seeing the evolutionary process continuing to some sort of fulfilment in the Universe. In Peacocke's words 'we appear to be rising beasts rather than fallen angels' (Peacocke 1998: 18). While not going as far as some climatic Omega point he does share a picture of unfolding fulfilment within the present process. Gunton notes the great appeal in such 'optimistic, immanentist, progressive eschatologies' but points that they have little to do with the cross, sin or evil. He comments:

'the dynamic of evolution is not coterminous with the dynamic of the Spirit ... a theological account of creation must say it has a destiny other than a continuing, if finite, progression to entropy and increasing complexity'. (Gunton 1991: 163)

Here is one of Peacocke's main weaknesses in relation to Christian theology.

Does Peacocke mock eschatology because he is a biologist with little interest in the far future Universe? This may be part of the problem but others who have written widely in the area of physics also lack a positive interaction with the end of the Universe. Ellis, a distinguished cosmologist and fierce critic of Tipler, nevertheless argues for continuity as a source of hope based on the Platonic nature of physical laws, human knowledge and forms with very little working out of what that means (Ellis 2002: 316–351).

On the other hand there are a few scientist theologians who have begun to take seriously the end of the Universe. In particular, Sir John Polkinghorne has touched on it in earlier works but has given a fuller treatment in three recent works (Polkinghorne 2002a: 43–55; Polkinghorne 2002b: xix; Polkinghorne and Welker 2000). We shall need to interact with Polkinghorne throughout the following discussion but it will be helpful to give a broad outline of his argument here. It is interesting that Polkinghorne makes no mention of the evidence of an accelerating Universe, even though all the above works were written after the evidence was published. He uses the two possibilities of either an ever-expanding Universe or a Universe of a Big Crunch. Nevertheless he takes seriously the pessimism of the picture which science presents. Implicitly in most of his work he parallels the futility of the end of the Universe and the futility of the end of human life in death.

The hope that he sees in the face of futility is that of the resurrection of Jesus. Using 1 Corinthians 15 he sees the resurrection of Jesus as the first fruits of not only our own resurrection but also the new creation. Throughout his work he does not explore the biblical passages in any great depth. He also takes from the resurrection that the relation between this creation and the next will be one characterized by continuity and discontinuity. He then begins to explore the nature of the continuity and discontinuity. In terms of human life he suggests that continuity is in terms of human identity. While rejecting dualism, he sees our information-bearing pattern being re-embodied in God raising us up. In this he wants to re-use the concept of the soul in the way that Aristotle and Aquinas spoke of the 'form of the body'. We will need to ask whether this is necessary. In exploring discontinuity, he raises the question of the future of matter and the future of time. He sees the empty tomb as important as it speaks for a 'destiny for matter'. That matter will be in a different form but he does not develop this. In terms of time, he sees time as inherent to both human beings and God's work as God works through process in his world. This means that the new creation will have some temporality to it. He defends a process of purgation for the cleansing and healing of human beings.

In this picture he is able to ask what the point of this creation is. He sees the old creation as a place of freedom and growth for human beings as God creates with kenotic self-emptying. However, the new creation will be a place where creation is drawn into the life of God. In this way the new creation will be totally sacramental. Underlying the whole of this is the faithfulness of God.

Following on from Polkinghorne's work, Russell explores the resurrection in the general area of science and religion and its implications for the end of the Universe in particular (Russell 2002a: 3–30). He begins with the suggestion that:

'If the predictions of contemporary scientific cosmology come to pass ("freeze" or "fry") then it would seem the universe will never be transformed into the new creation.' (Russell 2002b: 267)

He also seems unaware of the new cosmological discoveries. Nevertheless he wants to approach the problem of the futility of the future of the Universe hypothetically, in what he calls in various places a 'worst case scenario' or the 'hardest case'. By this he means an emphasis that God will act to transform the Universe radically, with the resurrection understood to have physical implications.

He claims to use Polkinghorne as a point of departure, although it must be said that there is little difference in the journey. He is concerned with giving a rigorous framework for the relationships of science and religion, which unfortunately often obscures his valuable insights. He shares with Polkinghorne the significance of relationality and holism, the concept of information of a 'pattern-forming kind', and a dynamic view of reality as 'open becoming'. He wants then to push further in a more formal way that theological research programs can play a fruitful role in suggesting new directions to scientists for their research. This reflects a similarity to Pannenberg's questions to scientists. He sees theology as a source of inspiration in the construction of new scientific theories and of help in selection rules to choose between theories that explain the available data.

We can be reasonably positive in all of this. It may be that in trying to over formalise the relationship of theology and science, Russell underestimates the complexity of a more organic relationship. It can no doubt be argued that theology has been a source of inspiration in the construction of new scientific theories, but it often works in a general sense or within a complex pattern of influence which includes the personality of individual scientists, dynamics within the scientific community, and indeed the culture in general. It may be more helpful to see theology more in a questioning role alongside any of its positive contributions. In addition, if theology can play a fruitful role for scientists, then scientists have to be convinced by the value of the dialogue. As we have seen with Pannenberg, this is far from easy.

In fact, Russell adopts this questioning mode when he questions 'nomological universality', that is, will the same laws that govern the past and present govern the future? If the resurrection is a radically new kind of action by God, does this give theology the mandate to raise such a question? It is an interesting line of speculation. While we agree with the view that the scientific laws are descriptive rather than prescriptive, we need to be a little careful at this stage. It depends on what is meant by 'the laws of physics'. They can mean the laws in an ontological sense, or the laws in an epistemological sense. For example, our present laws of physics give us two successful theories, general relativity and quantum theory, which at present cannot be fully reconciled. The hope is for a quantum theory of gravity to do just that. Thus, what we often call the 'laws of physics' simply represents our best models and theories at the moment. However, critical realism assumes a deeper reality to which our present descriptions exhibit verisimilitude. Of course there is then debate over whether there exist laws in the Platonic sense apart from God, or whether the laws are better described as God's faithful relationship with and within creation.

If Russell is asking whether the laws of physics will be different in an ontological sense in new creation then there are obvious problems for the Christian theologian. Is God's faithful relationship different in new creation? In addition, how can we talk of continuity or transformation in the physical Universe if the very laws of physics are different? If the laws of physics are completely different does this suggest a picture of God's starting again in another creation ex nihilo? Or does Russell mean that our present understanding of the laws of physics do not encompass the full picture in terms of a new creation? The resurrection of course holds central place in this discussion, and while recognising its importance he does not fully work it through. Do we see new laws in the resurrection? In all of this he is a little unclear and inconsistent; claiming later that some laws may not change. The obvious question is how theology inspires us to know which ones might change and which ones might not. At times he seems to be introducing this suggestion in order to avoid his fear that the present scientific picture rules out new creation.

In spite of these weaknesses, Russell is to be commended for beginning to think about how this might work out in reference to specific insights into the Universe and its future. He suggests that God has already given the Universe precisely those conditions and characteristics that it needs to be transformed, in terms of 'elements of continuity' and 'elements of discontinuity'. In his view science can help sort out what is truly essential to creation, and these elements of continuity he sees as temporality, ontological openness and mathematics. While our initial sympathy will be towards this position, we must ask why these are the elements of continuity and what might be the elements of discontinuity? It is simply not enough to ask for science to decide. Science must be brought into dialogue with systematic theology, which Russell rarely does. In particular, he hints at continuity and discontinuity in terms of resurrection, kingdom and 1 Corinthians 15, but fails in any detailed engagement with such themes.

3.5 What does the theological future hold?

With the exception of Polkinghorne and Russell, theological work on the future of the Universe is quite disappointing. While Moltmann and Pannenberg have opened up themes of new creation and in particular the importance of the resurrection, they have shown virtually no engagement with contemporary cosmology and little engagement specifically with the biblical material which has traditionally been at the heart of Christian eschatology. This means that their bold ambitions for an all encompassing and non anthropocentric eschatology are severely limited.

Polkinghorne and Russell share the importance of the resurrection, but they also show a limited engagement both with the very recent cosmological discoveries and with the specific scriptural passages and the systematic tradition in general. In fairness, they are ready to acknowledge this, speaking of the need for further work and the 'long term undertaking' of taking questions of eschatology and resurrection forward. Polkinghorne in particular has laid effective foundations to enable further work to be done. He points forward to the need for an exploration of both matter and time in creation and new creation. He also raises questions about the soul and the nature of God's relationship with new creation that will need more careful examination. Following his lead, Russell stresses the significance of relationality, the concept of information of a pattern-forming kind, and a dynamic view of reality as open becoming. Each of these issues raises profound theological implications, which the community of systematic theologians need to take seriously.

In the light of this, our agenda is clear. We need to explore the biblical literature in detail especially in terms the images of new creation and resurrection. Do they speak to some of these issues in ways that are both fruitful and as yet unexplored? We will attempt to do this in Chapters 4 and 5. Then we need to look at the nature of time and matter in the new creation as a key way of relating eschatology to the physical Universe. This will enable a more detailed exploration of the speculations raised by Polkinghorne and Russell. This will be presented in Chapters 6 and 7. Finally, in Chapter 8 we will begin to open up some of the implications not just for eschatology and the physical Universe, but how the insights we have developed might apply to the future of the non-human biological creation, the doctrine of providence, and the role of hope in stewardship, ethics and apologetics.

Chapter 4

Cosmological Hope in the Eschatologies of the Bible

In eschatology, the systematic theologian will be looking for internal and external coherence of the Christian tradition (Hart 1995: 103). In terms of internal coherence, the theologian must engage with the themes and images of hope contained in the Christian story, asking how they can be translated into the contemporary context of the community of faith. In terms of external coherence, this particular Christian story must be brought into engagement with the wider field of human knowledge, and to explore how they might question each other. Many theologians have looked for external coherence in eschatology in relation to economic and environmental issues, but few have explored the future of the physical Universe.

If the nature of both science and theology is best seen in terms of critical realism, then this gives the basis for pursuing external coherence as both science and theology share a commitment to truth and an exploration of a common reality, a Universe which is created by God. Of course, this dialogue of science and theology occurs in a whole variety of ways. However, we noticed in the theme of cosmic salvation in the theology of John Wesley an interesting approach. He brought the biblical texts into conversation with the insights of science. While our understanding of the biblical texts and indeed the world of science is now very different, might this still be a way of exploring issues of the end of the Universe for systematic theology?

In this chapter we will therefore focus on such an engagement with biblical texts. We might defend this for a number of reasons. First, we need to examine the use of the biblical texts by those who have explored the theological issues concerning the future of the physical Universe. For the authors of the *Left Behind* series and others who share a fundamentalist reading of scripture, do the biblical texts actually say what they want them to say? Or are there more insights from the texts that would be helpful in our dialogue than someone such as Peacocke is willing to acknowledge? Is the use of scripture in the systematic structures built by Moltmann, Pannenberg and Polkinghorne as secure as they think it is? Second, across the broad sweep of Christian theology, scripture functions authoritatively in the church. For all Christian traditions they are the foundation of Christian theological reflection and for some traditions they are supreme authorities of revelation of the nature and purposes of God. This is especially the case for the evangelical wing of the church which has explored the biblical texts in eschatology in a number of different forms, from the popular novels to major controversies surrounding body/soul duality, millenniarism and soteriology. Third, in the history of the dialogue between science and theology, it has been our experience that such a dialogue has helped in the task of a better interpretation of the biblical texts. Whether Galileo's emphasis on the importance of observation, Darwin's account of the evolution of the natural world, or Hawking's model of the origin of the Universe, scientific insights have provoked the Christian community to re-examine the scriptures and ask questions of interpretation. Can the scientific insights of the end of the Universe help us in our interpretation of eschatological passages?

Systematic theology of course is dependent upon biblical scholarship although the extent of that dependence is controversial, expanded in the last two centuries by debates concerning the nature of the biblical text. Is meaning (and the subsequent authority that this conveys) to be located in the events of history which the text records, or in the author's intention or in the reader's response or in the text's relationship to the canon of scripture or the overall narrative? (Thiselton 1992; Fowl 1998; Vanhoozer 1998) These questions are heightened in the area of eschatology because its primary texts are difficult to interpret and comprise a wide range of literary types. In addition in terms of the coherence question of systematic theology we find ourselves asking the question of how scripture relates to reality and in particular the insights from science.

While not belittling the importance or the complexity of such questions, I follow Barth in:

> 'theology has ... its position beneath that of the biblical scriptures. While it is aware of all their human and conditioned character, it still knows and considers that the writings with which it deals are holy writings'. (Barth 1963: 32)

Thus good systematic theology has to be based on good biblical exegesis. Yet it is more than that. While we may not share all of Brown's conclusions on the role of continuing revelation through tradition, he is surely right to recognise in the history of the church 'a community of faith in continual process of change as fresh contexts trigger fresh handling of inherited traditions' (Brown 1999: 57). Brown is concerned with how theology handles God's revelation of himself. If the supreme revelation of God in the Christian tradition is Jesus, then the incarnation implies a revelation within the limitations of a specific cultural context. Therefore we are faced with the question of whether that revelation is trapped within one particular epoch. Thus in the area of eschatology, are the scriptures of any use at all in bringing into dialogue with scientific pictures of the future very different to that of first century Palestine? Indeed, if it is argued that Jesus himself expected his own imminent return within the lifetime of the disciples, can we gain anything at all from the scriptures?

While Brown acknowledges that the Bible is an 'indispensable part of that story' (Brown 1999: 1), he argues that God takes our historical situatedness seriously and therefore revelation continues beyond scripture in the tradition of the church. Alternatively those from a more evangelical view of the text might argue that within the scriptures themselves you can see God at work in a process of revelation which involves event, meaning, application and hermeneutical community. Hart states that 'its very nature reminds us that the message to which it bears witness must be rearticulated (and hence reinterpreted) in every age afresh' (Hart 1995: 160). He helpfully characterises the Bible as understood in the Christian tradition as 'sermon in narrative form', recognising God has acted in history, but that the scriptures combine events and interpretation within a framework of the overarching interpretation of history as the theatre of God's creative and redemptive acts. In this way, the Christian theologian can stand under the text in the sense it is an objective given, but its meaning is to be found in the interaction between the world of the reader and the world of the text. This has similarities to the critical realist view of science, for the event of interpretation must be repeated, as its results are only provisional.

This reflects the characteristic practice of Methodist theological reflection which has held together the Bible with experience, reason and tradition as the focus of God's revelation in the so-called Wesleyan quadrilateral (Gunter et. al. 1997: 174). There remains much debate in terms of the interaction of this quadrilateral and its history, in particular the part played by scripture. Nevertheless it opens the way for a fruitful dialogue with other sources of truth such as science, while maintaining the central importance of the scriptures. On this basis there has been a significant contribution by Methodist scholars to the science/religion field, in particular the area of psychology, perhaps due to the emphasis on religious experience. However there has also been an increasing contribution in the biological and physical sciences (Coulson 1953, 1955; Green 2004).

I come to systematic theology with this Methodist perspective to participate in the 'roundtable discussion' with the biblical voices and other contemporary and historical perspectives (Turner 2000: 58). This naturally intensifies certain theological emphases and also has the danger of being too selective. Nevertheless if I recognise that it is one voice in the wider discussion then it has much to contribute (Thiselton 1992: 237–47; Wall 1995: 50–67). I offer it as a contrast to the more Reformed voices of Russell, Moltmann, Pannenberg and the Anglican voice of Polkinghorne.

In contrast to those who place a strong emphasis on reason and tradition, I want to argue for the rediscovery of the importance of the biblical material in dialogue with our experience of God at work in the world. While valuing the insights of reason and tradition, it seems to me that systematics has too long been held captive by philosophical theology. Systematic theology's philosophical framework means that it has difficulty in doing justice to much of the biblical material. For example, as Goldingay has argued, it is concerned with the unequivocal and presupposes a quest for unity. Thus starting from its Greek framework, traditional systematic theology affirms God's power and knowledge in terms of omnipotence and omnipresence, and then tries integrate these with the biblical narratives. In fact, it could be argued that philosophical theology has acted within the Western context as a filter for systematic theology (see diagram overleaf).

However, the nature of systematic theology needs to be much more dynamic in terms of its conversation with its sources (McGowan 2006: 365). The value of the biblical narratives is that they can question philosophical assumptions and continually critique the non narrative form of systematic theology. The biblical

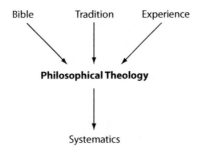

material can drive systematic theology to think more in terms of narrative and to be driven away from its rationalistic base. As Goldingay notes:

> 'Traditional systematic theology's strength is its analytical rigor and its emphasis on the law of noncontradiction, but that is also its limitation. Taking biblical narrative seriously has the capacity to release it from this limitation'. (Goldingay 2000: 131)

Thus concepts such as omniscience, omnipotence, omnipresence and timelessness need to be challenged by stories of answered prayer and God experiencing surprise, frustration, grief or anger. At the same time, systematic theology can address questions to the text (Wright 2000: 207). In particular a Christian approach to the text involves acknowledging its authority, gives us rules for reading the text, attending to scripture as a whole and a dependence on the Holy Spirit (Hart 2000: 183–204).

We have seen already the influence of certain philosophical assumptions in the approach of certain systematic theologians to questions of the end of the physical Universe. The biblical and scientific material can push our understandings beyond the confines of Western common sense, by engaging the imagination as well as the intellect. So we will attempt to bring the Bible and science into dialogue, not to map one onto the other, but to allow the dialogue to both critique current systematic models and to generate insights for new models.

This sort of dialogue between the scriptures and science questions the dominance of philosophical theology in views of eschatology within systematics. Until recent times, biblical exegesis has become disconnected with systematic theology, in part due to the influence of modernity and the separation of the Bible and theology within the academy (Childs 1992: xvi; O'Collins and Kendall 1997: 2; Green 2000: 24; McGrath 1990: 81; Hart 2000: 183). This separation was attempted to be addressed in the biblical theology movement but the diversity of the canon and the complicated nature of theology meant that it was impossible to maintain that the sole role of scripture was to provide theology's content. However, now a number of convergent trends are enabling a more fruitful dialogue to take place. There has been a shift of focus to treating the text in itself rather than what is behind it, coupled with a move from historical criticism to methodological pluralism, and a growing interest in relationships between biblical studies and contemporary theology. We hope to extend and model this relationship in what follows.

In diagrammatical form we therefore the see the process more like this (and if space allowed we would also add tradition, reason and experience into the model). As well as generating insights for systematics, there are also mutual conversations going on, for example between the Bible and science.

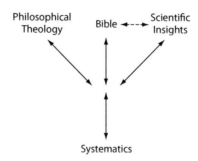

It is with this understanding of the role of scripture that we will proceed. It challenges us to rearticulate and reinterpret the eschatological passages within scripture in dialogue with contemporary scientific insights, attempting to understand the events and interpretation of the text as pointers to and in the light of God's creation and redemption for the whole Universe. It is a position where insights of natural theology can be valued within a framework of revealed theology and revealed theology must be worked out in a theology of nature. Of course this is not the only approach to these questions within systematic theology, but it will be offered as a contribution to the wider discussion. In particular we will not engage a great deal with tradition. This is not to ignore its value, but simply to limit the scope of the discussion.

However, does eschatology bring its own unique difficulties in using the biblical images and stories in this form of dialogue? Calvin of course reminds us that God in scripture accommodates his communication to the abilities of the audience. Yet even with this in mind the gap between images of the Bible and contemporary science seems huge. For example, the history of the interpretation of Revelation shows how badly it has been misunderstood. Yet the challenge remains to recontextualise it for the church and the world (Bauckham 1989: 85–102). While this been attempted in the political sphere, is it possible to do in the sphere of the end of the Universe? While eschatology is generally thought of to refer to a branch of theology concerned with the 'last things', it is not simply predictions about the future. If this was the case then the fundamentalist approach of using biblical narrative to predict future actual events, whether they be the French revolution or the creation of a European superstate, would be relatively easy.

To avoid this trap we need to understand more about biblical eschatology. The distinction between eschatology and 'apocalyptic' argued by Rowland is now widely accepted (Rowland 1982). Apocalyptic is a particular genre, found within sections of Judaism during the period 200 years before and after Christ. It generally has an interest in the last things but is not specifically identified by this interest. It concerns the revelation of heavenly mysteries, sometimes in reference to the last things but also the nature of the cosmos, questions of theodicy and the divine plan of history. Its purpose is often to sustain faith in times of crisis. Within the New Testament canon only the book of Revelation belongs to the tradition of Jewish eschatological apocalypses as a whole. Nevertheless, apocalyptic images are often used to give an assurance of God at work in history and the hope for the achievement of God's purposes in the future. This is focused in the Kingdom preaching, the life, death and resurrection of Jesus. Bauckham comments that it is 'primarily a means of expressing the significance of Jesus for the future destiny of the world' (Bauckham 1988: 428–430).

The error of 'future fundamentalism' is to identify apocalyptic as the only genre that addresses the future. As we look at the various biblical passages, which have been traditionally used in eschatology, we will need to be clear and sensitive about the different genres in both Old Testament and New Testament.

Yet can the biblical passages say anything to the world of an accelerating cosmos? The dialogue is not as easy as some would think. For example, one commentator on 2 Peter 3.10–13 identifies the biblical verses literally with the scientific picture of the end of the Universe:

'The solar system and the great galaxies, even space-time relationships will be abolished ... All elements which make up the physical world will be dissolved by heat and utterly melt away. It is a picture which in an astonishing degree corresponds to what might actually happen according to modern theories of the physical universe'. (Reicke 1983: 138)

This commentator does not seem worried that the writer of 2 Peter would be astonished to be told that 100 billion years would have to pass before these events occur! As well as issues with timescale, a second problem is the degree to which these eschatological images are anthropocentric. Moltmann suggests that 'the images of the future in the eschatology of the Bible all expect that the end of the world will coincide with the end of the human race' (Moltmann 2002: 252). This is an important cautionary word but is not totally convincing, as we shall see when we study the images themselves.

A third problem for some is that when we come to eschatology we enter the realm of narrative and image. McClendon points out that much New Testament teaching on the last things are in 'word pictures' that present visual scenes. These pictures should be understood primarily as life-changing rather than giving us the ability to specify all of the spatial, temporal and causal connections (McClendon Jr. 1994: 75–77). Murphy follows this route and ignores the questions of cosmology and concentrates on human identity (Murphy 2002: 202–218). Again this is an important cautionary word, but it does not mean that the narratives and images are of no use to thinking about the future of the physical creation. They should not be rejected out of hand as Peacocke is prone to do. In attempting to understand the relationship of the present state of the world and a future state of complete fulfilment, we do not need to be reduced to what Oberdorfer calls a kind of 'slim eschatology' which concentrates on the destiny of the individual self without taking into account the Universe itself (Oberdorfer 2002: 166). Fergusson rightly comments:

> 'Faithfulness to the insights of the prophets and apostles demands that we continue to employ their eschatological imagery. This is because their testimony to Jesus is inextricably bound up with hopeful expectation of the future … the eschatological representations of Scripture cannot be abandoned but must be seen as real though imaginative discourse which is analogically related to the content of hope. This side of eternity hope cannot be conceptualized in any other way.' (Fergusson 2000: 5)

Green reinforces the point arguing that images are indispensable as the only vehicles available to our imaginations for expressing a vision of the world to come (Green, G. 2000: 73–88). We will encounter images, symbols and narrative but that is to be welcomed. They may point to new ways of expressing eschatology and help us to understand the limits of what systematic theology is able to say. Of course the apocalyptic images are intended to be taken metaphorically and not literally, but as Schloss comments, 'even in their figurativeness, metaphors are metaphors of something, not nothing' (Schloss 2002: 58). To reflect on these metaphors and images is to reflect on the issues of continuity and discontinuity at the heart of eschatology.

Our approach to these images will recognise their limitations in terms of timescale, cosmology and anthropocentric nature, but we will use them to attempt to tease out more of the sermon in narrative form, as a way into the principles of creation and redemption at the heart of the Christian tradition. We will also acknowledge that there is no one uniform 'eschatological model' within the Bible, but many expressions of eschatological hope related to the context in which it is applied. The question then is whether there are common themes which relate to the work of creation and redemption within these eschatologies?

We would expect some common themes if we make the hermeneutical assumption of the underlying unity of the biblical revelation. This is not to ignore the diversity in different eschatological images in the Bible, but the presumption of the Bible speaking with one voice.

Biblical eschatology ultimately attempts to give an interpretation of the future in the light of the past and present with an invitation to live in the light of that. Following Forsyth, Hart characterises Christian theology as 'faith thinking' (Hart 1995: 1), for it is a reflection by the community of faith to explore, live and proclaim the shape of the truth. We will use the eschatologies in the Bible in order to shape our theological thinking in this way. Therefore this chapter examines a number of passages in the Old Testament and the New Testament, asking the question of whether there is anything to help with systematic questions of eschatology and the physical Universe, beyond these passages simply stating that the final condition of things fully expresses the will of God. In all of this we will need to be open to a better interpretation of the images. While biblical theology has much to offer to models of eschatology and the physical Universe, it is not a one-way process. Gilkey has commented, 'Biblical theology must take cosmology and ontology more seriously ... cosmology does make a difference in hermeneutics' (Gilkey 1961: 203).

Following Wesley we will see the theme of new creation becomes a focal point in the biblical passages and a fruitful place of dialogue with cosmology. However, it is worth dealing with the biblical passages first in their context and diversity.

4.1 'Heaven'

Before moving to particular passages we need to note the background of the concept of heaven, which has become intricately entwined with Christian hope for the future. 'Heaven' is commonly contrasted with earth in terms of the spatial sense of 'the heavens' and also in the metaphysical sense of the realm of gods or spirits or indeed the post death experience. However, in scripture the concept is much more complex.

While the Old Testament lacks 'a single, definitive and comprehensive cosmogony' (Bietenhard 1976: 189), heaven has a cosmological use, becoming part of the cosmic picture of underworld/earth/heaven, which is similar to many ancient oriental ideas. It is the firmament above the Earth (Gen 1.8) and above it there is the heavenly ocean (Ps 148.4–6). Other heavenly spheres are echoed in the phrase 'heaven of heavens' (Deut 10.14; 1 Kings 8.27; Ps 148.4). Heaven is also used in a theological context. It is the embodiment of permanence (Deut 11.21; Ps 89.29), and the host of heaven can mean the stars (Deut 4.19) or supernatural beings (Job 1.6). Under Assyrian influence it became the object of worship against which the prophets protested (2 Kings 21.3). There is a sense that the whole eschatological order of salvation is prefigured and already exists or has happened in heaven so that it precedes the earthly event (Zech 2f). Indeed, the Son of Man is seen as the personification of the eschatological people of God already present in heaven (Dan 7.13f). Central to the Old Testament is the understanding that the Lord created the heavens and the earth, that is, the whole Universe (Gen 1.1; Is 42.5; Ps 33.6). Israel took from the cult of Baal a description of Yahweh as God or king of heaven and earth to express his total sovereignty (Ezek 5.11; Dan 2.18; Deut 4.39).

In late Judaism, contact with the ideas of the ancient East meant a variety of cosmological speculations. Heaven became a place that one could see through a revelation or journey. There was detailed speculation about God's throne and the names, classes and functions of angels. Some believed that everything corresponds to an archetype and all earthly existence and events are prefigured in heaven.

In the New Testament, the primary interest is not a definite geography of heaven as in some Rabbinic writing but theological. However it builds on the Old Testament use. 'Heaven and earth' means the Universe (Mt 5.18, 34f; 11.25; 24.35; Lk 12.56), with an occasional reference to the sea in a tripartite formula (Acts 4.24; 14.15; Rev 14.7). In the world picture, heaven is above, and the stars are set in it so that in some of the eschatological discourses about the Parousia it is the stars which fall to earth (Mk 13.25; Mt 24.29; Lk 21.25; Rev 6.13; 8.10; 9.1; 12.4). God is acknowledged as Creator and Lord of heaven and earth (Acts

4.24; 7.49; 14.25; 17.24; Rev 10.6; 14.7; Mt 5.34; 11.25). He is said to dwell in heaven without there seeming to be any reflection on the difficulties inherent in this situation. Heaven is also a place where treasure and inheritance is kept (Mt 5.12; 2 Cor 5.1f) and where the names of the disciples are recorded (Lk 10.20).

In common Christian spirituality, the hope of deliverance from this world to the 'shadowlands' of heaven, has often ignored the link in the biblical material of the link between heaven and earth and the stronger image of the future in new creation. On the positive side, heaven is a reminder that there is more to God's purpose than just the Earth. Could it be that Moltmann's limited view of eschatology in terms of planet Earth and his view that the biblical images are anthropocentric are due to not taking heaven seriously?

4.2 Isaiah 11.1–9

With a few exceptions (e.g. Is 26.19; Dan 12.2) the Old Testament when speaking about the future generally concentrates on this world in terms of justice, prosperity and the blessing of God. Yet it expresses principles of God's nature and work that are applicable both to the short term and the long term.

This is the case with this passage, which is often quoted as a picture of God's new creation, and follows the devastation of Jerusalem (Is 10.27b–34). However, the prophet then announces that Yahweh will do something new and whatever the circumstances his people are to keep their hope. In contrast to the failure of the Davidic dynasty, a new royal figure will emerge who will bring justice. Verse 6 changes the images to that of a transformed creation. These images portray a radical reordering of the natural world to a world of peace. Their setting is in the custom of a child herding the sheep, goats and calves out in the morning and back at night. Natural enemies are at peace and the image of young children suggests a world without danger. This is a vision of promise for the weak and vulnerable. Brueggemann suggests that verses 6–8 are linked to verses 1–5 by virtue that the distortion of human relationships is at the root of all distortions in creation (Brueggemann 1998: 102). Thus the new scenario for creation is made possible by the reordering of human relationships. However the canvas is wider as the prophet links the Davidic king to Adam. This king becomes the steward of God's creation and cosmic agent of a new peace in creation.

The messianic interpretation of this passage has allowed Christians to see Jesus as the king and the new scenario of peace as a picture of the 'new heaven and earth'. Yet two important questions need to be answered. Can this passage really be applied to a 'new heaven and earth' and second, how does this figurative description relate to the biological and physical world? Brueggemann attempts an answer:

> '... aggression and domination belong to the animal world, and it was ever thus. Therefore this poetic scenario is unreal. However, this poem is about the impossible possibility of the new creation! The coming king will not only do what the world takes to be possible, but will also do what

the world has long since declared to be impossible. ... This poem is about deep, radical, limitless transformation.' (Brueggemann 1998: 103)

Certainly this passage seems to look beyond the mere political dimension. Verse 9 seems to address the whole of creation. In fact the passage is echoed in Isaiah 65 in the context of a new heaven and a new earth. Yet it is imagery based in the concreteness of our experience. Volf comments:

'If the text had not referred to wolves and lambs, to the needy and the wicked, little children and cobras, we would have been tempted to think that it is about a world that has nothing to do with our own. But it is a vision of our world – our world freed from injustice and destruction.' (Volf 1996: 305)

We therefore need to hesitate before reading too much into this passage. The hope is based on the coming king and it is he who is centre stage in the prophet's message. Some may argue that the bloody process of survival of the fittest and animals killing each other for food is a result of the Fall which will in some way be corrected in the new creation. Yet that process seems to be essential for the emergence of animals of higher complexity and human beings. Will God suspend such a creative process in the new creation?

4.3 Isaiah 65.17–25

This passage is important not only in its own right but because of its influence on later Jewish and Christian eschatological thought. It is part of a prophecy into the 5th Century BC, portraying the time of Ezra and Nehemiah and the rebuilding of Jerusalem after the exile. The bright hope portrayed in Isaiah 60 had not yet been fulfilled in terms of stable economy or government. Here the fulfilment of that hope is described, as part of Yahweh dealing with opponents (Is 65.1–16) and confirming his servant in his new city (Is 66.6–24).

The exclamatory 'Behold' (v. 17) indicates a change of mood and pace and introduces a key verse:

'I will create new heavens and a new earth.
The former things will not be remembered, nor will they come to mind'.

The verb 'create' is a rare word in the Old Testament found primarily in Genesis 1–2, a few psalms and Isaiah 40–66. Here in verses 17–18 it is used 3 times. A personal pronoun places the emphasis on Yahweh who calls attention to himself in the process of creating. The God who is Creator of all things is the restorer and redeemer (Watts 1987: 94). Certainly, the word 'create' links the new creation to God's original creative work.

What then is 'new'? It may mean a temporal newness in the sense of something that has never existed before and therefore is unknown in this time. Alternatively it can be used to distinguish what is different from what has already existed. Or it may mean something that is 'fresh, pure, young ... or sharp, polished, bright' (Fürst 1867: 1404; North 1974: 225–44). The word here is contrasted here with 'the first' or 'the former', something that is done in a number of places (Is 42.9; 43.9; 43.18; 46.9; 48.3; 61.4; 65.7; 65.16; 65.17).

Westermann sees these words echatologically in the sense that only after the old present order has gone can a new age be created (Westermann 1969). Yet we need to be careful in not reading later Jewish and Christian interpretations into these verses. Are the 'old order' and 'new age' simply the political and economic situations of the people of Israel and the city of Jerusalem? In addition, are these verses more concerned with God as creator rather than the nature of the new creation? The emphasis on 'new' and 'create' point to continuity with the God who created the present Universe. Yet this God is at work now. In fact the centrality of God as creator gives the 'new creation' a wider canvas than just the socio-political circumstances of Israel.

'New heavens and new earth' here may not be a reference here to the totality of creation. Watts argues that 'new heavens' may represent a new order, divinely instituted in which Persian Empire has Yahweh's sanction and Israel is called to be a worshipping and pilgrim people with Jerusalem as its focus. In addition, he sees 'the earth' as 'the land' suggesting that it is primarily referring to Palestine. The 'new creation' may therefore refer to agricultural fertility or a new political or social reality for Palestine (Wats 1987: 354).

What is the relevance of this for eschatological thinking about the physical Universe? The force of Watts' argument has to be taken seriously. The passage is so based in its historical, political and literary setting that it is difficult to apply it beyond them. However, in its own setting it emphasizes that an understanding of God as Creator has relevance to the future whether it be in the realm of nations or cosmology. Just as the passage sees hope for a new era for Jerusalem and the people based on the sovereign work of the Creator, so we today can apply the understanding of God as Creator to hope in terms of the future of the physical Universe.

The new creation is to be enjoyed with God (v. 18–19) and a contrast to the 'former things' (v. 19b–25):

'The former things'	'The new creation'
Crying, distress	Rejoicing
An infant dying a few days old	A child living to be a hundred
An elderly person dying prematurely	One hundred deemed an early age to die
Build and another live there	Build houses and live in them
Plant for another to eat	Plant vineyards and eat their fruit

The new creation promises security and longevity in contrast to the history of some three centuries past. It paints a picture of an idyllic existence with no violence (v. 25). Does it point to the perfection of nature like that in Garden of Eden? That is pushing it too far. Here is a vision of peace set in the real world of rulers, questions about worship, the return to Palestine after the exile and the building of the temple (66.1–5).

God is not simply restoring the Garden of Eden. His new creation based on his faithfulness as Creator is worked out in the context of political and social reality. In addition, God is able to do something new, that is, he not confined to processes of this world. It is worth emphasizing that the new creation, whether in the short political term or in the longer term, does not involve the abolition and replacement of the old creation. The new creation is described in terms of a renewed and reordered earth. Thus Westermann comments:

'The words, "I create anew the heavens and the earth" do not imply that the heaven and earth are to be destroyed and in their place a new heaven and earth created ... Instead, the world, designated as "heaven and earth" is to be miraculously renewed.' (Westermann 1969: 408)

4.4 1 Thessalonians 4.13–5.11

If heaven as a future escape from the reality of this world has dominated some Christian thinking, the second coming of Jesus with an associated rapture of believers has also directed thinking away from the image of new creation. We have already seen in the prophecies of some US fundamentalists which have become mass market reading, the centrality of 1 Thessalonians 4.13–5.11. In fact this passage has been of central importance throughout US fundamentalism in the 20th Century (Walvoord 1964: 8; Crutchfield 1992: 172–4).

Here Paul presents a view of the future and how that future will arrive. He develops the sense of what happens to those who die before the Lord comes again. The extent to which apocalyptic images are used here is debated (Käsemann 1969: 131; Sanders 1977: 543), but what is clear in verse 14 is that the resurrection of Jesus will be the model for that which is to come in the future. Indeed as Morris argues the centre of Paul's gospel lies in his apocalyptic interpretation of the Christ event (Morris 1982: 88). The concentration of Paul is on the incarnation and resurrection as interpreting the future.

Wright uses this passage to suggest that, 'Resurrection is something new, something the dead do not presently enjoy; it will be life after "life after death"' (Wright 2003: 215). For Wright, early Christians held to a two-step belief concerning the future: first, death and a 'blissful garden of rest'; second, a new bodily existence in a newly remade world (Wright 2007: 53). We will return to such a characterisation of resurrection in the next chapter, but it is important to note in passing that this is dependent on interpreting 'fallen asleep' as a distinct state (v. 14–15). Wright however concedes that Paul is using the language of sleeping and waking simply as a way of contrasting a stage of temporal inactivity, not necessarily unconsciousness, with a subsequent one of renewed activity.

Whether having already died or whether still alive, this resurrection occurs at the coming of the Lord from heaven (v. 15–16). The dead will rise and those who are still alive 'will be caught up together with them in the clouds to meet the Lord in the air' (v. 17). The obvious parallel here is with 1 Corinthians 15.51–52 with the resurrection indicating transformation of the physical body, modelled on the transformation of the risen Christ. Far from going up on a cloud in a spatial sense, the image evokes Daniel 7.13 to convey a sense of the covenant people after suffering and a joining of heaven and earth in the Lord's reign (Wright 2003: 215).

There is little explicit here in terms of the non-human Universe. Perhaps that is why the US future fundamentalists interpret it in terms of the rapture of human beings. Yet we do see the themes of transformation modelled on the resurrection of Jesus, and the bringing together of heaven and earth. Wright suggests that apocalyptic language was always poetic and metaphorical and therefore needs to be interpreted in accordance with the literary conventions of its own time (Wright 1991: 280–338). Thus Paul's imagery of trumpets and clouds draw on the images of biblical apocalyptic to assure us that God has plans for this creation, and that he will not simply destroy it. Hays comments that the images 'refer to real events in the future (i.e., the return of Christ, the resurrection of the dead), but the details of the description are imaginative constructs that should not be pressed literalistically' (Hays 2001: 130).

What however is introduced is the concept of the second coming of Jesus, a feature central to the church's liturgy in 'Christ has died, Christ is risen, Christ will come again'. It is interesting that this features little in the eschatologies of Pannenberg, Polkinghorne or Russell, while in Moltmann the stress is on the millennium. Can the second coming say anything to us in terms of contemporary eschatology or is it merely an apocalyptic image of relevance to the first century?

Central to the New Testament is an expectation of the return of Jesus although quite what role it fulfils theologically is complex (Bauckham 1998: 97–110; Dunn 1997: 42–56). Borg and others in the 'Jesus Seminar' have questioned whether Jesus was expecting his imminent return and the end of the world. They conclude that Jesus must be reconstructed along non-eschatological lines, and that the second coming texts were created by his followers (Borg 1994: 7–8; Funk et al. 1997). Robinson had gone further to suggest that there was no evidence in the teaching of Jesus or in the preaching of the church that there should be a second coming (Robinson 1957: 138). While the concept of when Jesus expected his return has been at the heart of eschatological debate, the weight of New Testament scholarship is clear that Borg goes too far to dismiss the authenticity of Jesus' own understanding of his return (Ladd 1974; Hoekema 1979: 112; Travis 1980; Sanders 1985; Witherington 1992: 28; Koester 1992: 14; Sanders 1993; Allison 1998; de Jonge 1998; Ehrman 1999; Schwarz 2000: 118; Hays 2001: 113–131; Hill 2002b). Diversity remains concerning Jesus' own understanding and the understanding of the gospel writers. Wright, in particular, has argued that all of the apocalyptic sayings in the synoptic tradition were spoken by Jesus as symbolic descriptions of concrete events taking place in his own activities, but he does acknowledge that elsewhere in the New Testament we do find an expectation of Christ's coming again (Wright 1991: 461; Wright 1996: 635).

When we set 1 Thessalonians 4 alongside other Pauline material, we see that Paul looked for a climactic event to God's plan in a return of Christ. It has become a standard mantra to repeat that Paul expected the end of all things and the Parousia to happen in his lifetime. The actual position is far more complex. While Dunn suggests that the expectation of an imminent Parousia 'was a prominent feature' in 1 and 2 Thessalonians, he denies that such a Parousia is expected in 1 Corinthians, Romans, Philippians or Ephesians (Dunn 1977: 325, 345–6). There is clear evidence that Paul considered the possibility that he would die before the Parousia (Kümmel 1974: 240). It is also obvious that the future is often talked about in terms of immediacy, in a different way to how it is viewed with hindsight. Cranfield makes an important observation:

> 'In one sense the interval between the Ascension and the Parousia might be long or short; but there was a more important sense in which it could be only described as short; for this whole period is the "last days" – the epilogue, so to speak of history – since it comes after the decisive event of the life, death and resurrection, and ascension of Christ'. (Cranfield 1959: 275)

Leaving aside these debates about 'when', we can ask the question of what role does the second coming play theologically? Bauckham and Hart see the Parousia as part of images of hope (Bauckham and Hart 1999: 117), and it certainly is a reminder that the future is not the result of history, but depends on the sovereign act of God in bringing something new. This is a theme that will come out of all of the passages that we will consider in this chapter. However, there are a number of other important reminders.

First, the second coming reminds us that biblical eschatology has a focus on Jesus Christ. Barth commented that 'Christianity that is not entirely and altogether eschatology has entirely and altogether nothing to do with Christ' (Barth 1933: 314). In fact we might add to this by saying that eschatology that is altogether and entirely not focused on Christ is not Christianity. Thus the Parousia shows that Christ 'has a future with the world which is really both his own and the world's future' (Bauckham and Hart 1999: 118).

Second, the images used are suggestive of an eschatological event, which is both in space and time, and yet transcends space and time. Hope is focused in a future great event. The fact that 'every eye shall see him' is not meant to invite us to imagine worldwide TV coverage, but to suggest that the limitations of space and time no longer apply to this eschatological event. Robinson and Dodd saw the final encounter with God occurring beyond space and time (Robinson 1950: 68–69; Dodd 1951: 74), but this ignores the importance of an event in space and time. The incarnation affirms this physical Universe with its space, time and matter. The danger of an 'otherworldly' eschatology is that such an affirmation is devalued. The Parousia and the resurrection work with the incarnation in exploring the value but limits of this creation.

Third, the second coming is a reminder of the importance of the particular action of God within God's more general activity of sustaining and transforming. This is often an unresolved tension within the New Testament, yet it needs to be held. God is not the endpoint intervener whose only work within the Universe is as deistic Creator and then as 'deistic' Judge. At the same time God is not simply the source of the process without having the freedom or will to do the unusual act. The second coming is an imaginative affirmation of God's unusual yet particular actions within the Universe, especially in the transition to new creation.

Fourth, the Parousia is a strong reminder of the role of God's judgement in this transition (Mt 25.31–46; Acts 10.42). Some, such as Wilder, have argued that the urgency of Jesus' ethics cannot be expressed by 'an anachronistic and literal Second Coming' (Wilder 1959: 193). Wilder is correct to stress that the ethics of the Kingdom are closely linked to seeing God at work in the ministry of Jesus now. However, it is not an either/or situation. O'Donovan has commented that apocalyptic eschatology allows us the confidence of 'confronting a false political order with the foundation of a true one' (O'Donovan 1986a: 90). While making this comment in the context of the book of Revelation, the same could be said of the Parousia. The second coming questions all idols and reinforces the ethics of the Kingdom. Indeed, with the church it warns against complacency, empowers mission and gives comfort in the face of suffering and death (Hays 2001: 126).

Fifth, there is a strong sense to the second coming of the appearing or making visible of the Lord Jesus (1 Tim 6.14). In contrast to the Jesus who is hidden by the ascension, here he is seen. This could be linked to images of judgement as we have seen, but is there something more to it than that? Within the resurrection narratives there is the importance of the risen Jesus being seen. This functions as a source of intrigue, puzzlement and realisation of who Jesus is, alongside (as we shall see in the next chapter) the affirmation of the body and the hope of new creation. The second coming is a statement of the permanence of these things.

It is of course important to recognise that what we have in the second coming is not necessarily history written in advance but the work of the eschatological imagination. That imagination relates to themes of creation, incarnation and resurrection, and then points forward. Yet as Wright points out:

> 'though the early Christians did indeed hope for a future great event … they rested their weight of their theology on the event which, they firmly believed, had already happened. It was because of the bodily resurrection that the second coming meant what it did'. (Wright 2003: 582)

4.5 2 Peter 3.10–13

In this passage, the translation of verse 10 as 'the earth and everything in it will be burned up' has been used to justify total destruction of this creation. This 'burning up' has been identified in various scenarios ranging from the fireball of the Big Crunch to utter destruction of the cosmos by fire and replacement by a new one. On this view the physical universe has no ultimate place in God's purposes. We need to examine this in some detail.

The letter of 2 Peter is written to a specific church or groups of churches (2 Peter 3.15) with an apologetic content directed against specific objections to Christian teaching and a group of false teachers (Bauckham 1983; Chester and Martin 1994; Hillyer 1992). At the same time it is seems to be a 'farewell speech' or 'testament' which contained the characteristics of ethical admonitions and predictions of the future.

Its central theme is eschatological scepticism, and it responds to a number of attacks. First that the Parousia was invented by the apostles as instrument of moral control (1.16–19); second that Old Testament passages had been mistakenly interpreted (1.20–21); and third that without the Parousia or the promise of judgement life would be morally liberated (2.3b–10a). The final attacks are addressed in 2 Peter 3.3–14. It was claimed that the Parousia was expected during the lifetime of first generation Christians but this had been a mistake as these Christians were dying (3.4, 9a). In addition, based on a common sense view of the world, there would be no judgement or divine intervention because the world continues without interruption (3.4). It is interesting to note these attacks in the light of our comments on the Parousia in the context of 1 Thessalonians 4. In particular, if there is no prospect of divine intervention the world goes on without interruption and without new creation. To develop the theme, the Parousia is a reminder that the world is not a closed system.

The reply to the attack that the world continues in a regular pattern is twofold (3.5–7). First, the continuance and regularities of the world are not self-explanatory. It continues to depend on the will of God. Second, the world has not continued without intervention. The word of God acted in creation and flood, and it is the word of God that decrees that judgement will come. Here is a link directly between eschatology and creation. The false teachers ignore, overlook or forget the creation and flood (v. 5). The writer links these together through 'water' and 'word'. Various Old Testament passages tell of how the sky and the earth emerged out of a primeval ocean (Gen 1.2, 6–9; Ps 33.7; Ps 136.6; Prov 8.27–29). It is in this sense that the earth was 'formed out of water and by water'. It was by water also that judgement came through the flood (v. 6). The allusion here is to Genesis 7.11 which describes the cause of the flood to be the waters of chaos, confined at creation above the firmament, pouring through to the earth. Bauckham suggests that phrase 'world of that time' (v. 6) indicates that the flood has a cosmic dimension in the mind of the writer (Bauckham 1983: 299).

This cosmic dimension comes from the influence of contemporary Jewish apocalyptic sources, which we will return to later. At this point we can simply note that 2 Peter is similar to 1 Enoch and other writings of the period in viewing history in three periods – the world before the flood, the present world to be judged by fire, and the new world to come. The word of God is active in the transitions between these periods. By his word and water God created and destroyed the world. By his word and fire he will judge the present world. As he has already created by his word, destroyed by his word, then future judgement that is decreed by his word will happen, contradicting those who say that the world will continue without intervention (v. 7).

Though apocalyptic in its language and character, this argument has relevance to our understanding of eschatology and the future of the Universe. Scientific predictions of the future of the Universe are based on the assumption of the regularity of the Universe shown in the laws of physics. Within their own realm such predictions are useful. However, it is not valid to build a philosophical or theological picture of the future simply on the scientific predictions. Such 'scientism' does not recognize that the laws themselves may be the description of God's faithful upholding of the Universe or that the God who in creation gives regularity to the Universe may at the same time allow himself freedom to work within the Universe in acts which go beyond those regularities. The same principle that 2 Peter uses in terms of the flood could be used more positively in terms of the resurrection. The resurrection gives evidence that God can go beyond the constraints of the normal pattern of human life and death to new creation. Indeed this is the argument that is foundational to 1 Corinthians 15, which we will examine in Chapter 5.

Yet 2 Peter does not help us much in relating just how the new creation will be different from this creation. Verse 6 says that the world of that time was 'destroyed'. However, destruction by the flood does not mean total annihilation. The world was created out of the primeval ocean and then submerged again. It was a cleansing process of judgement without any change in the nature of the world (unless of course one was to follow some of the claims of seven-day creationists). The flood is simply being used to illustrate that God can intervene in judgement, or that God is in sovereign control of the forces of destruction and judgement.

Some have argued that the use of the image of fire for judgement (v. 7) is dependent on the idea of an eschatological world conflagration found in Stoic or Iranian (Zoroastrian) sources. Greek philosophy had two main views about the end of the world. Plato, Aristotle, Philo and Heraclitus held to the indestructibility of the cosmos. However the Stoics believed in the periodic destruction of the world by fire. Thus a fragment of Zeno says, 'The Universe will be destroyed by fire. Everything which has something to burn will burn up its fuel' (van der Horst and Mansfield 1984: 74). The destruction of the world by fire was part of infinite cycle and looked on in positive light. The new world was the same as the old world and there was no sense of judgement (von Arnim 1921–24: 1.510–511). However, was the writer of 2 Peter influenced by these sources?

Bauckham argues convincingly that the main influence is Jewish apocalyptic. In contrast to dissolving and renewing fire of the Stoics, and the Zoroastrian view of purification, here in the emphasis is on judgement. The idea of destruction by fire is widespread in the Old Testament, its function being to consume the wicked not to destroy the world (e.g. Deut 32.22; Ps 97.3; Is 30.30; Ezek 38.22; Amos 7.4; Zeph 1.18; Mal 3.19). As the theme of universal judgement developed it became widespread in Palestinian and Hellenistic Jewish eschatology in the post biblical period, and in Christian writing. It was often paralleled with the flood.

It is in this context that Bauckham comments that the image of fire is an:

'apocalyptic image, it is an image which remains powerful today, evoking both the threat of nuclear holocaust and the eventual reabsorption of our planet into the expanding Sun.' (Bauckham 1983: 302)

It is interesting in the first place that he feels the need to make such a comment. He is not alone among commentators in trying to link the biblical picture to the future of the Universe as science pictures it. However his link is unconvincing. The image used in 2 Peter, as Bauckham himself has pointed out in reference to the context and Jewish apocalyptic background is primarily about judgement rather than cosmology. While nuclear holocaust in the popular mind may be an image of fiery judgement on the technological arrogance and violence of human beings, the eventual reabsorption of our planet into the Sun has no relation to judgement at all. As we have seen in Chapter 2 technological development of human beings in the next few billion years may allow them by travel to another planet avoiding any 'fiery judgement'! This careless comment by such a careful commentator illustrates the need to better relate Christian eschatology to the physical Universe. (It is also worth noting that in fact fire is not the important factor in nuclear holocaust. More destruction would be caused by nuclear winter and longer-term radiation damage. The better image of nuclear holocaust is of a never-ending cold dark night.)

Verses 8–10 now pick up the second line of attack, that of the delay of the Parousia. The first response is to point out that this delay is not serious from the Lord's perspective, using Psalm 90.4. Some have argued that this verse in 2 Peter refers to the Day of Judgement lasting a thousand years, based on many Jewish and 2nd Century Christian texts, in which eschatological chronology uses the formula 'A day of the Lord is a thousand years' (Allmen 1966: 262). However, this is a very different context to where such an exegetical formula is used. There are parallels in Jewish literature where Psalm 90.4 is used to contrast the brevity of human life and God's eternity, and this is often used in apocalyptic contexts. Thus the argument is that those who complain of delay do not understand that from the perspective of eternity it is only a short time.

This does not mean that time becomes unimportant or that God is understood to be totally separated from time. If time means nothing to God then the very idea of the delay of the Parousia becomes meaningless. Are these temporal gaps within 'Christ has died, Christ is risen, Christ will come again' significant in reminding us of God's serious commitment to the nature of time in this creation?

While recognizing God's perspective, the author of 2 Peter encourages Christians not to discard its immanent expectation. As Bauckham has pointed out elsewhere, the holding in tension of immanent expectation and delay was a characteristic of Jewish and Christian apocalyptic (Bauckham 1980: 3–36). The writer then goes on to contradict the scoffers in terms of a classic text (Hab 2.3) that was a key verse for reflection on the problem of delay in Judaism. But then a theological understanding is offered for the delay. The delay reflects God's patience in deferring judgement and giving an opportunity for repentance (v. 9).

The image of the thief (v. 10) is taken from the parable of Jesus and is used to convey the unexpectedness and threat of the judgement (Mt 24.43; Lk 12.39). It is linked with the heavens disappearing 'with a roar'. This image of disappearing or 'pass away' is used in the gospels (Mt 5.18; Mt 24.35; Mk 13.31; Lk 16.17; Lk 21.33). 'With a roar' is an onomatopoeic word communicating hissing, whizzing, cracking or roaring of flames. It could also refer to God's thunderous roar that announces his coming and if this were the case it would place more emphasis on judgement rather than physical effects.

The 'elements' (v. 10) may better be translated as 'heavenly bodies'. Although the word may reflect the belief that the Universe is made out of the four elements of water, air, fire and earth, 'heavenly bodies' referring to sun, moon and stars is a meaning well attested for in the second century AD. For example, Apoc Pet E5, which follows 2 Peter 3.12 or Isaiah 34.4 or both, took the reference to be to the stars. Some have argued that the 'heavenly bodies' are in fact angelic powers. This may be an additional meaning but does not detract from 'stars', as stars were believed to be controlled by spiritual beings.

Yet all of this uncertainty of meaning is overshadowed by the last part of the verse 'the earth and everything in it will be laid bare'. The basic meaning of the words in English is 'the earth and the works in it will be found', and the uncertainty of what this means has led to numerous varieties of translation and interpretation. Some English translations use variant readings in alternative manuscripts to suggest 'will be burned up', 'will vanish' or 'will be found dissolved', but there is little evidence that these were original. The phrase 'will not be found' has 2 occurrences in ancient versions but not in the Greek MSS. This makes sense of the verse but it can only be a later emendation of text. Some argue that 'not' was missed out in an early version of the copying of the letter. Other scholars argue for various emendations to give the meanings 'will be burned', 'will be consumed by conflagration', 'will flow together', 'will be singed', 'will be judged', 'will be healed', 'the earth and the works which are found in it', 'the earth and the works in it will be found useless', 'the earth and all that is in it will be found as chaos' or 'it shall be found to the earth according to the works in it'. Others question the reading, arguing that it is in fact a rhetorical question 'will they be found?'

Such diversity cautions against any hasty conclusions as to the meaning of the phrase. Yet the most attractive solution is to take the words simply as 'the earth and everything in it will be found' in the sense of will be made manifest before God's judgement. The Old Testament usage does not seem to support the absolute use of 'to find' meaning 'to subject to judgement'. However, as Bauckham suggests, general familiarity with that usage could have influenced the choice of words in 2 Peter. The verb 'to find' is used in contexts concerned with moral or judicial scrutiny where sin or righteousness is found (e.g. 1 Sam 25.28), someone is found righteous (e.g. Dan 5.27) or where a criminal is detected or found (Ex 22.8). This interpretation is supported by the suggestion that the passive form perhaps indicates a divine passive, that is, these things will be discovered or found out by God (Wenham 1987: 477–9; Wolters 1987: 405–13). It is an interpretation with a long history (Wilson 1920–21: 44–45) and fits with the context that is of the Parousia as a time of judgement. Bauckham rightly comments that 'the destruction of the universe is of interest to the author only as the means of judgement on men and women' (Bauckham 1983: 319). In relating these biblical images to the future of the physical Universe we must always keep that as a primary concern.

Verses 11–16 now turn to a description of the new heaven and earth. The 'day of God' (v. 12) is a reminder that the new heaven and earth is a direct work of God. The phrase 'the heavenly bodies will melt in the heat' picks up verse 10 and derives from Isaiah 34.4. The verb 'to melt' is also used of the melting of the mountains at the eschatological coming of God (Is 63.19–64.1). The link with Isaiah is developed also in the promise of a new heaven and earth. It is found throughout Jewish apocalyptic (e.g. 1 Enoch 45.4–5) and in early Christianity (e.g. Mt 19.28; Rom 8.21; Rev 21.1).

What do we make of this cosmic dissolution (v. 10–12)? We have already pointed out the parallel to the flood (v. 4–7). The writer sees such events as demonstrating a creator God who is able to work in human history in a dramatic and physical way. Within the context of the apocalyptic images and the difficulty of recovering the original meaning, some intervention of God in the physical Universe accompanying a time of judgement is envisaged. Therefore, total destruction of the present creation cannot be justified by these verses. Bauckham concludes that such passages 'emphasise the radical discontinuity between the old and the new, but it is nevertheless clear that they intend to describe a renewal not an abolition of creation' (Bauckham 1983: 326). The passage is not written for the purposes of cosmology but to give Christians hope and urge them to live lives consistent with the new creation 'in which righteousness is at home' (v. 13). Once again we have a passage that speaks of a renewal of creation, alongside judgment with the action of God being central.

4.6 Revelation 21.1–8

This passage once again uses Isaiah 65.17 and has also been used to justify the picture of God destroying the old creation before bringing in a new creation. This form of apocalyptic literature does not give us history of the future, but imaginative theological insights into the purposes of God (Robinson 1950: 34; Hill 2002a: 128).

It is a carefully crafted passage. The angelic speech from the throne is framed by the verbal parallels of 'the first heaven and earth had passed away' (v. 1) and 'the former things had passed away' (v. 4). The main elements of John's vision in verses 1–2 are referred to in reverse order by the voice from the throne (v. 3–5a). In addition, 'new' (v. 1a), 'first' (v. 1b), 'passed away' (v. 1b) and 'no longer exists' (v. 1b) occur in reverse order in verses 4b and 5a. Verse 5a is the transition verse leading to verses 5b–8 which is a speech from God, of which the only other instance in is Revelation 1.8.

The 'new heaven and new earth' is 'introduced abruptly and enigmatically' (Aune 1998: 1116). This renewal of creation in ancient Judaism is referred to in a variety of ways in Jewish apocalyptic literature as the final eschatological act (1 Enoch 45.4; 91.16; Bib Ant 3.10). A number of other passages refer to the recreation or transformation of an eternal heaven or an eternal earth or both. It is difficult to distinguish between creation and transformation in these passages. Some passages refer to the creation of a new heaven and earth (1 Enoch 72.1), 'new nature' (Sib Or 5.212), 'new creation' (Jub 1.29), and a transformation or renewal of heaven and earth (1 Enoch 45.4–5; 2 Apoc Bar 32.6; Apoc Bar 44.12; Bib Ant 32.17; Jub 1.29; 4 Ezra 7.30–31, 75).

However we get a better picture of the meaning of Revelation's 'new heaven and earth' if we see it in context with the second part of the verse, 'for the first heaven and first earth had passed away, and there was no longer any sea' (v. 1b). Some scholars put this together with the earlier verse, 'Earth and sky fled from his presence, and there was no place for them' (20.11b) to argue for a complete destruction of the physical Universe (Vögtle 1985: 301–33). However, a majority of scholars think that a renewal or transformation of the cosmos is in view (Caird 1966: 260, 265–66; Bauckham 1993: 49–50). We note the following reasons.

First, destruction of the cosmos by fire is not mentioned anywhere in Revelation. As we have seen 2 Peter 3 speaks of the flood and future judgement of the world by fire. This was also a tradition in early Judaism with two destructions of the world by water and fire (Adam and Eve 49.3). This is quite different from the cyclic destruction found in Greek sources. The Old Testament and early Judaism demonstrate a link between divine judgement and fiery destruction but it is often difficult to determine whether this is complete or partial destruction of the world (Kittel and Friedrich 1964–76: 6.936–41). The eternity of God is sometimes contrasted with the temporary existence of the heavens and earth (Ps 102.25–26), while destruction of the Earth by fire is predicted in Zephaniah (Zeph 1.18; 3.8) but this probably refers to the destruction of nations, not the Earth itself (Berlin 1994: 133). At least a partial destruction of the world by fire is expressed or implied in Isaiah 51.6 and 66.15–16. In several early Jewish apocalyptic texts, complete destruction of the cosmos is clearly in view (e.g. Sib Or 2.196–213; 1 QH 11.32–33). These texts originate from the 2nd Century BC and earlier, and may show the influence of Stoicism although the infinitely repeated destruction of the cosmos is never adopted. Other texts show some evidence for the belief that heaven and earth are stable (2 Apoc Bar 19.2; Tg Jer 33.25). The apocalyptic theme of the destruction of the heavens and the earth occurs occasionally in early Christianity (e.g. Justin 1 Apol 20.1–4). It has been argued by some that it is present in the teaching of Jesus (e.g. Lk 16.17), however the disappearance of heaven and earth here is simply a metaphor of contrast for the permanence of the Torah. Thus, the writer of Revelation 21.1 has a host of images of the destruction of the cosmos to use yet no reference is made to them. This strengthens the case for believing that transformation of the cosmos is being pictured.

Second, Bauckham suggests that the apocalyptic writing of Revelation 21.1 shares an understanding of other new creation passages also based on Isaiah 65.17 which have parallels referring to the renewal rather than destruction of creation (e.g. 1 Enoch 72.1; 91.16; 2 Bar 32.6; 44.12) (Bauckham 1993: 48).

Third, the contrast between 'new' and 'first' (v. 1) means not a literal new creation but a figurative prediction of a radically changed cosmos (Beale 1999: 1040). The word 'new' (kainos) usually indicates newness in terms of quality rather than something new which has never been in existence (Harbeck, Link, and Brown 1976: 669–74; Mullholland 1990: 315; Beasley-Murray 1974: 312). This change is about ethical renewal but also a 'transformation of the fundamental cosmic structure including physical elements' (Beale 1999: 1040). Beale does not specify what those physical elements might be but he points to the contrast between 'there will be no more night' (Rev 22.5) and Genesis 8.22 'While the earth remains … day and night will not cease'.

Fourth, some commentators argue that the allusions to Isaiah probably understand Isaiah as prophesying the transformation of the old creation rather than an outright new creation ex nihilo. A transformation of creation is necessary to provide the correct environment for the eternal kingdom (Black 1976: 15; Aune 1998: 1133).

If then there is a good basis for believing that Revelation 21.1 portrays a transformation of creation, what part does the final part of the verse play, that of 'there was no longer any sea'? The sea is represented in many different contexts in the Old Testament. The Lord is its Creator and controller, he compels it to contribute to human good, it utters his praise and there are many manifestations of the Lord's power against it (Gen 1.9f; 49.25; Ex 14–15; Deut 33.13; Ps 77.16; 104.7–9; 148.7; Is 17.12; Jer 6.23; Jonah 1–2). However, one of the major themes is the Lord's combat with the sea (Kloos 1986: 81–83). He sets borders or guards on the sea (Jer 5.22; Job 7.12), rebukes or is angry at the waters (Is 1.2; Nah 1.4; Hab 3.8; Ps 18.6; 29.3) and dries up the waters (Is 19.5; Jer 1.38; 51.36; Ezek 30.12; Nah 1.14; Ps 18.16; Job 12.15). Underlying this is the belief that the sea personified the power that fought against the deity, a negative symbol for chaos and evil.

Against that background, Beale points out that in Revelation the sea is identified in a number of ways, as the origin of cosmic evil (4.6; 12.18; 13.1; 15.2), the rebellious nations (12.18; 13.1), the place of the dead (20.13), the primary location of the world's idolatrous trade activity (18.10–19), and a literal body of water sometimes used with 'earth' to represent totality of old creation (5.13; 7.1–3; 8.8–9; 10.2; 14.7). He suggests that in Revelation 21.1 it probably carries all these five meanings. Therefore new creation with no longer any sea means no threat from Satan, other nations, death, no more idolatry, and no more chaos.

Other commentators have also suggested that the sea represents separation between groups of people and nations and so such a separation will be no more, since all are in new community with God and one another (Boring 1989: 216; Hughes 1990: 222). Mealy has even suggested that primary reference is to the heavenly sea which served as veil in the sky separating God's presence from earth but will be eliminated from the new creation (Mealy 1992: 192–212). The force of all of these suggestions is that there will be no more tribulation for God's people in a renewed creation where there is direct fellowship with God and one another.

However, Bauckham goes further in suggesting that 'no sea' means that the new creation is characterized by one feature that makes it really new different to the old creation (Bauckham 1993: 53). With no sea, the waters representing destructive evil and chaos are finally no more. The judgement of the old creation and the inauguration of the new are not so much a second flood but a final removal of the threat of another flood. The new creation is thus eternally secure beyond the threat of evil. This is supported by Revelation 11.18 alluding to Genesis 6.11–13, 17 so forming a parallel between the flood and eschatological judgement.

The emphasis then of Revelation 21.1 is not on the passing away of material elements of the old world but on the passing away of evil. That is not to say that the verse does not portray discontinuities between the old creation and the new creation. However, the 'newness' of the new cosmos will have maintained continuities and will be a renewal of the old creation (Harrisville 1960: 99–105).

This is the position argued by some commentators not only on the text itself but also on the basis of parallel with the resurrection (Farrer 1964: 213; Sweet

1979: 297). Indeed, the parallel with the resurrection raises some important questions. If resurrection can only occur after the death of the body, does this mean that renewal of the cosmos can only happen after destruction of this present cosmos? This understanding of new creation following the pattern of Christ's resurrection can be demonstrated by the exegetical link between new creation and resurrection (Beale 1999: 298). First there are allusions to Isaiah 65.16–17 in 2 Corinthians 5.14–17 and Colossians 1.15–18. Second, Revelation 3.14 is also an allusion to this the new creation prophecy which has begun to be fulfilled in the physical resurrection of Christ who is described as 'the Amen, the faithful and true witness, the ruler of God's creation'. Beale suggests that this is a literary development of Christ's title in Revelation 1.5 'the faithful witness, the firstborn from the dead, and the ruler of the kings of the earth'. The second part of 3.14 is better translated, 'beginning of the creation of God'. This does not link Jesus to the original creation but is an interpretation of the resurrection from 1.5. That is, his resurrection is viewed as the beginning of a new creation in parallel to Colossians 1.15b, 18b. While this link between new creation and resurrection is strong, the parallel is not strong enough to support the conclusion that this creation needs to be completely destroyed before transformation can completely take place. We might expect this creation to bear the marks of death, that is, it is destined to futility. At the same time the context of transformation gives new creation some difference to individual human death and resurrection.

Returning to the rest of the Revelation 21 passage reinforces the above conclusions about the nature of the new creation. God is pictured as coming to live with his people paralleling Old Testament passages with similar themes (Lev 26.11–12; Zech 2.10b–11; Ezek 43.7; Ex 29.45). Verses 4–5a fill out the nature of the new creation as a place of peace and re-emphasize that the previous things have passed away because God is making everything new. This is a claim to the certainty of the future age and its all-encompassing nature. The central message of Revelation is then summarized in the portrayal of God as Alpha and Omega, Beginning and End (v. 5–8). The latter phrase is a widespread Hellenistic divine title which has cosmological rather than temporal significance emphasizing the totality of the sovereignty over the created order and history (van Unnik 1976; Beale 1999: 1055).

What then are we to take from Revelation 21.1–8 in terms of its eschatology as it may relate to the physical Universe? First, we see the relationship between resurrection and new creation as key in understanding the passage and indeed the wider eschatological implications. Second, the vision focuses not on the physical universe but on the glorified community of believers. It is interesting if not striking that such an important cosmic event is referred to so briefly and with the mention of the sea. It is yet another reminder that cosmological speculation is of little importance compared to the hope for the individual believer or Christian community in these passages. This has to be an important cautionary word for any work on the physical Universe. Third, the universality of the eschatological new beginning derives from an understanding of God as creator of all things. Bauckham comments that this understanding:

'was not only integral to Jewish and Christian monotheism; it was also essential to the development of Jewish and Christian eschatology. If God was the transcendent source of all things, he could also be the source of quite new possibilities for his creation in the future. Creation is not confined for ever to its own immanent possibilities.' (Bauckham 1993: 48)

Just as the resurrection was based on God giving new life, so eschatology was based on God as creator. Creation and new creation must be held together. Bauckham extends this and attacks models that make God dependent on the Universe:

'A God who is not the transcendent origin of all things but a way of speaking of the immanent creative possibilities of the universe itself cannot be the ground of ultimate hope for the future of creation. Where faith in God the Creator wanes, so inevitably does hope for the resurrection, let alone the new creation of all things'. (Bauckham 1993: 51)

Thus, this passage from Revelation fits into the apocalyptic tradition in giving a radical attitude to the future. Yet it does not warrant a complete destruction of this creation. Here we have again the renewal of the old by a radical transformation, not its abolition. This is in line with the view of Chester (Chester 2001: 73) and Rowland's view that this is an ultimate rejection of a detached other worldly spirituality. Instead heaven comes down to earth where the created reality becomes one (Rowland 1985: 292–4).

4.7 Romans 8.18–30

In the history of the relationship of science and religion it can be argued that with Galileo, Darwin, and Freud, human beings are 'mere fragments in a world that appears to be neither about us nor for us' (Durant 1985: 9). So far in this chapter we have considered biblical passages that have focused on the future of creation. We might ask whether Durant's comments could be extended to eschatology. Are human beings irrelevant to the whole picture? In the last section we noted the centrality of the future of the human community, but is that true elsewhere? Indeed, what is the relationship of the future of human beings with the future of the physical Universe? As we have seen Rees, Dyson and Tipler are fascinated with such a question.

Inevitably one of the biblical passages which is immediately employed in this area is Romans 8.18–30. Yet it is not an easy passage to interpret. It has a long history of interpretations (Rudrum 1989: 34–54), but very few relate to the physical nature of the Universe and its future, even when commenting extensively on such a 'cosmic' passage. We therefore need to look at it in some detail being sensitive to questions about creation.

Romans 8 needs to be seen in its context of its place in Romans but also in its general context of Pauline eschatology, which in turn is set in its own context of Jewish and Christian eschatology. In this we need to be clear of the complexity of Pauline eschatology. As Johnson comments,

'Paul's eschatological language is made up of several not entirely reconcilable elements that are put together in a variety of ways depending on
the circumstances ... he deploys aspects of eschatological expectation as
its fits paraenetic needs, rather than as it fits within a system' (Johnson
2001: 433).

Having said that, there are still some broad themes that we can note.

The first is that creation and consummation are held together (Dahl 1964:
422–443; Bridger 1990: 297). Paul reflects the Jewish sense of the linear
nature of history that is dependent on the purposes of God being worked out
between creation and consummation. Second, the link between creation and
consummation is Christological, that is, it is Christ who is both Creator and
Consummator (Wright 1986: 70). Third is the idea of transformation of this
creation into new creation:

> 'The fundamental idea here is not the conformity of the eschatological
> salvation with the original creation but that creation as described in
> Genesis prefigures the whole history of the world, including its eschato-
> logical fulfillment.' (Dahl 1964: 429)

The new creation is not a return to Eden. It is better than the old since it is
freed from the corruption of sin. This is shown in the Adam/Christ contrast
(Rom 5) where the curse of Genesis 3.17–18 is lifted by the obedience of the
second Adam. This sense of discontinuity between the old and new creation
is also present in Paul and Messianic Judaism in thinking about the physical
universe. The resurrection is to incorruptibility (1 Cor 15) and even the light of
the heavenly bodies in new creation exceeds that of the old (Is 30.26).

In the light of this we now turn to Romans 8.18–30. It is preceded by Paul's
discussion of the problem of sin and the concepts of liberation, sonship, resurrection and the role of the Spirit. Already we encounter some key questions.
What does it mean for creation to be 'liberated'? How does sin affect the physical
creation?

Paul has been setting out that we are 'heirs of God and co-heirs with Christ'
(v. 17) but now has to ask how this relates to our earthly existence. If we have
been given such a privileged position, then does this mean that we will be
protected from suffering and further is there any point to our earthly existence?
However, the sufferings of this world are real and Paul interprets them as sharing
in the sufferings of Christ as a necessary part of sharing in his glory. Here we
have a strong link between the sufferings of this creation and the glory of the
new creation. Indeed, one seems necessary for the other. Thus, on this view, the
futility of the present Universe is necessary for the emergence of new creation
brought about by the action of God.

Paul wants to get this into perspective pointing out that the present suffering
is outweighed by the future glory (v. 18). Paul's use of 'I consider' signifies strong
assurance. Cranfield speaks of 'firm conviction reached by rational thought on
the basis of the gospel', while Dunn rightly qualifies this by effectively adding
'and experience of the Spirit'. The present sufferings may be from a number

of sources such as sin, the persecution of Christians, or life in this fragile world. Commentators generally see in reference to the 'present' a reference to the era between the first and second comings of Christ. This tension between the beginning of the new creation and the end of this creation leads to some disagreement on 'the glory that will be revealed in us'. Cranfield sees this revelation already real in some sense, a revelation of God's glory in the lives of the persons transformed by it. Dunn however sees it as something future, belonging to the transition to heaven (Dunn 1988: 468). Dunn's argument, although rightly stressing the future revelation, does not do sufficient justice to the sense of the glory now (2 Cor 4.7–5.5).

On the basis of verses 17 and 18 we are left with the important question of whether suffering is a necessary preliminary to the coming glory. Sanders has pointed out that it is difficult to document the belief that suffering must precede the coming of the kingdom in Jewish thought before AD 135 (Sanders 1985: 124), and indeed the best parallels come from post AD 70 literature shaped by the trauma of fall of Jerusalem (Strack and Billerbeck 1926: 3.244–45). However, Dunn argues that the idea follows directly from Daniel 7.21–22, 25–27; 12.1–3, and is already implicit in other writings (Jub 23.22–31; T Mos 5–10; 1 QH 3.28–36; Sib Or 3.632–56). He then quotes Matthew 3.7–12 to support this. However, this is primarily an image of judgement. Dunn is quite right to link this to the coming glory, but it is not valid to immediately identify the present sufferings with judgement. In fact the rest of the passage speaks of these sufferings not as judgement but linked with the 'pain throughout creation'. As Gore put it, 'here we have, as nowhere else in the Bible ... a man who feels with the pain of creation' (Gore 1902: 305). Of course it could be argued that the futility of the creation is part of God's judgement on it, but this is slightly different to claiming that there was a widespread belief that suffering precedes the glory. Paul certainly recognizes that this creation involves suffering in a way that the new creation will not, but stops short of claiming that such suffering is necessary to glory.

In fact the creation waits in expectation for the revelation of that glory (v. 19). Ἀποκαραδοκία is an unusual word signifying the persistent expectation of stretching the head forward or craning the neck. While some suggest that this involves both curiosity and some uncertainty (Fitzmyer 1993: 505), most commentators interpret the image as confident expectation (Denton 1982: 138–40).

More disagreement has been about what Paul means by 'creation'. The most obvious meaning would be the sub personal creation (Morris 1988: 320). However, other commentators find the personification of creation and its need for liberation difficult and so think 'creation' refers to human beings, for example 'the world in so far as it is distinct from the church' (Leenhardt 1961: 123) or the 'non-believing human world' (Gager 1970: 329; Schlatter 1959: 269–75), or simply 'mankind' (Manson 1962: 946). Christian tradition has also given a variety of interpretations including Origen's 'mankind both believing and unbelieving and also the angels', 'angels only' (Fuchs 1949: 109) and 'sub human nature together with mankind in general' (Barth 1959: 99f).

None of these interpretations are convincing. Ambrosiaster, Cyril, Chrysostom, Calvin and the majority of recent commentators have argued strongly that it refers to 'sub-human nature only' (Käsemann 1980: 233; Cranfield 1975: 411; Sanday and Headlam 1902: 212; Fitzmyer 1993: 505). Believers must be excluded since they are contrasted with creation (v. 23). The phrase 'not by its own choice' (v. 20) seems to rule out human beings as this includes Adam, and the suggestion that Paul is referring here to angels seems very unlikely. Perhaps Paul did not intend a precise definition, but it does seem clear that Paul was speaking of the sum total of sub human creation both animate and inanimate.

The personal language when referring to creation is not unusual in the context of the Old Testament (Is 35.1–2; 55.12–13; Ps 96.11–13). This raises an interesting parallel that has relevance to our understanding of creation. The personification of nature is often used to view creation pointing towards the glory of the Creator God (e.g. Ps 19.1). Indeed Paul has already emphasized the way that God reveals himself through the natural world (Rom 1.20). Such a biblical base is often used by those who speak of a revival of natural theology within the dialogue between science and religion (Polkinghorne 1998). Such a revised natural theology does not fall into the traps of the classical proofs for the existence of God but identifies insights into the nature of the world revealed by science that point to something beyond the scientific description of the Universe. Thus, the anthropic fruitfulness of the Universe, its intelligibility and the awe it invokes can be pointers to a Creator God. They are not proofs and they fall short of any full and reliable description of the nature of such a God, but they point to transcendence.

The image of creation craning its neck forward is helpful in suggesting that the nature of this creation points forward to its own limitations and the coming of new creation. Just as some aspects of the Universe give pointers back to a Creator God, other aspects may point forward to new creation achieved by the sovereign act of God. These aspects include the 'present sufferings' but also the sense of futility concerning the future of the Universe revealed by science. The Christian doctrine of creation would expect certain pointers forward to new creation. The futility of the future of the Universe is therefore not a problem for Christian eschatology. Thus Russell is misleading to argue, 'If the predictions of contemporary scientific cosmology come to pass ("freeze" or "fry") then it would seem the universe will never be transformed into the new creation' (Russell 2002b: 267). The fact that at the moment the Universe seems destined to 'freeze' is a pointer to new creation.

Barrett suggests that Paul 'is not concerned with creation for its own sake' (Barrett 1957: 165). This is correct in that Paul sees creation as a stage in God's purposes which has already within it pointers towards a better future. This is in line with the expectation in Judaism of a renewal and transformation of nature. However, creation is important in pointing forward to new creation and the importance of redeemed human beings as key to that new creation. This passage does not say that this creation is worthless, for as Dunn rightly comments, 'redemption embraces the material creation … as the climax to a divine purpose, pursued from the beginning of creation, now nearing its fulfilment' (Dunn 1988: 470). The link between creation and the 'sons of God' is a clear allusion to the Genesis narratives. So Dunn continues, 'as creation in the beginning had its role in relation to man, the crown and steward of creation, so creation's rediscovery of its role depends on the restoration of man to his intended glory as the image of God' (Dunn 1988: 487).

This challenges those who would underestimate the importance of both human beings and the material creation. It also questions any eschatology that stresses too much continuity at the expense of discontinuity between creation and new creation. The very nature of this creation points forward to a qualitative difference in the new creation. Yet just as this Universe cannot be understood as creation without God's revelation and the response of faith, the pointers to new creation also need interpretation by God's revelation and faith. The 'eager expectation' of creation is for the 'children of God to be revealed'. The revelation of the sons of God is likened by Dunn to a play when the final curtain is drawn back to show actors in their real characters. Such reality of sonship is only recognized by faith at this time. As Cranfield comments, 'they ... have to believe in their sonship against the clamorous evidence of much of their circumstances and condition which seems to be altogether inconsistent with the reality of it' (Cranfield 1975: 413).

The creation waits in eager expectation because it has been subjected to 'frustration' (v. 20). This word is found 37 times in the LXX of Ecclesiastes and has the sense of emptiness, futility, purposelessness, and lack of permanence. What does this mean for the physical creation? Fitzmyer suggests that it refers to the chaos, decay and corruption to which humanity has subjected God's noble creation (Fitzmyer 1993: 505). However this has the sense of human beings doing the subjecting. More helpful is to think of the subjection being the result of the relationship between God, human beings and nature being corrupted.

Cranfield sees the frustration as the ineffectiveness of that which does not attain its goal. Thus he states, 'the sub-human creation has been subjected to the frustration of not being able properly to fulfil the purpose of its existence, God having appointed that without man it should not be made perfect' (Cranfield 1975: 414). Paul's point is that as long as we refuse to play the part assigned to us by God, that is to act as his stewards, then the entire world of nature is frustrated and dislocated. That is, 'an untended garden is one which is overrun by thorns and thistles' (Berry 1995: 39). Cranfield helpfully uses the following picture:

> 'What sense is there in saying that "the subhuman creation – the Jungfrau, for example, or the Matterhorn, or the planet Venus – suffers frustration by being prevented from properly fulfilling the purpose of its existence?", the answer must surely be that the whole magnificent theatre of the universe, together with all its splendid properties and all the varied chorus of sub-human life, created for God's glory, is cheated of its true fulfilment so long as man, the chief actor in the great drama of God's praise, fails to contribute his rational part ... just as all the other players in a concerto would be frustrated of their purpose if the soloist were to fail to play his part'. (Cranfield 1974: 224–30)

Such musical illustrations are widespread. Kidner comments, 'leaderless, the choir of creation can only grind on in discord' (Kidner 1967: 73). Dunn prefers a satellite not functioning in the way it was designed. He sees the frustration as the futility of an object that does not function as it was designed to do.

In Chapter 2 we noted that the futility of the Universe as revealed by contemporary cosmology in its prediction of heat death or Big Crunch is a difficult issue for scientists who dismiss theism. Thus Stephen Weinberg's 'the more Universe seems comprehensible the more it seems pointless' is a reflection of seeing the Universe solely in relation to human beings. The desperate scientific eschatology of Tipler and Dyson is also based on seeing the Universe solely in relation to human beings. At the other extreme those who would deify the Universe also have a major difficulty in relation to the futility of the Universe.

Paul's view is helpful in that it cuts across both these positions. The Universe is not futile if seen in the purposes of God of creation and new creation. Creation is caught up in the human fallen state, as human beings are not able to play their part. Once again allusion is made to Genesis 1–3. The subjecting of creation may refer to the dominion given by God to human beings (Ps 8.6), but more likely refers to the consequences of sin (Gen 3.17–18).

The question is then 'who subjected it?' Some have suggested that Paul is referring to Adam, idols, or even celestial powers (Robinson 1979: 102; Byrne 1986: 166–67). However, the majority see Paul referring to God as the one who subjected the creation to futility (Dunn 1988: 471). Why should God do this? Dunn suggests:

'God followed the logic of his purposed subjecting of creation to man by subjecting it yet further in consequence of man's fall, so that it might serve as an appropriate context for fallen man: a futile world to engage the futile mind of man ... There is an out-of-sortedness, a disjointedness about the created order which makes it a suitable habitation for man at odds with his creator'. (Dunn 1988: 488)

However, this process draws out and destroys the destructiveness of sin so that creation can be restored.

Thus creation, as it now is, is both necessary to new creation and a pointer to new creation. The 'disjointedness of creation' is testimony that it was not always intended to be like this and that it will not always be like this in the purposes of God. The present fragility and suffering of this world has been used to point backwards to the seriousness of the fall. Here Paul also points forward to the seriousness of new creation. For it was subjected 'in hope', that the judgement itself included the promise of a better future. Once again we have found in a major eschatological passage in the Bible a stress on discontinuity and indeed hope grounded not on human beings but on God. These are essential in the dialogue of science and religion concerning the end of the Universe, and indeed in Christian eschatology in general.

The hope for creation is that the effect of sin will be no more and creation will be set free to be what God wants it to be (v. 21). Creation itself will be redeemed rather than human beings will be simply redeemed from creation. Paul images it as 'liberation from its bondage to decay'. He has already used this image in liberation from sin (6.18, 22) and from the law (7.3; 8.2). But what does it mean for the Universe? Fitzmyer suggests:

'Physical creation is thus not to be a mere spectator of humanity's liberation and triumphant glory, but is also to share in it by being released from its own material corruption and decay. Phthōra denotes not only perishability and putrefaction, but also powerlessness, lack of beauty, vitality, and strength that characterize creation's present condition'. (Fitzmyer 1993: 509)

Contemporary cosmology points forward to a decay of heat death. However, it also shows the beauty, elegance and faithfulness of the cosmos in the physical laws. Fitzmyer does not reflect such a balance in characterizing the creation's present condition. While recognizing the reality of the bondage of decay, Cranfield nevertheless acknowledges:

'If the sub-human creation is part of God's creation ... and if he is going to bring it also (as well as believing men) to a goal which is worthy of himself, then it too has a dignity of its own and inalienable, since divinely appointed, right to be treated by us with reverence and sensitiveness'. (Cranfield 1974: 229–30)

The tension between creation and new creation must be maintained. In trying to interpret what 'decay' means for the physical Universe, some have suggested mere 'transitoriness' (Jones 1987: 132). This is not adequate either in the light of this passage from Paul or in thinking about the physical Universe. Of course, the Universe is time dependent and part of its decay in the second law of thermo-dynamics is due to the arrow of time. Yet that arrow of time is also key to the growth of complexity, life, organization and creativity. There is deterioration in the Universe, but part of that deterioration can point forward to new creation. The new creation is not necessarily time independent. The liberation is from decay, to provide a new environment for redeemed human beings. The key feature of that environment is the freedom of the incorruptible setting for resur-rected embodiment (1 Cor 15.42–50), not at the mercy of sin, deterioration or death.

Paul now appeals to common knowledge among believers that the creation is in trouble (v. 22), but again sees this groaning as a process and sign for the future. As Calvin pointed out this is meaningful pain in the sense not of death but birth pangs. Some controversy surrounds the use of the metaphor of child-birth. It is an image used much in Christianity and Judaism (Is 66.7–8; Jer 22.23; Hos 13.13; Mic 4.9–10; 1 QH 3.7–18; Mk 13.8; Jn 16.21; Acts 2.24; 1 Thess. 5.3; Rev 12.2) and therefore it may have been common in contemporary apocalyptic and rabbinic Judaism as well as in Greek thought to speak of a period of suffering until new creation (Zeisler 1989: 218; Allison 1987; Vermes 1975: 157). However, as we observed earlier there are those who object to this link of suffering and new creation (Sanders 1985: 124, 130).

Nevertheless, it reemphasizes the important point that creation both prepares for and points to new creation. Does this mean that we should expect to see aspects of creation which can be interpreted not just as a result of alienation from God but also as signs of what is to come? The problem of natural evil has often been explained by a consequence of the fall or a consequence of inherent freedom given to the Universe. Might it also be a sign which points this creation beyond itself to new creation?

The groaning of creation is echoed in the groaning of believers (v. 23). Believers are part of this creation with its present sufferings, frustration and decay, but they have been given the 'firstfruits of the Spirit'. Jewish custom was to bring the first of the harvest to the temple and offer it to God. This would consecrate the whole harvest and would also be a sign that there will be later fruits. This harvest image may be an allusion to the final resurrection of believers (1 Cor 15.20, 23), with the firstfruits being the gift of the Spirit. The image further means that just as the firstfruits are of a piece of the whole harvest, then there is continuity between the gift of the Spirit, the Spirit's work in the believer and the final product of resurrection.

Here we encounter again the importance of holding a tension between creation and new creation in terms of continuity and discontinuity. The Spirit does not free the believer from such a tension but in fact heightens it. The experience of sonship and calling 'Abba Father' (Rom 8.15) is held in the frustration that the life of the Spirit cannot find full expression in this creation. The groaning is a sign of the Spirit's presence, his work within us and a sign of the new creation to come. Paul uses the same 'wait eagerly' as in verse 19 to highlight both the parallel and the link between the future of the believer and the future of creation.

This passage is helpful in eschatological thinking as it constantly challenges views that see creation as meaningless compared to future glory or new creation as meaningless compared to present experience. New creation is not an escape from a fatally flawed creation; it is the completion of God's original purpose in and for creation. Thus new creation is part of God's purpose from the beginning but creation is necessary for that purpose to be fulfilled.

Paul then has to defend against any sense that this eschatological perspective on creation might lead to dualism which values spiritual experience over against present reality (v. 24–25). The hope for the future is based on the work of salvation and the present experience of the Spirit, but in the light of all that Paul has already said cannot ignore this creation. Yet the Christian perspective is not determined by the frustrations of the present, but by its future hope. This means that the believer must wait for the new creation patiently, with positive endurance rather than quiet acceptance. As Grundmann comments, 'In virtue of the reception of the Spirit the Christian attitude is one of burning expectation in conformity with the divine plans' (Grundmann 1964–76: 56). The groaning of creation and the believer is also linked to the groaning of the Spirit (v. 26–27). The Spirit helps believers in their weakness, when not just words fail but when they do not know fully God's will in the transition and tension between creation and new creation. Paul then turns again to the certainty of Christian hope (v. 28–30). Hope is based on the confidence of the outworking of God's purpose, despite the present experiences of contradiction and frustration. Behind this view is the characteristic Jewish thought of God's purpose moving history to its intended end.

The importance of this passage should not be underestimated. First, one of the strongest insights is that hope for the future must be based on the action of God the creator. Without the redeeming purposes and actions of its Creator, creation is destined to futility. Second, creation and new creation must be held together in tension, and discontinuity must not be sacrificed at the expense of continuity. Third, we have developed the idea from the passage that creation is not just a process towards new creation, but also has within itself pointers to new creation. That is creation and new creation existed together in the mind of God from the beginning. Furthermore, the very suffering, frustration and decay that result from the sin of human beings can become pointers to God's future purposes.

In this there are certain parallels to the revival of natural theology that has focused on the nature of the Universe and pointers to a Creator. I have argued elsewhere that such natural theology is limited but significant (Wilkinson 1990: 95–116). It is significant because it demonstrates that science itself has limits in understanding the Universe and points to something beyond itself. However, as Kant and Hume argued, it is limited as a means to prove the existence and nature of God. When encompassed within a framework of revealed theology, such insights from science concerning the origin of the Universe can be seen to be consistent with the existence of a Creator God. Thus anthropic fruitfulness and intelligibility of the Universe are both pointers to and consistent with the God who is revealed in the life, death and resurrection of Jesus.

Is there an eschatological version of such revised natural theology? I suggest that there is, as long as it is encompassed within a framework of revealed theology. The futility of the future of the physical Universe, the disjointedness and present sufferings of the natural world can point beyond themselves. By themselves they can be interpreted in different ways (not least in the problem of evil type arguments against the existence of God) but seen from the perspective of the resurrection of Jesus they point forward to a new creation. The recognition that creation is both a process towards and pointer to new creation has implications for providence, ethics and apologetics that we will explore in Chapter 8.

Fourth, Romans 8 also asks us to take seriously the corrupting influence of human sin. Mascall noted the difficulty of this area when he wrote, 'The fact of original sin is undeniable, but its adequate formulation is the despair of theologians' (Mascall 1956: 43). I share such despair in terms of its dialogue with the end of the physical universe, yet it is something we cannot dismiss altogether if we are going to develop systematic theology in this area. As Gunton points out, a robust doctrine of sin and redemption guards against an over-optimistic view of human evolution as advocated by Peacocke and others.

Finally, we need to continue asking what is the link between God's purposes for the Earth and God's purposes for the whole of the Universe? Is the redemption of humans a part of wider redemptive work? Does this mean that humans have some part to play in the renewal of the cosmos as well as the renewal of the Earth? It is easier to see how renewed human beings may join in with God's purposes of cleaning and caring for the environment. It is harder to see this in a cosmic perspective.

4.8 New creation and this creation

We have surveyed a variety of eschatological images in both the Old and New Testaments. We have adopted this rather detailed examination of scripture as part of our exploration of systematic theology for a purpose. Too often systematics, because of its very nature, has oversimplified the complexity of its themes. The use of a controlling principle such as predestination or one controlling passage or even verse has led some theologians to a very limited view of eschatology. It may have been simpler and shorter in this chapter to have presented a number of biblical themes instead of the focus being on the biblical passages. But the approach we have adopted has illustrated a number of important issues.

At a foundational level, there is diversity and complexity in the eschatological images presented within the Bible and traditionally used in eschatology. We have encountered images of 'fire', the second coming and the new heaven and earth. Systematic theology needs to reflect that diversity and complexity. It is easy to criticise the *Left Behind* authors for their naïve use of scripture and concentration on only one or two passages, but they are not alone in this. Even in Moltmann's comprehensive work, a reliance on 1 Corinthians 15.22–28 is sometimes overstressed. Systematic eschatology may not be as tidy as some would like. Thus, the biblical passages can be used to question theological constructions.

At the same time we need to be sensitive to the handling of such passages. What is challenging to systematic theology is their common attempt to do eschatology in 'the real world'. The new creation is discussed in the context of worship, temples, nations, false teachers and persecution. This encourages us to do our eschatology in our contemporary context of which the scientific predictions of the future of the Universe are part. Very few of the biblical commentators take this seriously, simply ignoring questions of the future of the physical Universe. On the other hand, the temptation to draw science and apocalyptic insights too closely together can affect even distinguished commentators. There is however another way. In the process of attempting to allow the biblical passages and the insights of science to speak directly to each other, we have generated some important considerations for systematic theology.

First, we note the centrality of new creation. Recognition of the various dimensions scripture ascribes to God's work of new creation has led Beale to argue recently that the theme of 'new creation' should be seen as the controlling conception for all of eschatology, and the integrative centre of all the major theological ideas of the New Testament (Beale 1997: 11–52). That may be pushing it a little too far, and as we have pointed out may be due to the way that the imagery of Isaiah 65.17 has been so influential in New Testament eschatology. However, we can agree with Moltmann that, 'Christian eschatology is not about "the end" at all, but about the new creation of all things' (Moltmann 1996: xi). In our theology of the 'last things', there needs to be this strong theme of new creation. Of those theologians we reviewed in Chapter 3, this is certainly true of Moltmann's work but less so in Pannenberg and Russell. Of the 'eschatological scientists', Dyson and Tipler have no conception of new creation. They simply want to keep this creation alive for as long as possible. There is an interesting parallel here with contemporary views of human death. There are those who want to avoid death, even to the extent of being frozen until a time they can be resuscitated and cured in the future of this world. Without resurrection in a new creation, technology is their only hope.

Second, all the passages build their eschatology on an understanding of God as Creator. God is constantly at work sustaining the Universe and new creation is only possible because of this. The passages are about hope based not on the individual's influence or on the ordering of the nations, but that God will act. Hope is based on a transcendent creator God working in his creation. Whatever the circumstances, creation is not limited to its own inherent possibilities. The Creator God can always do a new work. Therefore we can urge that creation and new creation are mutually interdependent in any theological understanding of God's work. Creation needs to be seen in the light of new creation, and new creation needs to be seen in the light of creation. Indeed we have proposed a new pointer for a revised natural theology in the future futility of the physical Universe. The creation is both necessary and points forward to a new creation, in the purposes of God. This is similar to Hardy's point that creation keeps the Universe from ending, but also brings it to an end.

Third, the nature of new creation is hinted at in these passages without any full or consistent answer to how it is related to the present creation. However, the new creation is a transformation, renewal or purification of the present creation rather than a total annihilation and beginning again. Further the relation of the new creation to the old creation is one of both continuity and discontinuity. The images, though concentrating on the theme of the judgement, picture a radical effect on the cosmos. From the reordering of the biological world to cataclysmic events in the sky, the passages in different ways emphasize that that the new creation involves and changes the physical Universe. The new creation is not simply the present order with a renewed humanity. There is something essentially 'new' both for human community and the physical Universe.

Fourth, we see a consistent theme of judgement. Jackelén gives an important reminder that an obvious but often unstated characteristic component of biblical eschatology is a 'getting rid of the bad' (Jackelén 2002). This is in great contrast to the scientific eschatologies of Tipler and Dyson which seem to be all about a simple accumulation of information. As Peters comments, 'The apocalyptic horizon within which intertestamental and New Testaments texts became written and interpreted prompts an acute sense of divine justice' (Peters 2002: 306). This sense of justice and judgement runs throughout the texts. It provides hope for the here and now. Setzer, commenting on the Jewish idea of resurrection, illustrates this, 'Resurrection of the dead serves as an implicit protest, against the world as it is, against Roman hegemony, and against the powerlessness of Israel. These, it says, will not prevail' (Setzer 2001: 96). Finally, all the passages have an ethical focus. They are about moral judgement by God and this is used as a motivation to live a life of righteousness. The new creation becomes an important part of living in this creation.

Fifth, questions of the relationship of human beings to the rest of the Universe, and of the nature of sin are raised. However we formulate the origin or cosmic effect of sin, its importance is that it undercuts all claims of human ability to save ourselves and so establishes our radical need of God's grace as the single source of any possible salvation (Outler 1968: 102). This sense of dependence is central to these biblical passages but missing from a great deal of contemporary eschatology. The future of human beings is intricately bound up with new creation, that is, the future of God's redemptive work for the whole of the physical creation. Perhaps this is similar in the way that both anthropic insights and the early chapters of Genesis see human beings intricately bound up with creation. The role of Jesus Christ in incarnation, resurrection and Parousia then moves to centre stage in this discussion. Both our origin in creation and our future in new creation are related to God's action in Christ, and at the heart of understanding both of these things are the cross and the resurrection. Within this, the understanding of the relationship of the Earth to the Universe is raised by these passages but the focus remains the future for human beings. The terminology of 'heaven' and 'the heavens' and its relation to earth has a number of different meanings, and therefore one must proceed with caution on this question. Yet Romans 8 in particular does question a view that sees God simply transforming planet Earth as a new habitat for his redeemed creatures. Creation and new creation have a much bigger canvas than that.

Sixth, God is at work towards new creation both in the process and in the particular event. The redemption of this creation is pictured in terms of a long process, working through contemporary structures as well as a specific event of judgement such as in the 2 Peter passage. What is common is that both are acts of God. This is of course is always the case. In terms of revelation, we acknowledge God's communication in many and various ways including the faithful processes of creation, alongside the particular of the life, death and resurrection of Jesus. We would also see God at work in the creative processes of the laws of physics and biological evolution, alongside particular actions, which are often called miracles. Just as the incarnation is an unusual space-time event within God's sustaining of the Universe, the second coming is an imaginative reminder to see the particular event of God acting in addition to his more hidden work of trans-formation. It is interesting that the question of providence is addressed directly in 2 Peter 3 in an argument against an early form of the mechanistic universe, which exists without any intervention from God. The understanding of God as Creator is used against such a picture, and new creation suggests a God who not only sustains the regularities of the present creation but also is prepared to work in a radical way beyond those regularities.

Therefore by bringing our scientific picture into dialogue with the biblical passages, we have as Gilkey hoped, begun to tease out some important questions. What does the scientific view of the end of the Universe mean for the doctrine of creation, the doctrine of new creation, the relationship of the Earth to the Universe, providence, our present hope, and our practice of ethics and apolo-getics? We will need to explore these themes in greater detail in the chapters to follow. However, before we do there is one major biblical theme that we have not yet covered, but already highlighted its importance. That is the resurrection, and it is to this that we now turn.

Chapter 5

Reclaiming the Resurrection in Its Cosmological Setting

In the previous chapters we have continually touched on the significance of the resurrection. Yet the resurrection raises its own questions, two of which have seen some significant work in recent years. The first is the relationship of the resurrection to the physical sciences (Peters 2002: 297–321). Russell claims that few theological views of the resurrection have engaged carefully with scientific cosmology, and that in the dialogue of theology and science 'over the past forty years, the resurrection has received little sustained attention' (Russell 2002a: 4). Yet 'the physical sciences, including cosmology, raise tremendous, perhaps insurmountable, challenges to the intelligibility of "bodily resurrection"' (Russell 2002b: 273). Russell's own strategy has been to take the 'worst case scenario' of bodily resurrection and see what that means for physics and cosmology. He provides some insights but acknowledges that his work encourages more thinking in this area. In particular, he does not engage with the biblical texts in detail or recent New Testament scholarship and does not apply his insights to an accelerating Universe. Polkinghorne is much more positive about bodily resurrection, claiming, 'I believe that a downplaying of the empty tomb and of bodily resurrection, is a severe impoverishment of our eschatological understanding' (Polkinghorne 2002a: 49). Once again he provides some useful insights, but shares some of the same limitations as Russell. Is Polkinghorne right to be positive about bodily resurrection, and can Russell's challenge be met in the context of cosmology?

These are interesting questions especially in the light of the second area of significant work, that is, New Testament scholarship on the resurrection. Of particular interest is Wright's thesis that the resurrection, denied by pagans but affirmed by many Jews, was both reaffirmed and redefined by the early Christians. The pagan world assumed it was impossible, the Jewish world believed it would happen eventually, but Christians said it had happened to Jesus (Wright 2003). Further, in the early Christian community there was no spectrum of belief but an almost universal affirmation of resurrection, and that this was seen in terms of bodily resurrection. The future hope of Christians was based on their firm belief that Jesus had been raised from the dead. Wright sees this open to historical study, which he carries out in some detail.

As we have already noted, he stresses the importance of understanding resurrection as 'life after "life after death"' to stress a definite content (some sort of re-embodiment) and a definite narrative shape (a two step story involving death and a period of death as a state) (Wright 2003: 31). This he argues is its constant meaning throughout the ancient world until the second century. He wants to emphasise this to avoid a loose usage of resurrection which is sometimes used as a disembodied 'heavenly' life or continuation of the soul (Porter 1999: 68; Davies 1999: 93), or the claim that the sense of Jesus being raised on the third day is that he was exalted into heaven (Evans 1970: 83; Harvey 1994: 74; Carnley 1987: 18; Perkins 1984: 86), or that it simply means an experience of his risen life (Schillebeeckx 1979; Goulder 1996: 48).

The importance of Wright's work is twofold. First, the tendency to see resurrection as simply the experience of spiritual life or the continuation of the soul has serious consequences for Christian eschatology. I will argue that unless the resurrection of Jesus is seen in terms of physicality, then the creation becomes unimportant and indeed irrelevant to thinking about the future. The resurrection needs to be seen in its cosmological setting rather than simply a picture of individual soul survival. Second, he points us back to engaging with the New Testament texts. The value of this for systematics is that too often the resurrection has been limited in its application. Christian history has offered various implications of the resurrection including its demonstration that Jesus is Lord, hope of life after death, and apologetic proof of the truth of the Christian faith. Yet has it anything to say about the future of creation, in particular the end of the Universe?

The Nicene Creed links the resurrection to the 'the Resurrection of the dead, And the life of the world to come' and many contemporary theologians are quick to link resurrection with eschatology. The resurrection was central for Moltmann in the whole re-discovery of eschatology so that he characterizes the Christian hope as directed 'towards a new creation of all things by the God of the resurrection of Jesus Christ' (Moltmann 1967, 36). However, Moltmann limits his 'all things' to the future of the eco-system and ignores any engagement with the rest of the physical Universe. Likewise, a large number of authors speak of the resurrection as the crucial act in the cosmic drama wherein God will 'transform, redeem and renew all of creation' but then say nothing about 'all of creation' (Perkins 1984: 28–29).

The vast amount of literature within systematics on the resurrection reveals very little thinking of the relationship of resurrection to all of creation. Is this due to the fact that there is little to say about the relationship, or has the understanding of the resurrection been unduly limited? Stendahl and Barr have criticized those who characterized immortality and resurrection in overly individualistic terms motivated by selfishness (Stendahl 1984: 199; Barr 1992: 95). Such individualism means that the resurrection has not been thought about in a cosmic setting, or if it has it has been limited to 'the world' rather the Universe.

If we approach our systematic theology through the richness of the New Testament texts on resurrection in dialogue with the questions of the scientific predictions of the end of the Universe, will that once again generate some fruitful insights in a similar way to the last chapter? In particular will it enable our understanding of the resurrection to reclaim its cosmic dimension and setting? We will therefore suggest that the resurrection is crucial to any Christian understanding of the future of the Universe, and then outline some of the questions and insights that it raises. In particular it will be argued that the biblical literature concerning resurrection questions a 'this worldly' eschatology and encourages us to see more discontinuity between creation and new creation than is represented in current theological thought. We will begin with the key biblical passages of Colossians z5–20, 1 Corinthians 15 and the accounts of the resurrection in the gospels.

5.1 Colossians 1.15–20

Some disagreement continues between biblical scholars over the Pauline authorship of this letter and both the nature and existence of a particular 'heresy' that the writer was responding to (Dunn 1996: 76; Wright 1986; Patzia 1995; O'Brien 1982). My own view is that the evidence for Pauline authorship is strong and that there were a number of ideas attractive to the Colossian Christians from both Jewish and Gentile sources which questioned the supremacy of Jesus (Wilkinson 2002: 142).

Since the work of Norden it has been widely accepted that Paul borrowed an already existing piece of a hymn or liturgy. There is not enough information for us to be sure of its original purpose and setting, but we can be clear about how Paul used this passage. Paul's argument is simply that because Jesus is supreme in all things he is also sufficient for all things. In order to do this Paul uses parallels within the passage to stress the supremacy of Christ in both creation and new creation (Norden 1923; Robinson 1957: 270–87; Hay 2000):

- 'who is' the image of the invisible God (v. 15a) and the beginning (v. 18b)
- 'he is the first-born' of all creation (v. 15b) and from the dead (v. 18c)
- 'he is pre-eminent' as he is before all things (v. 17a) and he might be pre-eminent in all things (v. 18d)
- the Son unifies as in him all things hold together (v. 17b) and he reconciles all things (v. 20a)
- everything is related to him in creation (v. 16b) and in new creation (v. 20c)

In addition the sequence of 'in him … through him … to him …' is paralleled in both verses 16 and 19–20a, implying that the same agent accomplishes both creation and new creation. Jesus is not simply an historical human being or even a mediator of present religious experience; he is both Lord of creation and new creation.

The parallels link creation and new creation. Burney suggested that this hymn in Colossians applies to Jesus everything that could be said of the figure 'Wisdom' (Burney 1925–6: 160–177). He argued that Paul combines Genesis 1.1 with Proverbs 8.22 to suggest that the divine Wisdom has been fully embodied in human form. The one who is creator is also redeemer. The agent of creation is also the goal to which the creation tends, its eschatological purpose. Of course this is based on the Old Testament view that Israel's God, the one who delivered them from Egypt, is also the creator of the whole Universe (Is 40.12–31).

One of the key aspects of this new creation is reconciliation. Sin is overcome by Jesus' death on the cross and Paul's use of 'blood' (v. 20) gives a model for this reconciliation in the idea of sacrifice. However, his canvas is large. Another parallel between the One who creates 'all things' and reconciles 'all things' emphasizes the universal scope of God's action. In fact this is further emphasized by yet another parallel between verses 19 and 20. His argument is that because 'the fullness' of God was in Christ then there will be a fullness of 'all things' redeemed. The image of reconciliation also has the sense of bringing the entire Universe into a new order and harmony, a fulfilment of God's plan for it (Wright 1986: 68).

At the heart of the parallels is the phrase 'first born'. It is used as 'over all creation' (v. 15) and then 'from the dead' (v. 18). Jesus is not only the beginning of the creation; he is also the beginning of the new creation. This is demonstrated by his resurrection. His resurrection is the beginning not only of the new age, but will be followed by the resurrection of believers.

Therefore, in the many parallels that the writer uses, we see again the centrality of Christ, and we have a clear understanding of the link between the resurrection of Jesus and the reconciliation of all things. As Wright puts it, 'with the resurrection itself, a shock wave has gone through the entire cosmos: the new creation has been born, and must now be implemented' (Wright 2003: 239). But we may ask what does it really mean for a shock wave to go through the entire cosmos? In what sense is the new creation born? Perhaps the image of birth is not a bad image in this context. The birth of a child is a dramatic event which has both immediate effects and points forward to a new phase of family life. We can see the pointers to the future in the resurrection. But what are the immediate effects of the resurrection on this creation? The gospel writers interestingly enough see little immediate effects on creation in the aftermath of the resurrection. Indeed, Matthew's earthquake and associated upheavals happens at the death of Jesus (Mt 27.51–53). The immediate effects are of course on transformed, hopeful and puzzled people. The birth of the new creation is seen in the power of the gospel to change lives. However, the dramatic and immediate effects should not blind us to the longer term consequences. In terms of our systematic theology, this passage of Colossians always asks us to expand our horizon in these consequences.

5.2 1 Corinthians 15

Being one of the earliest parts of the New Testament, this passage raises questions of the historicity of the empty tomb and resurrection appearances, and whether Paul's understanding of resurrection differs from that of the gospel writers. In addition, it links the resurrection of Jesus to a bigger eschatological picture.

There remains disagreement over the precise nature of the problem over the resurrection of the dead which Paul addresses here (Thiselton 2000b: 1172–1176). Some argue that it was the belief that there was no life after death at all (Schmithals 1971: 156), some that it was the belief that the resurrection had already happened (Martin 1984: 109–10), some that it was over difficulties of the resurrection of the body (Market 1995: 104–36) and some that they were attempting to produce a mixture of Christianity and paganism (Hays 1999:

391–412). However, it may be that there was a complexity of a number of the above problems at Corinth. What was common was that they were not following through the consequences of the resurrection of Jesus (Mitchell 1992: 284). Wright further suggests that, as Genesis 1–3 is a frequent point of allusion and also provides some of the key structural markers of the passage, Paul intends this entire passage to be an exposition of the renewal of creation (Wright 2003: 313).

5.2.1 *The empty tomb*

What is immediately striking in the short summary of the gospel (v. 1–11) is there is no reference to the empty tomb. This has been used to argue that the empty tomb was not important to the early Christian preaching or was consciously ignored to promote the authority of the male disciples over the women who were first at the tomb (Radford Ruether 1983: 10–11; Borg 1999: 117–28). Marxsen and others have suggested that Paul's description here could be simply interpreted in existentialist terms (Marxsen 1970; Patterson 1998: 218). Of course the gospels are clear about the empty tomb (Eckstein 2002: 115–123), but did Paul share this belief?

Barclay cautions against narrowing our options at this point, due to the breadth of meaning in the noun 'resurrection' (anatasis) and in the verb 'to raise' (egeiren) and the jumble of views about the afterlife held by first century Jews (Barclay 1996: 18). However, the juxtaposition of 'he was buried' and 'he was raised' surely implies an empty tomb especially in the context of first century Judaism where resurrection would always be thought about in physical terms (Sider 1977; Pannenberg 1991–98: 358–360; Fee 1987: 725; Hays 1997: 256). This cannot therefore be interpreted simply as 'Christian experience' (Thiselton 2002: 1197–1202; Wright 2003: 318). Paul sees the resurrection as a public event with witnesses of a specified number, and an implied empty tomb.

Is the empty tomb important for eschatology? The resurrection of Jesus is seen as the 'first fruits' of God's purposes for all creation (v. 20–28). If the resurrection body of Jesus is the model being used for the relationship of old and new creation, then the question is whether the empty tomb means anything for the nature of Jesus' resurrection body. The tomb being empty does not in isolation immediately imply anything about the nature of the resurrection body. However, as we shall see Paul's discussion later in the chapter does explore the nature of the resurrection body (v. 35–58). He uses the image of body but distinguishes between two kinds of body (v. 44). Some commentators take this to mean that Paul did not believe in a bodily resurrection and therefore whether the tomb was empty or not was irrelevant.

Against this it can be strongly argued that that empty tomb is necessary in demonstrating the transformation rather than replacement of the body, and therefore by implication that God's purposes for the material world are that it should be transformed not discarded (Pannenberg 1996: 70; Torrance 1976: 81; Wright 2003: 233). However Pannenberg goes on to qualify the significance of the empty tomb. He notes that the analogy between the resurrection of Jesus and our own resurrection cannot be extended too far. There is a short timescale between Jesus' death and resurrection with his physical body preserved from decay while in our case the timescale is extended and our physical body has decayed. Pannenberg writes,

'There, the transformation occurs through participation of whatever is remembered of our earthly lives in the life of God's eternal life, and when a new life of their own is given to them, it will be something entirely new'. (Pannenberg 1996: 70)

We can expand this point. The resurrection of Jesus occurred in history, exalts him to his rightful place as God's Son, and has universal redemptive significance. This is quite different to the general resurrection which occurs at the eschaton (O'Collins 1987: 180; Davis 1993: vii). In this sense we need to remember that the first fruits indicate the harvest is coming but are different from the harvest in certain respects. While the empty tomb stands within the space-time history of this creation, the resurrection body of Jesus is better suited to the fullness of new creation. Indeed, it is only until the discontinuity of God's action in the Parousia to transform fully this creation that Jesus in resurrected bodily form can return. The empty tomb is the demonstration of God's purposes in transforming creation, while the ascension and Parousia are the confirmation of the limited extent of this creation.

Yet the empty tomb provokes another question. Why was it empty on the third day rather than the first? If there are differences between Jesus' resurrection and the general resurrection, what is the significance of being buried until being raised on the third day (v. 4)? While for the early church it may have been 'in accordance with the Scriptures', the often-used theological explanation that during this time he went to preach to those who had already died, is far from satisfactory. It rests on a notoriously difficult verse (1 Peter 3.19), which cannot support the speculative theology built upon it. Rather, the three days timescale surely supports the bodily nature of resurrection. If the resurrection of Jesus had been thought of only as glorification in heaven, then we must ask why three days at all? Further, the three days point to the importance of time in the transformation of new creation. If the transformation of the body of Jesus occurred in time, we should not be surprised if the corresponding transformation of creation does not happen outside of time.

5.2.2 *The resurrection body*

In the light of this we now consider verses 35–58. These verses have been at the centre of much discussion in terms of the relationship of continuity and discontinuity in new creation (Gillman 1982: 309–33). This revolves around how much continuity there is between the resurrection body and our present bodies, and in particular the meaning of 'natural body' and 'spiritual body' (Schmithals 1971; Pearson 1973; Horsley 1976: 269–88; Sellin 1986).

Those who stress discontinuity are concerned that there is nothing about continuity that could be associated with some kind of eternal entity. Thus the soul has been used to provide the continuity between this life and the next, but in doing so has raised the problem of whether it is an eternal entity in itself. Lindemann suggests that Paul's uses the 'seed' imagery to convey the idea of something newly created both in terms of its matter and its form. We can represent this in the following way

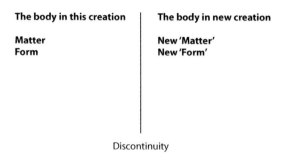

The body in this creation	The body in new creation
Matter	New 'Matter'
Form	New 'Form'

Discontinuity

This is to emphasize that the continuity is located in the 'action of God' (Lindemann 2000: 357). The danger of such a position is whether it does justice to the text and also whether it opens the door to a completely non physical 'spiritual body'. Indeed, in such a picture can we talk about matter or form at all? Yet, whatever discontinuity is indicated, Lincoln is right to see that the heart of this passage is the issue of the nature of the body of the resurrected Lord, and therefore of our bodies in the resurrection (Lincoln 1981: 39–42).

Further, we can note that throughout this passage Paul brings together images from the natural world and images of the resurrected Jesus. It is suggestive that resurrection is already seen in the natural world, stressing a degree of continuity between creation and new creation. Wright points out that Paul alludes to Genesis 1–2 in terms of the major themes of this passage, including plants and animals (v. 39), the heaven and earth (v. 40), the heavenly bodies (v. 41) and the contrast between Adam and Christ (v. 45). His aim is to give a 'deliberate and careful theology of new Genesis, of creation renewed' (Wright 2003: 341). While this focuses attention on the work of God as Creator, it also stresses that new creation comes forth out of this creation. Indeed, there are images in this creation which point forward to new creation.

Those who stress continuity look for contrasts between different kinds of bodies described by Paul (Gooch 1987: 52–84; Martin 1995; Johnson 2003). Gundry suggests that the resurrection body 'is a physical body renovated by the Spirit of Christ and therefore suited to heavenly immortality' (Gundry 1976: 165). Yet part of the problem here is one of language. The term 'physical' can be used of this present human body or can be used of materiality, and it is not often clear how Gundry uses it. He is on safer ground when he argues that Paul's use of the image of 'body' does indicate real continuity between states of creation and new creation.

Johnson points out that Paul's twofold use of 'natural' psychikos and 'spiritual' pneumatikos (1 Cor 2.6–16 and 1 Cor 15), is to distinguish between what is characteristic of 'this age' and of the 'new creation' (Johnson 2003). In the earlier passage the psychikos/pneumatikos distinction is one that has to do with epistemology (Martyn 1997: 89–110), that is they describe two different classes of people who have opposite paradigms for understanding reality. Then in 1 Corinthians 15 Paul uses these same two adjectives in a corresponding way in the context of ontology, that is, to distinguish between a body characteristic of this age and a body that will be truly changed by the Spirit to make it appropriate for the new creation at its consummation.

Martin has suggested that the Corinthians would have viewed the cosmos as a hierarchy that 'ranges from fine, thin, rarified stuff down to gross, thick, heavy stuff' (Martin 1995: 116). Indeed, he argues that what was disparaged was not the general category of embodiment or of materiality, but this present fleshly body composed of heavy elements at the bottom of a hierarchy that has no place in the afterlife (Martin 1995: 3–37, 104–23; Riley 1995: 23–34, 48–58). That was then the problem for the Corinthians in terms of the future. How can the 'thick' human body be resurrected in a 'fine' form? It is a problem with the type of materiality of the resurrection body. Asher disagrees with Martin concerning a hierarchy but does suggest a polarity between the celestial and terrestrial realms. Thus the problem is how the human body is transformed to be able to cope with this celestial existence (Asher 2001: 103).

Johnson follows Martin in that it is this hierarchical view of the cosmos that Paul attempts to 'turn upside down' by arguing that lower status elements like flesh will be transformed and incorporated into the new creation at its consummation. Thus the 'naked' (gymnon) seed (v. 37) that is buried in the ground, Johnson sees as Paul's reference to the corruptible and decaying body of low status flesh which needs to be 'clothed' (v. 53–54). In terms of our diagram above, this picture would be represented by

The body in this creation		The body in new creation
Matter in the body	———————	Transformed 'Matter'
	Continuity	

The question now is how far one can push the seed analogy? Witherington is cautious about how much material continuity can be implied between seed and plant as an analogy for the resurrection body (Witherington 1995: 308). However, Johnson is surely correct that the analogy suggests that the seed's material is somehow incorporated into or 'clothed' with the material of the stalk of wheat. Some material continuity is implied. Nevertheless, Johnson may go too far in claiming that this implies that God does not abandon even the decomposed fleshly material, but somehow redeems and transforms it so that it becomes capable of being the material of the new creation.

In fact the picture is far more complex and subtle than either of the above pictures allow. Verses 39–41 are interesting at this point in the use of 'flesh' and 'body' in terms of animate and inanimate parts of creation. The diversity and continuity is being stressed (Robertson and Plummer 1916: 371–75). 'So will it be with the resurrection of the dead' (v. 41) surely broadens the canvas. The resurrection body will have material continuity but it will not necessarily be redemption of the material of this body. For an individual's resurrection body, God may use the atoms of this Universe but not necessarily the atoms that make up the individual's body now.

This is reinforced through a series of antitheses (v. 42b–44a) using the imagery of sowing:

- perishable (phthora), it is raised imperishable (aptharsia).
- in dishonour, it is raised in glory.
- in weakness, it is raised in power.
- a natural (psychikon) body, it is raised a spiritual (pneumatikon) body.

Verse 42b provides difficulty of translation. The initial term, phthora, has the general meaning of 'dissolution, deterioration, corruption.' Some prefer the term corruption. However, the danger of that is that it is too static a term. Thiselton has rightly argued that a better translation is more dynamic in terms 'in a state of decay' (Thiselton 1964: 229). Thus the second term aptharsia, rather than 'immortality' or 'incorruption', is better expressed as 'non-decaying' or even 'decay's reversal' (Thiselton 2000b: 1272).

Verse 44a then raises the question of whether the natural body that is sown is left behind and does not participate in being raised. Johnson suggests that the rhetorical effect of these verses is that the psychikon body and the pneumatikon body act in an adverbial sense to describe how 'it' is sown and raised. Hence, what is sown, namely a decayed/decaying fleshly body, is also raised, albeit in a changed form that can only be described as a pneumatikon body. However, this is not generally accepted (Fee 1987: 785; Gillman 1982: 327). In addition the continuity has to be limited by the preceding verses 39–41.

The reference to the first and last Adams develops the theme (v. 45–49). Genesis 2.7 is used to justify that the 'natural' body came first and indeed all of us have such a body. It could also convey the sense that this human body was subject to death and decay through Adam's sin. In contrast the last Adam is 'a life giving Spirit' (v. 45). This leads the contrast between natural and spiritual away from the material of what they are made of to a much more dynamic relational concept. The first Adam received the gift of life in a natural body, while the last Adam has the capacity to actively generate the life characteristic of the new creation.

Verse 46 has been used to claim evidence for a realized eschatology at Corinth but this can be overstressed (Johnson 1996: 461; Martin 1995: 105; Hays 1999: 391–412; Thiselton 1978: 510–26). Thiselton also points out that it was used by a surprising number of late nineteenth century commentators to speak about a 'law of progress' perhaps reflecting an evolutionary influence (Edwards 1885: 445; Meyer 1884: 95; Findlay 1961: 938). The movement from natural to spiritual was seen as a development that emphasized continuity.

This illustrates another oversimplification with little evidence in the text. Yet the prevailing philosophy controlled the interpretation. It completely ignores any sense of eschatological discontinuity and marginalises the action of God.

The body in this creation   **The body in new creation**

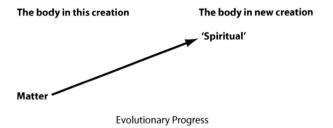

'Spiritual'

Matter

Evolutionary Progress

Johnson makes the important point that Paul's rhetoric here implies that the nature of the discontinuity between the psychikon body and the pneumatikon body has to do with the presence or absence of the effects of sin. While this may involve a supplementing of Paul's thought here with Romans 5.12–21, it does resonate with Jeremias' interpretation that 'flesh and blood cannot inherit the kingdom of God' as an idiom referring to living, but frail and sinful human beings (Jeremias 1956: 151–59).

In the light of this, how do we characterize the continuity and discontinuity present in the resurrection body? Is it, as Johnson argues, that the human body of flesh is not annihilated but rather the 'making alive Spirit' transforms its 'this age' (psychikon) characteristics into pneumatikon ones enabling that person to participate in the new creation at its consummation? We may agree that it is a body characterized by freedom from the ravaging effects of sin, a body so pervaded by the influence of the 'making alive Spirit' that it has no propensity to death and decay (Barrett 1994: 372). However, the difficulty lies in the 'human body of flesh is not annihilated'. This seems to be overstressing continuity and based on a static view of the body.

The question is what is this natural body? In fact the atoms within our bodies are constantly changing, being exchanged with the rest of the Universe (Prokes 1996: 45). This means a continual changing with time and in relationship with its physical surroundings. Therefore to speak of it not being totally annihilated is very difficult. Indeed, post death this interchange of material with the surroundings is accelerated, a point highlighted by Pannenberg with regard to the difference between Jesus' resurrection and our resurrection. Dabney is right when he suggests that in the resurrection of the body, God will redeem 'not just that body, the locus of our existence, but the entirety of our embodied life: the whole of our relationships, our experiences and our encounters, all that makes up our identity' (Dabney 2001: 61–62). However, as we saw earlier with Moltmann this does not necessarily mean that God has to redeem every diachronic extent of a person's life.

Thiselton sees more discontinuity than either Martin or Johnson in the image of seed and plant (Thiselton 2000b: 1259). He helpfully sees the natural body and the spiritual body in much more dynamic terms. The natural body is in a state of decay with 'decreasing capacities and increasing weaknesses, issuing in exhaustion and stagnation' (Thiselton 1964: 229). He uses the illustration of a person who is suffering from the weakness of a wasting disease. This person may be transferred into the medical care of the hospital at which point a decisive change has occurred. However en route to a full recovery the patient remains beset with weakness until the process of care is complete.

The resurrection body is then characterized by decay's reversal, that is, a purposeful flourishing. This is a more helpful image than that of immortality, and gives the sense of some form of temporality to the resurrection body (Collins 1999: 567). Thiselton goes on to stress on the basis of verse 38 that the sovereign power of God is able to enact far-reaching transformation of his own devising however unimaginable it may be to human minds now. The continuity is provided not by the 'stuff' but by the 'identity' resurrected by God in a different mode of existence.

However Thiselton goes too far. He rightly wants to stress a discontinuity by seeing Paul addressing the mode of the resurrection body rather than the substance. But the question of substance still remains. We can agree with Fee that 'the transformed body is not composed of "spirit"; it is a body adapted to the eschatological existence that is under the ultimate domination of the Spirit' (Fee 1987: 786). But we are still left with the question of what is the 'stuff' of the new body. Of course we cannot answer that question in isolation. Thiselton is indeed right that for Paul 'what counts as a body … depends precisely upon its immediate environment and purpose' (Thiselton 2000b: 1278).

Padgett suggests that for Paul body is always form-plus-substance (Padgett 2002a: 155ff). He comments that some have 'pushed' Paul into believing that the resurrection body will have 'light' or 'glory' as its substance, which does not do justice to the text (Lietzmann 1949; Weiss 1910). Nevertheless he asserts that a body has substance which is the main point of this passage from Corinthians. In the case of the spiritual body, the substance is 'of heaven', but that does not permit us to assume that it is made of 'light' or 'glory.'

While there are useful insights here, the tendency of commentators is to reduce the complexity of the pictures that Paul is using. This must be resisted, as the complexity is very useful for the dialogue with science both in terms of human identity and the future of the Universe. We must hold to body being substance-form-mode-context for Paul in dialogue with the assumptions of his Corinthian listeners. In the contrast of the natural and resurrection body we must consider continuity/discontinuity in all four of these aspects. The resurrection body is more than physical but not less, it is animated by the Spirit, dynamic in the sense of purposeful flourishing and freed from the decay associated with sin. Its context is new creation.

Barrett characterizes Paul's view as 'resurrection means transformation' (Barrett 1994: 372). But we need to see transformation not just of substance but also of substance-form-mode-context. On this basis Paul is implying not the exchange of one body for something completely different, but transformation (Davis 1993: 50; Hawthorne 1983: 172–173). Yet we must hold the importance of discontinuity in this picture. The old body is subject to death and decay, while the resurrection body is characterized by growth. The key to both continuity and discontinuity is to be found in the action of God in this transformation

This complexity needs to be maintained as we attempt to relate to science. Jeeves and Berry comment:

'there is no suggestion of a physical continuity between our present body and the resurrection body ... (the) continuity is essential at the level of our personal relationship with God; our personality will be re-expressed in this new embodiment, with the same essential relational structure that identifies and distinguishes us as individuals here and now.' (Jeeves and Berry 1998: 148)

They then use an interesting illustration which is of metabolic change during a night's sleep. Although our body changes during the night we wake up to find ourselves as same individual. The continuity to life in this creation is provided by the same reason for continuity between this life and the new creation, that is, God's divine sustaining of all life moment by moment. While underestimating the physical continuity implied by this illustration and the passage itself, it is helpful in highlighting the importance of God's work in all of this.

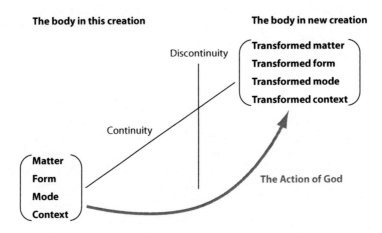

Here the doctrine of providence enters the discussion. For those who overstress continuity in new creation, it has often been the doubting of any providential action by God within the Universe that has meant that the continuity needs to be found in something 'natural'. Yet central to Paul's view is the action of God. Kennedy comments that the only organic link between this body and the glory to come is 'the sovereign power of God' (Kennedy 1904: 243). This gives hope even when the future cannot be conceived fully. Resurrection therefore distinguishes Christian eschatology from secular futurology and introduces the unexpected into the unfolding of the Universe (Thiselton 2000a: 9–10).

Thus we see again the complexity of description of the future state within the biblical literature but the over-riding theme of transformation through the action of God. There is no support for a swing to continuity that neglects discontinuity. The key to resurrection and new creation is not the importance of the material but the action of the creator God. The crucial point is that all things in creation and new creation are dependent on the Creator's power. While there are different types of physicality throughout creation (v. 39–41), they are there because of the creative action of God. Likewise, there may be different kinds of physicality in the new creation because of the resurrection action of God by the Son's authority and in the power of the Spirit. Whatever the images of continuity and discontinuity, the fact that images are used from creation is a reminder of where the tension is located, that is in the sovereign act of renewal by the Creator God. It is gift.

5.3 The Gospels

The diversity in the gospel accounts of the resurrection needs to be taken seriously (Mt 28.1–20; Mk 16.1–8; Lk 24.1–53; Jn 20.1–21.25). The gospel accounts apparently disagree on who came to the tomb, what they found there and where the resurrection appearances happened. Barclay characterizes four positions in regard to the gospel accounts (Barclay 1996). First, there are those who attempt to harmonize all the material into a single historical account (Harris 1983; Wenham 1984). Second, there are those who do not attempt such a harmonization but view both the empty tomb and appearance stories as containing a reliable historical core (Dunn 1985: 63–9; Brown 1993). Third there are those who consider the empty tomb as legendary but uphold the veracity of the appearances (Lindars 1983: 116–35). Fourth and finally, there those who reject any historicity at all (Lüdemann 1994; Goulder 1996: 48; Crossan 1998: 550–73; Patterson 1998: 213).

While the details of the historical arguments both for and against the empty tomb and the resurrection appearances are extensive (Marxsen 1970: 68; O'Collins 1978: 49; Fuller 1980: 115; Beasley Murray 1999: 367–370; Wright 2003: 587ff), we should not neglect the representation of the tension of continuity and discontinuity when these passages are taken together. Whether at the stage of when the Canon of scripture was formed or at an earlier stage when independent accounts of the resurrection were in circulation, part of the diversity of the narratives reflects such a tension (Welker 2002: 35).

The continuity between the body of Jesus before and after resurrection is reflected by:

- the risen Jesus is recognized by the disciples (Jn 20.19–20)
- he can be touched (Mt 28.9; Jn 20.17; Lk 24.39)
- he eats fish (Lk 24.42–43)
- he shows them his hands, feet and side (Lk 24.39; Jn 20.24–31)

These passages emphasise physicality (Gundry 1994: 204–19). Of course central to the gospel accounts was the tradition of the empty tomb. Theologically this acts to rule out any re-interpretation of the resurrection that makes it indistinguishable from mere immortality (Carson 1991: 638). Yet there is more than just physicality. These things have often been so overemphasized that expressions of Christian belief in popular piety and apologetics have bordered on physical resuscitation rather than resurrection. However, discontinuity is also stressed within the gospel accounts. Although they know that this is the same Jesus he seems to have different physical characteristics:

- the disciples have trouble recognizing Jesus and some continue to doubt (Jn 20.14; 21.4; 21.12; Mt 28.17; Lk 24.37)
- he did not seem to be limited to space and time, appearing in rooms with locked doors (Jn 20.19–20)
- there is a real sense of mystery to the resurrection appearances (Mk 16.1–8)

Fletcher-Louis points out that these appearances have some similarities but also differences with the appearances of angels in Luke-Acts. Jesus disappears and appears suddenly, but Luke presents the risen Jesus as both more divine and more human than the angels (Fletcher-Louis 1997: 62–70). While we agree with this, the similarities with angels are not in terms of the 'spiritual nature' of the risen Jesus, but in terms of his unexpected appearances and sense of transcendence.

The account of the disciples on the road to Emmaus gives an interesting example of how exegesis has been dominated by continuity more than disconti-nuity. The two disciples walk miles with Jesus without seeming to recognize him (Lk 24.13–35). Commentators give many suggestions why, including the Sun was in their eyes, their eyes were filled with tears or that they were too frightened to look around! Others more convincingly see the revelation of Jesus in the scriptures and in the breaking of bread being key to the passage (Crüsemann 2002: 89–102). However, the obvious point is that Luke is telling us that Jesus was somehow different. Jesus in some way has transcended the constraints of his earthly life. He is the Jesus that the disciples knew but he is different (Marshall 1978: 892–900).

Yet again we see an undervaluing of discontinuity in interpretation of the resurrection. Wright has characterized the 'modern consensus' among critical scholars to be around the claim that the resurrection narratives grew up following a belief in Jesus' exaltation (Wright 2003: 588). These narratives produced the 'apologetic legends' of an empty tomb, 'bodily' stories of the risen Jesus to combat docetism, and a second stage ascension (Bultmann 1968: 290; Robinson 1982: 5–37). In addition, the diversity in the narratives come out of rival claims for apostolic authority in the early church (Riley 1995: 78–126).

This will not do as an adequate explanation. There is a surprising lack of reference to other biblical passages and indeed a lack of application to personal hope in the resurrection narratives (Williams 2000: 195; Wright 2003: 599) which might be expected if the stories had been created for theological reasons. Further we might have expected that the risen Jesus of the gospel writers was the vision of a dazzling figure of Jewish apocalyptic tradition (Dan 12.2–3), and that the first witnesses would not be women (Bauckham 2002: 268–77) As we have argued above, it is not the case that Paul did not believe in bodily resurrection and an empty tomb. Finally, if the stories had been created then we would expect them to be much tidier and consistent (Wedderburn 1999: 37).

It is the discontinuity of the transformation of the body and how to represent this discontinuity that adds to the 'untidiness' of the gospel accounts. As Williams says of the resurrection narratives:

'They do not fall tidily into familiar genres; they do not easily present themselves as fulfilments of prior expectation ... They are painfully untidy stories, reflecting sometimes all too plainly the various political interests at work in the formulation of the tradition, yet containing more than those interests can manage. The central image of the gospel narratives is not any one apparition but the image of an absence, an image of the failure of images, which is also an absence that confirms the reality of a creative liberty, an agency not sealed and closes, but still obstinately engaged with a material environment and an historical process.' (Williams 1996: 100)

5.4 Resurrection and the future of the Universe

Extensive surveys of the material show that, with some minor variations, the bodily resurrection of Jesus was the foundation of thinking about the future in the early church in 1 Clement, 2 Clement, Ignatius of Antioch, Polycarp, the Didache, the Letter of Barnabas, the Shepherd of Hermas, Papias, the Ascension of Isaiah, the Apocalypse of Peter, 5 Ezra, the Epistula Apostolorum, Polycarp of Smyrna, Justin Martyr, Athenagorus, Theophilus, Minucius Felix, Tertullian, Irenaeus, Hippolytus, and Tatian (Hill 2002b; Daley 2002: 136–164; Wright 2003: 480–552). Much of this was worked out in an apologetic context in dialogue with pagan contemporaries and a wide range of beliefs concerning human survival after death. It is also interesting to note that in many of these writers the resurrection was based on a strong understanding of God as Creator, and this led to a strong sense of God's purposes for this material creation and its goodness. We also see in many places the importance of the theme of judgement linked with resurrection and an apologetic usefulness of the theme of God as creator linked to the God of the resurrection. The link broadens the implications of the resurrection beyond a simple existential description of experiencing the life of Christ or of evidence to convince the individual of the truth of the gospel.

It is only in the third century in the Acts of Thomas and the Nag Hammadi treatise Epistle to Rheginos that we see bodily resurrection rejected and Gnosticism developing. However, Daley points out that around the same time, we see the development of the conception of resurrection as the reassembly of scattered material fragments, a conception which was to remain powerful through to Augustine. Origen, although sometimes characterized as denying bodily resurrection, introduced the important concept of resurrection as trans-formation. He disliked resurrection as reconstitution as he saw the human person in terms of continual psychosomatic change. Here we begin to see the resurrection beginning to open up a dialogue with the kind of questions that science would pose. Yet too often those questions have concentrated on the fate of an individual after death. Often neglected has been the cosmic dimension of the resurrection.

We have seen in the biblical passages above, the centrality of the resurrection for creation and new creation, whether in the reconciliation of all things or in the imagery of 'firstfruits' which signifies the pledge of that which is to come (Hamilton 1957: 19–25, 31–33; De Boer 1988: 109; Holleman 1996: 49–50). The tradition of Western philosophy reflecting individualism, the mechanistic Universe of Newton and the belief that all things are under the tyranny of logic has led to systematic theology devaluing the cosmic dimensions of a resurrection which is characterised by discontinuity as well as continuity. It is interesting that often biblical scholars have been more ready to see the cosmic implications even if they have been unable to then allow them to interact with the insights of science. Yet from detailed exploration of the biblical passages we begin to see some important areas of fruitful dialogue emerging. We group these cosmic implications of the resurrection under the following points.

5.4.1 Resurrection and the doctrine of creation

Morgan comments on the empty tomb:

> 'However unhistorical, it expresses Christian claims that God really vindi-cated Jesus ... It further symbolizes the Christian belief that human flesh and bones are precious'. (Morgan 1994: 18)

Morgan does not seem to see the inconsistency of this statement. If flesh and bones are precious then surely the tomb should be empty. He is right to stress that the empty tomb is one of the strongest indications of God's commitment to this creation, but we have argued above that the historicity of the empty tomb leads to this, rather than the empty tomb being read back as a symbol of God's commitment.

O'Donovan further suggests that resurrection is God's vindication of creation and our created life. Using the parallel between Christ and Adam, he argues that the resurrection is the affirmation of the initial gift of life and a transformation of that gift of life (1 Cor 15.22, 45):

> 'It might have been possible ... before Christ rose from the dead, for someone to wonder whether creation was a lost cause. If the creature consistently acted to uncreate itself, and with itself to uncreate the rest of creation, did this not mean that God's handiwork was flawed beyond hope of repair? ... Before God raised Jesus from the dead, the hope that we call 'gnostic', the hope for redemption from creation rather than for the redemption of creation, might have appeared to be the only hope.' (O'Donovan 1986b: 14)

It is important to understand that O'Donovan sees creation not as the raw material of the Universe but as the 'order and coherence' in which it is composed. The resurrection 'assures us that the very thing which God has made will continue and flourish' (O'Donovan 1986b: 31). However, God's plans go further than just this creation. The resurrection vindicates the created order in that it redeems it and transforms it.

Therefore, the resurrection opposes the view that simply because the Universe is destined to heat death that it is without value. At the same time it also opposes the view that this Universe is an end in itself. The resurrection reminds us that God acts in this creation for its renewal and transformation. The 'order and coherence' of the Universe, embodied in the faithfulness of the scientific laws of the physical Universe, will not be totally rejected by God in the new creation.

This may be of importance in how we view the future of time. Jones argues that it is a common misconception to see Bultmann as uninterested in bodily resurrection (Jones 1996: 32). This is because Bultmann sees the resurrection as revealing the full meaning of what it means to be human in the sight of God and to be human is to be embodied. Thus Jones suggests the bodily resurrection is important for it locates the risen Jesus in time. This is an affirmation of created time. As Rahner states, Christian faith 'must contain an eschatology which really bears on the future, that which is still to come, in a very ordinary, empirical sense of the word time' (Rahner 1966: 326). We therefore need to oppose any suggestion that the new creation is 'timeless' and the subsequent undervaluing of the gift of time in this creation. Time is not a mistake or an imperfection in creation. Moltmann's view of 'eternal time' comes close to this and must be resisted.

If this creation is affirmed and yet shown to be in need of transformation, the resurrection also discloses the nature of the Creator. The resurrection in body and time speaks of the immanence and transcendence of God's presence in the world. Peacocke rightly comments that his Jewish followers encountered in Jesus:

'especially in the light of his resurrection, a dimension of that divine transcendence which, as devout monotheists, they attributed to God alone. But they also encountered him as a complete human being and so experienced an intensity of God's immanence in the world different from anything else in their experience or tradition.' (Peacocke 1990: 343)

However, we note that Peacocke prefers 'personal resurrection' to bodily resurrection (Peacocke 1990: 332). This leads to a view of new creation where the purposes of God for human beings will 'finally achieve their fulfilment beyond space and time within the very being of God himself' (Peacocke 1979: 353). This is inconsistent. The immanence of God in this creation is a very important affirmation of the value of the space-time structure of the Universe. Holding the resurrection alongside this, means that an immanent and transcendent God is able to affirm and offer transformation to a Universe destined in scientific terms to futility. Talk of 'beyond space and time' is unhelpful and misleading.

We may also suggest one other implication of the resurrection for the doctrine of creation. That is, the resurrection implies that this creation is destined to end. Paul sees the eschatological process already begun (Witherington 1992: 28). The resurrection is a sign that in Thiselton's translation of 1 Corinthians 7.31, 'the external structures of this cosmos are passing away' (Thiselton 2000b: 585). Paul's eschatological frame indicates a dynamic cosmic process, with an end to this creation. This not only resonates with the insights from science that the end of this Universe is futility but also with Hardy's suggestion that creation keeps the Universe from ending, but also brings it to an end. The stress on discontinuity is important here. Too much continuity between this creation and new creation does not take seriously the ending of this creation. The resurrection acts as a reminder of the discontinuity.

5.4.2 *Resurrection and the doctrine of new creation*

Peters, in noting some of the scientific picture of the end of the Universe, puts it bluntly when he states, 'Rather than consonance, it appears that we have dissonance between physical cosmology and Christian eschatology' (Peters 2002: x). He goes on to suggest that physical cosmology has the potential for falsifying Christian belief in the resurrection, if in the future the whole of the creation is not renewed. Now this seems to be a profound statement, but what does it actually mean? At what point in the future might such a judgement be made? If intelligent life itself is destined to death in an accelerating Universe, then does the last person standing make such a judgement before switching out the lights! Even then it is not impossible for the full renewal of this creation to be after that time. Peters is making a meaningless statement. However the link he is making can be stated in a much more positive and meaningful way. Christian belief in the resurrection gives us knowledge now of the future of the renewal of the whole of the creation. Indeed, seen in this way, we do not see dissonance between physical cosmology and Christian eschatology.

For if resurrection affirms creation, then it also points forward to new creation. Moltmann points out that it in the experience of the futility of this creation that:

> 'Faith in the resurrection is the faith in God of lovers and the dying, the suffering and the grieving. It is the great hope which consoles us and gives us new courage.' (Moltmann 1996: 73)

Rather than seeing the resurrection in the perspective of history, Moltmann argues that history needs to be seen in the perspective of Christ's resurrection, that is, the resurrection gives a new framework to history. Thus the future should not be focused on heat death as an inevitable end to God's purposes, but should be focused on the resurrection. He uses Romans 8.11 to illustrate the link between Christ's resurrection in the past with the present experience of the Spirit with the future promise of resurrection from the dead. Therefore resurrection is experienced now and the resurrection hope is for this world. The resurrection is God's eschatological act in history but it is also 'the first act in the new creation of the world'.

This is a very helpful description of the implications of the resurrection for new creation. As we discussed in Chapter 3, Moltmann sees the resurrection of Jesus as the paradigm for the new creation of all things. This does not mean just human beings but the whole of creation, that is 'animals, plants, stones and all cosmic life systems' (Moltmann 1990: 258). Yet we saw that the phrase 'cosmic life systems' is not expanded in any detail and is not worked out for the Universe as a whole. This is due to the lack of detailed biblical engagement and indeed dialogue with contemporary science in the work of Moltmann.

In the light of our engagement with both the science and the biblical literature we can now push further our critique of Moltmann's view that the resurrection is the paradigm for the new creation. First, the exploration of what the resurrection means for cosmic life systems is both possible and necessary. The biblical material, while having its own limitations in terms of its anthropocentric and cultural horizons, nevertheless encourages a questioning of the implications for the whole of creation. This comes in part from the centrality of God as creator within its thinking. Systematic theology must take both the scientific insights and biblical material more seriously in thinking about new creation. Moltmann's inability to expand seriously his thinking to the Universe means that his view of the resurrection as hope for this world can easily become a 'this-worldly' hope. While important in inspiring Christian action in areas of justice and environment, it does not translate well to questions concerning the end of the Universe. He attempts to hold discontinuity but then because his theological horizon is so limited to human beings and the environment of the Earth, it subtly collapses into continuity. In the light of the end of the Universe the discontinuity in the resurrection appearances gives more ground for believing that God's actions will radically transform the physical Universe.

Second, Moltmann suggests that the continuity of old and new in the renewal of creation does not issue from the history of the old creation, but it is created by God's act of new creation. We have seen that the danger of positions that overstress continuity is that new creation can be seen to issue from old creation and we neglect the aspect of God's action. The resurrection stresses discontinuity and the action of God alongside continuity. Moltmann is therefore surely right to see the resurrection in this way. The strength of this picture of the resurrection is that it allows eschatology to be based on something beyond the natural physical processes.

Third, Moltmann suggests that the new creation is not a restoration to original perfection but a 'transformation in the transcendental conditions of the world itself'. As we have seen transformation is a key concept for the biblical literature. The world is not annihilated in order to be re-created, nor does some inherently eternal part of creation survive into new creation. The resurrection demonstrates the transformation of the whole, whether it be the body of an individual or the world. However, Moltmann then goes on to claim that the transformation is about the temporal creation becoming eternal creation just as the resurrection was transformation of the mortal into the eternally living Christ. At this point we must disagree. The New Testament does seem to picture the resurrection as something more than a restoration to original perfection, but Moltmann is unconvincing in suggesting that the transformation is characterized by the change from transient time to eternal time. There is no need to see the transformation in this way. Indeed our consideration of the resurrection body as discussed in 1 Corinthians 15 and the gospel narratives leads to the opposite conclusion. Transformation is not about transient to eternal time but about a process of decay to a process of growth. The resurrection appearances of Jesus speak of a strong relationship to historical time. Jesus spends a certain length of time with the disciples, he eats, he speaks, he develops relationships, and he teaches – all of which are time dependent. The key seems to be that Jesus is no longer bound by the constraints of time. He is no longer bound by the having to journey between different locations, and of course will not undergo the negative processes of the passing of time such as decay and death.

Fourth, Moltmann suggests that Christ's solidarity with the dead and the transfigured form of his temporally lived life means that the whole of what has happened in the lives of all creatures and in the whole of the time of this creation, will be gathered up, healed and transfigured into eternal life and eternal time. We have argued that this does not necessarily follow from the resurrection or the biblical literature. Thomas agrees, pointing out that the forty days of resurrection appearances and the time between resurrection and Parousia rejects a view of new creation as timeless eternity (Thomas 2002: 264–5). This is important to maintain. There is a tendency in Moltmann and indeed other systematicians to devalue the importance of time. Barth comments:

> 'For us, therefore the resurrection and the parousia are two separate events. But for Him they are a single event. The resurrection is the anticipation of the parousia as His parousia is the completion and fulfillment of the resurrection.' (Barth 1936–62: 490)

Now of course the resurrection and Parousia can be thought of a single movement including the ascension. But to term them as a 'single event' either runs the risk of the *Left Behind* writers of confusing the promise of the Parousia with the resurrection, or leaves us with the question of why is there a temporal gap between resurrection and Parousia? The very fact that Jesus appears as resurrected body, then disappears from view, in order to return again is important for holding in tension, the ending of this creation and its transformation to new creation. Further if the resurrection and Parousia are a single event, then what does that mean for the doctrine of the Spirit at work in the world? Pannenberg seems to notice this point, but then because of his emphasis on the proleptic nature of the resurrection falls into the same trap:

> 'The coming again of Christ will be the completion of the work of the Spirit that began in the incarnation and with the resurrection of Jesus. From the standpoint of eternity we have here one and the same event because the incarnation is already the inbreaking of the future of God, the entry of eternity into time'. (Pannenberg 1991–98: 627)

There is no need to collapse the incarnation, work of the Spirit, Parousia and resurrection into the same event. If we use the term 'single movement' as in Paul's parabola movement of Philippians 2.6–11, we maintain the interdependency but also see the space-time distinctiveness of particular actions of God in specific events.

We see through all of this that time is a much richer concept than simple models would indicate. Further, we need to make a distinction between the risen but present Christ and the risen but absent Christ. As Thomas helpfully notes, the primary absence expressed in spatial terms in the ascension is paralleled in temporal terms, that is he is absent until he comes (Thomas 2002: 265). In order to explore this more fully we will need to return to it in Chapter 6 when we examine the nature of time.

While Moltmann and Pannenberg raise issues of space and time, there is one other aspect of the resurrection which is important for the scientific picture.

Russell and Murphy question whether the resurrection of Jesus is the first instantiation of a new law of nature (Murphy 2002: 202–18; Russell 2002a: 3–30). Murphy suggests that the laws of nature can be read back into the elemental spirits of the Universe (Col 2.8), but the exegesis is unconvincing. Russell seems particularly keen on a new law in order to avoid his perceived sense that the present laws of physics predict a futile end to the Universe and that this is inconsistent with Christian eschatology. Thus a new law of physics, as yet unknown outside the resurrection, solves the problem. This appeal to an unknown law has been a classic appeal in defending miracles (Wilkinson and Frost 2000: 173). While this may be the case, it is not necessary to invoke such a view of the resurrection. Russell's pessimism is misplaced concerning the lack of consonance between cosmology and Christian eschatology. However, on the basis of the picture of new creation that we have been developing we need to be open to a transformation of the physical laws themselves. Of course if the transformation is characterised solely by discontinuity, then our ability to describe anything in physical terms in the new creation becomes almost impossible. However if there is both continuity and discontinuity in the transformation of the physical laws we should be able to speculate a limited yet significant amount. We have also been led to agree with Polkinghorne and Russell that God must have created the Universe with precisely those conditions and characteristics that it needs in order to be transformable by God's new creative and transforming act.

5.4.3 Resurrection and the relationship of the Earth to the Universe?

Anthropic insights from science and particular passages such as Romans 8 have raised the question as to the significance of human beings in creation and new creation. Typically however theologians have been content to explore the future of human beings in relation to the future of the Earth. Occasionally, a few theologians have speculated more widely, in particular in the whole area of the incarnation in relation to the search for extraterrestrial intelligence (Weston 1920: 128–129; Milne 1952: 153; Pittenger 1959: 248; Jaki 1980; Mascall 1956: 36). Indeed, as I have argued elsewhere the consideration of this scientific possibility raises interesting questions for biblical hermeneutics and systematics (Wilkinson 1997).

What is the relationship of the Earth to questions of new creation? One suggestion is that God transforms the Earth and leaves it in its place in the present Universe. That however will not do. In such a scenario, a transformed Earth would still be vulnerable to comet impact, the Sun going to a red giant stage and the accelerating Universe. Any transformation of life on Earth must be closely linked with a transformation of the whole Universe. As we have seen such a broad canvas is far more consistent with the biblical material.

Yet how do God's particular actions in incarnation and resurrection as historical events on the Earth relate to the rest of the Universe? The gospels see the resurrection of Jesus linked to the global task of evangelism (Mt 28.16–20), although a more universal significance is seen in the linked accounts of the ascension. However, Paul's understanding seems to be very clear that the events of death and resurrection in Jerusalem have far reaching effects for 'all things' (1 Cor 15.20–28; Col 1.15–20). Thus, the resurrection demonstrates that the purposes of God revealed in Jesus are consistent with his purposes for all creation. Therefore, we cannot envisage a renewed humanity or even a renewed Earth without a renewed creation as a whole.

We can see this link in two other doctrinal considerations which we have briefly noted in our discussion so far. The first is the work of the Spirit. The New Testament sees the Spirit involved in the resurrection of Jesus and is at work in the life of the believer before the final resurrection (1 Peter 3.18; Rom 8.11). The Spirit is also involved in the current reign of Christ and in the future resurrection of believers (2 Cor 13.4; 1 Cor 6.14). Therefore Thomas argues that the hope of new creation must be seen against the backdrop of the work of the Holy Spirit now (Thomas 2002: 255–276). Further, we have images of the Spirit as firstfruits or first instalment (Rom 8.23; 1 Cor 1.22; Eph 1.13–14). In this sense, the Spirit mediates the risen presence of the Jesus who is physically absent. The Spirit's work both in the church and the world is transformative. As it is the same Spirit at work we might expect parallels between the transformation of the individual believer and the community of the church and the transformation of creation as a whole. This is certainly highlighted by Paul in Romans 8 and raises some important questions for anthropology and mission. For example, the transformation of new creation is through both process and particular event. One might expect the same pattern within the life of the believer, or in the transformation of community.

Earlier in Chapter 3 we raised questions with Pannenberg's equating of the Spirit with a physical field. While problems of physicalizing and depersonalizing God remain, there is something in Pannenberg's conviction that the work of the Spirit needs to be seen as dynamic and as giving priority to the whole over parts. He wants to see the Spirit as giving cohesiveness to the Universe. Indeed, the work of the Spirit could be seen as giving cohesiveness to the work of new creation. Perhaps the Spirit is the ground and the redeemer of the relationality inherent in the Universe. Where the relationship between God and his creation is restored we see the work of the Spirit in new creation. Thus the signs of the Spirit's presence on the Earth from the community of the church to environmental regeneration are the firstfruits of the new creation of the cosmos. We will return to what this means for space-time and matter in the next chapters.

It is worth noting that in contemporary Wesleyan scholarship this movement of new creation through individual conversion to social change and then to a cosmic perspective has become very popular (Runyon 1998; Maddox 2002). In fact as we noted in Section 3.1, Wesley was one of the few theologians to take the cosmic significance of new creation seriously. This was surely the outworking of a strong sense of the Spirit being at work in the world. This aspect has perhaps not had enough attention from Wesleyan scholars.

The second aspect concerning the relationship of the Earth to the Universe as a whole is in the relationship of the ascension to the resurrection. Farrow has helpfully emphasized the doctrinal importance of the ascension, not least in the hiddenness of the resurrected body of Jesus (Farrow 1999). Does the ascension give us a sense of the hiddenness of the work of new creation? The fullness of the new creation which includes a transformed time and space and a lack of decay is hidden from us on the Earth. It is held back and only partially present through the Spirit (Torrance 1965: 98). The temporal gap between ascension and Parousia implies that God wants to take time to bring about the final redemption and at the same time unfold this creation (Thomas 2002: 266). The ascension also universalizes the resurrection for the whole of creation.

5.5 Continuity, discontinuity and transformation

The resurrection has always been linked to hope. Houlden notes that the setting of the resurrection in the New Testament is in apocalyptic expectations, and suggests that it may be 'an icon of the fact, inescapably involved in faith, that Jesus is the focus of hope and life' (Houlden 1986: 150). If there is going to be a focus for hope in the scientific picture of the end of the Universe it needs to be something outside of the scientific process and Houlden's emphasis on Jesus is helpful. Race commends Houlden's view as:

> 'rescuing the enterprise of hope from a rigid dependency on the outcome of sterile debates about, for example, what really happened at "the resurrection". It also has the advantage of opening up alternative possibilities for engaging in fresh explorations of the meaning of hope'. (Race 1994: 178)

Race attempts to apply this 'opening up' to ecology and militarism. He rightly points out that images of hope prevalent within contemporary society depend on the imperative for survival. However, rather than see the resurrection as providing a hope which goes beyond mere survival, he sees hope in the development of a global ethic looking for areas of agreement between different religions. In fact, to develop such a global ethic he jettisons the resurrection as historical event. Race's analysis of other religions borders on the discredited comparative religion approach in religious education of the 1960s-1970s. More importantly his hope is totally 'this worldly'. It lacks any moral or theological distinctive and as a number of leading scientists have recently pointed out the development of a 'global ethic' by itself is insufficient to make a difference to the environmental crisis (Berry 1994: 138; Prance 1996; Berry 2000: 2003).

We take a completely different approach. By allowing the insights of the biblical texts to inform a discussion of eschatology in the light of scientific predictions about the end of the Universe, we have defended the importance of the historical event and also developed some of the cosmic implications of the resurrection. Pannenberg has argued that history in all its totality can be understood only when viewed from its end point and the end of history is disclosed 'proleptically' in the history of Jesus Christ (Pannenberg 1968: 66–73). So what might be disclosed for us in the resurrection that will be important for the future of the Universe?

First, and in line with the previous chapter, the biblical texts point us towards the importance of the action of God as a basis for hope for the future. The resurrection of Jesus questions a view of the world as a closed system with no room for God's action. Indeed such a closed system gives little hope for the future of the Universe. Theologians who limit their engagement just to the individual or society or even to the Earth can give false hope by reliance on progress and evolution of human society. Stressing continuity in the future with what is happening in the present, considering a short time period and narrowing the focus to the Earth, it can be argued that you can see such progress. But these pictures rarely consider that the Universe is destined to decay and futility. The picture is far too simplistic. Creation is both about the development of complex life and about pointers forward to new creation. The resurrection becomes a reminder of the importance of the action of God not just at the beginning of creation but at every moment and towards new creation.

Second, the biblical texts concerning resurrection point us towards the transformation of matter. The empty tomb demonstrates that the physicality of this world does matter to God and will not be completely destroyed or discarded. Further, whatever the complexity of Paul's discussion of the resurrection body in 1 Corinthians 15, his central understanding is that of transformation. Thus in terms of the future of the Universe we expect God's actions to involve transformation of the physical Universe rather than annihilation and beginning again. The biblical passages do not see new creation as God's 'second attempt'. Polkinghorne summarizes:

> 'the new creation is not a second attempt by God at what he had first tried to do in the old Creation. It is a different kind of divine action altogether, and the difference may be summarized by saying that the first creation was ex nihilo while the new creation will be ex vetere. In other words, the old creation is God's bringing into being a universe which is free to exist 'on its own', in the ontological space made available by the divine kenotic act of allowing the existence of something wholly other; the new creation is the divine redemption of the old'. (Polkinghorne 1994a: 167)

Not only does this transformation point us forward to new creation, the resurrection points to the end of this creation. Moltmann comments, 'it is God's new beginning which brings this perverted world to its deserved and longed-for end' (Moltmann 2000: 131). The resurrection demonstrates God's new beginning and the fact that this creation is not all that there is or ever will be.

While agreeing with Polkinghorne on transformation, we differ however in emphasis on the source of transformation. Polkinghorne emphasizes the faithfulness of God as the source of transformation:

> 'the ultimate eschatological issue, and the only adequate ground of hope, is the everlasting faithfulness of God.' (Polkinghorne 2002b: 65)

It is interesting that he points to Mark 12.26–27 for the everlasting faithfulness of God as the ground for hope of resurrection. While there is much of value in this, the stress on faithfulness is only part of the story. It is the 'I am' God who interacts directly and specifically with the sign of the burning bush and through communicating to Moses. It is important to see that it is the faithfulness of God in acting that is important. In fairness to Polkinghorne, he does have a strong view of the resurrection and it is highly influential in his eschatology. However, he does not explicitly acknowledge the extent of its influence. The resurrection shows that God acts not just in the sustaining of the processes of the Universe, but also acts in a specific way within and at times beyond those processes. Some theologians would call this 'intervention', a term which is largely out of favour in contemporary systematics because of its imagery portraying God as capricious. We agree with this, but do not want to move to a picture of God who is unable to interact in specific and gracious ways with his creation. Yet the resurrection shows God's faithfulness to his creation together with an unusual sign of his activity promising new creation. It is only by holding together God's faithfulness and action in creation and new creation that Christian theology has a fruitful interaction with the end of the Universe. This is a weakness in Polkinghorne's position and may come from a shallow interaction with the biblical passages. We will attempt to stress both faithfulness and action in God's transformative work.

Third, the resurrection body gives us some insights into nature of transformation. McGrath has claimed that:

> 'Christian discussion on the resurrection body has attempted to explore the tension between the physical and spiritual approaches to this issue. It must be said however, that the debate is widely regarded as speculative and pointless'. (McGrath 1998: 560)

While taking the point about being cautious about speculation concerning the future, McGrath is mistaken to take this view. Careful exegesis of the biblical passages has led to a wealth of insights that are important for eschatology. We suggest that transformation has to be seen in substance-form-mode-context. Often the discussion has been limited to discussing transformation of substance, that is, what will the atoms of the new heaven and earth be like? Keeping all the factors together does more justice to the biblical passages and the nature of the body. The question then for the future of the Universe is how will God transform not just the matter, but matter in its relationship to form, mode and context? We will return to this in the next chapter.

Then we have suggested that the transformation from the natural to resurrection body is characterized by the transformation from a state of decay to purposeful flourishing. We do not see the transformation as being from transience to timeless existence. Indeed the resurrection body for Paul is dynamic rather than static and the resurrection appearances of Jesus are about being no longer limited by space-time rather than being totally isolated from it. Thus we are not surprised by the insights of contemporary science that the Universe is in a state of decay. The transformation will not be a timeless new heaven and new earth but a new creation that is dynamic and more temporal not less. In this creation, because of the second law of thermodynamics the flow of time is linked to greater entropy. In the new creation will that be reversed?

Fourth, the resurrection reminds us of the need of holding together continuity and discontinuity in any thinking about the future. We have seen that contemporary theology often overemphasizes a 'this worldly' eschatology. The resurrection accounts helpfully remind us of the importance of discontinuity between this creation and the new creation, which is necessary in the context of the heat death of the Universe. At the same time they stress a tension between continuity and discontinuity that if never clearly defined, needs to be maintained. It may be a difficult discussion but it is exactly in that tension that eschatology needs to locate itself (Pannenberg 1968: 66–73). The resurrection stops us from going to either extreme of complete continuity or complete discontinuity. It also in the complexity of the resurrection accounts reminds us of our limits in resolving the tension.

Fifth, we have highlighted the crucial role of the Spirit in the work of transformation. Salvation, as Bauckham comments, 'is both restorative (repairing the damage done by sin) and progressive (moving the work on to its completion)' (Bauckham 1986: 239). Can we therefore see signs of the Spirit restoring damage and progressing God's work on to completion? This may be an area which has had a lot of attention in terms of the Spirit's work in the life of the believer, but how do we see it in the cosmic context? We saw in Paul's discussion in Romans 8, that the Spirit works in the tension between creation and new creation, sharing in the 'groaning' of this creation and yet pointing forward to the hope of that which is to come. Yet the Spirit's work is more than that. If the damage of sin is the breaking of relationships between Creator, creatures and creation, then is the Spirit's work a restoring of those relationships in part as a sign of the final reconciliation of a new heaven and a new earth? Restored relationships now in terms of individual forgiveness, community reconciliation, the care of animals and responsibility for the environment then become signs of God's purposes for the whole of creation.

Having said that we can go on and ask the question of how might this transformation and continuity/discontinuity work out in terms of the physical Universe? The nature of space-time and the nature of matter in a new heaven and new earth seem to be key in answering this. It is to this that we turn next.

Chapter 6

Space-time in Creation and New Creation

If the resurrection of Jesus gives us the best model of the new creation, we can ask how this new heaven and earth will exhibit both continuity and discontinuity with the present creation? How might we characterize this theological continuity and discontinuity in terms of the scientific view of the Universe? Within many aspects that might be explored, two areas are crucial, that is the nature of space-time and the nature of matter.

In Christian history, space-time and matter have been important considerations in eschatology. Premillennialists like Irenaeus were the most likely to argue for the necessity of a renewed Earth in the future of God's purposes. However, we need to be careful in seeing too much continuity here. The renewed Earth was a staging post, a penultimate state, not the ultimate expression of God's deliverance. In fact both premillennialists and amillennialists in the early church reflected three key neo-Platonic assumptions about the world and the future. First, temporality was imperfect, so that any new heaven and Earth would be 'above' this temporal world in an Eternal Now, not in some awaited future. Second, matter was also inherently imperfect, only indivisible souls could exist in the ideal state of the Eternal Now. Third, the 'soul' was found only in rational beings, hence no non-human animals or plants, let alone the physical Earth, were candidates for this ideal state (McDannell and Lang 1988; Maddox 2004: 21–52). These assumptions have permeated much 'Christian' eschatology since. Time, matter and the non-human creation have been dismissed, leading to souls ascending to heaven as ghostly apparitions leading to an atemporal existence on some kind of spiritual cloud. This pushes discontinuity to an extreme and leaves this creation as useless and irrelevant.

However, if we hold together continuity and discontinuity in the way we have been arguing then both science and theology can be in dialogue about these things. Polkinghorne rightly suggests that if the new creation is the eschatological transformation of the old, then 'science may have some modest role to play in clarifying what will be the necessary degree of continuity required for this to be the case' (Polkinghorne 2002b: 13). Therefore we shall explore what science tells us about space-time and matter in this creation and bring it into dialogue with theology. We shall see that Christian theology has moved a long way since the three Neo-Platonic assumptions above in a way that makes the dialogue extremely fruitful.

When it comes to space-time, many contemporary theologians suggest that divine eternity should not be conceived of as sheer timelessness (Peters 1993: 175–6; Russell 2000: 46–55). Time is important for relationship and growth. The continuity may be that time is real in the new creation but the discontinuity is that time no longer limits us in the way that it does in this creation. In this creation time is associated with decay and growth, but in new creation might time be simply about growth?

The nature of time and space has fascinated scientists, philosophers, theologians and writers over the length of human existence (Achtner, Kunz, and Walter 2002). Theologians do not speculate about subjects such as time in a cultural vacuum. Assumptions and speculations about time are often greatly influenced by both science and popular culture. We therefore need to briefly review the main insights from these areas. We will then examine the philosophical and theological questions, in particular, whether time and space can provide the key to understanding the continuity and discontinuity of the relationship of creation and new creation? In addition, are there any models or new insights that can be transferred into the theological arena?

6.1 The shaping of time in contemporary culture

Speculation about time has been one of the main themes of the science fiction industry. Here the big questions of existence are explored in narrative form. At times it may be dismissed as 'pseudo-science' or indeed 'pseudo-theology' but it does serve an important purpose. Hawking comments, 'Science fiction ... is not only good fun but it also serves a serious purpose, that of expanding the human imagination' (Krauss 1997: xi). Perhaps on time it expands the human imagination most of all.

Of course, speculation about time is not new. From Wells' *The Time Machine* in 1895 to movies such as *Back to the Future*, science fiction writers have examined the consequences of time travel. Wells was a graduate of Imperial College and scientific language permeates his discussion. However he does not care about a mechanism for time travel. In contrast, scientists themselves have speculated about the means.

To travel forwards in time is very easy in terms of ageing. More difficult would be a person frozen in deep sleep who could emerge hundreds of years into the future to find a very different world. This demonstrates in itself that there exists in popular culture subjective perceptions about the nature of time. Time is coupled with ageing and decay, but at the same time there is the belief that time is coupled with change and progress. In the year 1900, science and technology were triumphant. Evolution had explained the diversity of the natural world and virtually all the questions of physics seemed to be answered. Western culture, represented by the engineering of the Eiffel Tower was to be exported as God's way of salvation. In such a picture, an eschatology that stressed the continuity of this creation and a new creation was popular. However, this dream of human progress turned into nightmare in the abuse of the environment and the horrors of war. In the new millennium, discontinuity is popular, represented in the best-selling *Left Behind* series. The view of time is interesting in these books. Believers disappear to a 'timeless eternity' while non-believers have another chance, being left in this world's linear time. Meanwhile the figures of evil are destroyed also in this time. Once again, time is associated with growth and change. Whether in science fiction, scientific optimism or in US fundamentalism we see a fascination with time, its linear yet complex nature, and how our human perception relates to reality. When we turn from popular culture to the insights of science, we see some parallels to this and yet some differences.

6.2 The shaping of space-time in the Universe

Two problems remained for physics at the end of the nineteenth century; the detection of the ether and the radiation from a heated body. These problems would in fact lead to major theories of twentieth century physics, general relativity and quantum theory, both of which would raise revolutionary questions for space and time.

The problem of the ether concerned the detection of the medium through which light waves travelled. Maxwell had united electricity and magnetism in an elegant theory showing that light could be understood as a wave motion of electric and magnetic fields. However, light travels through a vacuum, so there had to be something else to propagate these waves, the ether. Michaelson and Morley attempted to show that the speed of light would be different in two directions due to the Earth's motion through this postulated ether, but they found that the speed of light did not vary at all. In a brilliant insight, Einstein saw that talk about the ether was unnecessary, and the speed of light was the same however you measured it (Einstein 1905: 891). This was the basis of his Special Theory of Relativity. He argued that for observers not under-going acceleration, the laws of physics should be the same. The result was the abandonment of absolute time, that is, one's measurement of time depended on one's motion. Clocks travelling at speeds close to the speed of light would appear to run slower than those at rest. Other consequences were that as speed increases, so mass increases and length contracts. These effects only become obvious at speeds close to the speed of light, so that at an everyday level we do not notice them. In such a picture, time is not to be totally divorced from space, but the two are to be talked about together in a framework called 'space–time'.

Einstein's General Theory of Relativity went on to take gravity into account and give a radically new description of it (Einstein 1916: 771). He suggested that space–time was not fixed and permanent, but could be described as being shaped by the presence in it of material bodies such as stars and planets. The mass and distribution of matter in the Universe determines the geometry of space and the rate of flow of time. This complex interaction of matter and space–time was described by a set of equations, whose solution gave the geometry of space–time and showed how bodies moved within it. However, they were so difficult that they could only be solved in a few simple cases. One of these was for a uniform distribution of structureless points freely floating in space–time, which is in fact a good approximation to the Universe, since when taken as a whole, the clusters of galaxies have a relatively uniform distribution. Soon de Sitter and Friedmann showed that the theory predicted that the Universe was not static but expanding. Einstein, disturbed by such a conclusion, was tempted to modify the equations in order to make the Universe static. Little did he realise that this modification in terms of a cosmological constant would resurface in the accelerating Universe.

General relativity in connecting the rate of flow of time to the distribution of mass, also showed that time runs slowly not only if you travel at speeds close to the speed of light but also if you are in the region of a strong gravitational field such as that near to a black hole. While such effects have been experimentally demonstrated, other possibilities of general relativity remain theoretical. Could space-time be distorted in such a way that it bends back onto itself, forming loops in the four dimensional structure of space-time which could provide a route backward in time? In 1949 Gödel had found a cosmological model of a rotating universe satisfying the Einstein equations in which journeys into history were permissible (Gödel 1949: 447–50). However, this had no resemblance to the physical Universe in which we live. Nevertheless, a number of physicists including Tipler, Thorne, Morris and Yurtsever have suggested that such effects might occur close to a black hole, or in rotating black holes or in wormholes linking black holes (Wilkinson 2001: 111–112). While such situations would have to be carefully engineered and impractical to test experimentally, such speculation demonstrates the complex nature of time.

In particular, would such a time machine violate what seems to be a fundamental aspect of the Universe, that is, cause and effect? Could time travellers go back and kill their own grandparent? Is there a principle that forbids travel backward in time in order to maintain cause and effect? Or are our notions of cause and effect too simplistic? Most physicists, on the observational fact that we have not seen time travellers from the future, would argue that time travel is not possible. However, the theological consequences of time travel have never been seriously considered. Yet, it raises some interesting questions. Human responsibility and sin would not be possible in a Universe where time travel was easily done (Asimov 1955). We need to live with the past and indeed it is necessary for learning, growth and love. Yet the very possibility of time travel raises the question of God's relationship to time. Time may be subtler than we think.

This discussion may seem at first glance to be a long way away from the relationship of creation and new creation. However, questions of this sort demonstrate just how little we really understand the nature of time, even with the successful descriptive tools of special and general relativity. Further, contemporary physics has opened up a world where in Polkinghorne's phrase 'the tyranny of common sense' has been exploded. Torrance points out that because we cannot perceive the structure of space-time by our senses, it encourages a humility towards surprising aspects of our experience of the Universe as a whole (Torrance 1976). Rather than imposing our everyday experience of the world as the pattern for the nature of the Universe, modern physics has encouraged a sense of wonder and openness to novelty and the unexpected.

The final reflection from general relativity is that it superseded the Newtonian model of the absolute nature of space and time, which theologically had led to the mechanistic view of the Universe. Time and space are much more subtle. There is a subjective element in terms of how you measure them, and they are intricately woven into a complex relationship with the geometry and bodies of the Universe. Time is not isolated but is only seen in relationship to space, how you measure it, and the mass of the bodies around it. It is not difficult to move from there to the suggestion that time has to be seen in relationship to God. Much thinking about God has set up time as an isolated ontological concept and then asks how God can 'intervene' or be 'timeless'. Perhaps the relationship between God and time is much more organic, that is, the very existence of time depends on the sustaining creativity of God.

6.3 The arrow of time

If it is claimed on the basis of relativity that all time is relative, an inadequate picture of time is given. There is the further fundamental question of how time on the atomic level relates to time at the everyday level.

The arrow of time is a phrase coined in 1927 by Sir Arthur Eddington (Coveney and Highfield 1991). It means that at the level of the everyday world, time has a direction. This is shown by five important insights. First, the second law of thermodynamics states that the disorder in a closed system, characterized by a property known as entropy, increases with time. It was previously thought that if the force of gravity was able to halt and reverse the expansion of the Universe, then in a collapsing Universe entropy might decrease, so reversing the arrow of time. However, work by Hawking and Penrose showed this not to be the case. Time would flow in the same direction even in a collapsing Universe (Hawking 1988). However, the recent discoveries we described in Chapter 2 about the expansion of the Universe have made this irrelevant. We now know that the Universe will expand for ever and never collapse, thus time will always have the same direction as increasing entropy. Second and third, the Universe both expands in size and increases in complexity. We can make a distinction between the Universe now in terms of its structure of galaxies and the lack of structure when it had just emerged from its period of inflation (a rapid expansion of the Universe early in its history). Fourth, we experience cause and effect in the Universe and fifth, our psychological experience is that of a flow of time. We can distinguish between past and future.

However, at the atomic level and indeed in the laws of physics themselves, time is reversible. That is, Newtonian mechanics, relativity and quantum mechanics all work well with time running in reverse. For Newton, space and time were absolute and his laws of motion allowed predictions of both past and future. As we have seen, in Einstein's theories of relativity, space and time are linked, but the equations themselves do not distinguish between past and future. Indeed, Einstein attempted to comfort the grieving family of Michelangelo Besso in 1955 with, 'For us faithful physicists, the separation between past, present and future has only the meaning of an illusion, though a persistent one' (Jammer 1999: 161). Einstein was overstepping the case. The distinction may not be there at the atomic level, but it is not an illusion at the everyday level.

How does the arrow of time emerge from this reversible atomic world? It may be that the arrow of time emerges from the measurement problem of quantum theory (see page 138). Alternatively, Rees points out that the irreversibility of time may be linked to the cosmic expansion. In the early Universe, the time asymmetry would not show up in any local measurement because the density would be so high that microscopic processes would occur very fast compared to the expansion rate. However as the Universe expands these processes are affected allowing the emergence of structure and complexity (Rees 2000). Others including Prigogine point to the self-organization of complex systems where order emerges from disorder, while Penrose suggests that in a quantum theory of gravity the arrow of time would be explicit (Penrose 1989; Prigogine 1997). Nevertheless, there is no general agreement amongst physicists as to how to reconcile the arrow of time with the reversibility of time at the atomic level. Both the arrow of time and speculation about time travel demonstrate the ability of modern physics to engage with these questions, but also demonstrate that the nature of time and our perception of it are still somewhat mysterious.

This mystery and the philosophical difficulties of giving a coherent view of time have led some to doubt the reality of time at all. McTaggart argued that as time is riddled through by inconsistencies and contradictions, it cannot be real (McTaggart 1927). Are our perceptions of time simply socially determined? Yet our understanding of relativity and the arrow of time cannot allow such a position. Relativity does remind us that our perception of time is not absolute, as it depends on how we are travelling or where we are in a gravitational field compared to someone else's perception of time. Yet the arrow of time does enable us to make a distinction between past and future. The expansion of the Universe and in particular the temperature of the microwave background radiation give to us a sense of the history of the Universe and its timescale, which would be shared by different observers in different parts of the Universe.

These insights raise important theological questions for understanding creation and new creation. Is time real and how important is the arrow of time? Certainly within the Christian tradition, time has been viewed as both real and linear. Delumeau has noted that the notion of the end of time is a recurrent theme in literature and has fuelled innumerable millenarian movements. However, it is almost entirely confined to the Jewish and Christian contexts where time is viewed as linear (Delumeau 1995). This is in contrast to much Eastern thought in its emphasis on cyclical time, and belief that, after immense eras, everything will return to its original starting point. Certainly the tides, solstices, seasons, and stars suggested to ancient civilizations cyclical time, but as Eliade has commented, 'Christian thought tended to transcend once for all the old themes of eternal repetition' (Eliade 1969: 34). The reasons for this linear view of time come from a variety of Jewish and Christian sources. The Universe was viewed to have a definite beginning in the sovereign acts of God, God revealed himself to the people of Israel at specific times in their history, and such events as the death of Jesus were unique and could not be repeated. Augustine for example argues against the idea of cycles of time on the basis that Jesus could die only once.

However is time real and linear in new creation? If it has a direction and is an important constituent of this creation, will there be continuity or discontinuity in new creation? We have argued that complete discontinuity in the nature of time leads to a timeless new creation and an associated timeless God. We need to explore more how God relates to time before we return to the issue of continuity and discontinuity.

6.4 Imagining space-time at the beginning of creation

Part of the question of God's relationship to time is highlighted by the origin of the Universe. How does time behave at the beginning of the Universe? In one of Hawking's early papers he produced a theorem that asserts that space-time admits a global time function if and only if it is stably causal (Hawking 1968: 433–35). Stably causal space-time means that there are no temporal loops which would ruin the idea of a global time of the Universe. Yet is that all that can be said about time?

In his more recent work, Hawking aims for a single theory, a quantum theory of gravity, which would describe the initial conditions as well as how the Universe changes with time. Such a theory would, Hawking hopes, pick out one initial state and hence one model of the Universe. While acknowledging that a complete and consistent combination of quantum theory and gravity has not been achieved, Hawking nevertheless believes that some of its features are fairly certain. One feature he proposes, in order to describe the Universe by quantum theory, is that the calculations are done using imaginary time. The calculations would then use Euclidean space-time, where any distinction between time and space disappears.

This has the following important implication. The surface of a sphere is finite in size, but there is no edge to its surface. This same property of a finite size with no boundaries is possible in four dimensions of space, rather than the two dimensions of the surface of a sphere. But the Universe as we know it has three dimensions of space and one dimension of time. Hawking's proposal is that when the Universe is the size of the quantum scale, the ordinary concept of time is transcended and becomes like another dimension of space, thus giving four dimensions of space. As the Universe expands beyond the quantum scale, so time crystallizes out into a dimension distinct from space. It is important to stress that the use of imaginary time and hence Euclidean space-time is a mathematical device to calculate answers about real time.

The second proposed feature of a quantum theory of gravity is that gravity is indeed represented by curved space-time. If the Universe's space-time stretches back to infinity (that is, the Universe has no beginning in real time) or it starts with a singularity, the problem remains of specifying the initial conditions. However, using Euclidean space-time:

> 'It is possible for space-time to be finite in extent and yet have no singular-
> ities ... at which the laws of science broke down and no edge of space-time
> at which one would have to appeal to God or some new law to set the
> boundary conditions of space-time'. (Hawking 1988: 135–136)

That is, space-time is seen like the surface of a sphere, finite and yet without a boundary.

Now what does this mean? If, as in this proposal time becomes a superficial feature of nature, then as we go back in the history of Universe we approach but never reach time zero. Time has faded away before we reach a time zero singularity. The Universe has a finite past of 13.7 billion years, but no beginning in time with no temporal boundary. Hawking's theory therefore suggests that there would be no singularity of the Big Bang at which the laws of science would break down. In real time, some 13.7 billion years ago, the Universe would have a minimum size corresponding to the Universe having arisen by a chance quantum fluctuation from a state of absolutely nothing to a small, finite expanding state. While few philosophers and theologians have engaged with this, it raises some interesting questions. What is the ontological status of imaginary time? If time crystallizes out in the early Universe does this mean it is not real? Is time a 'superficial' dimension to the Universe? What does this mean for God's relationship with time?

It needs to be stressed that Hawking's views on quantum gravity are not widely accepted by the scientific community. Indeed there exist other quite different suggestions that attempt to answer the same problems of initial conditions (Heller and Sasin 1998: 48–54; Gibbons, Shellard and Rankin 2003; Penrose 1989). Further there are a range of scientific questions that have been directed at Hawking (Barrow 1988: 101; Gingerich 1988: 288; Tipler 1988: 23).

With the possibilities of string theories uniting gravity and quantum theory still having severe problems, Hawking has more recently examined the possibilities of M theory, where we live in a four-dimensional surface or brane in a higher dimensional space-time. There could for example be 11 dimensions, with 7 of these dimensions so small that you cannot see them. In this picture gravity would permeate the whole bulk of the higher dimensional space-time (Hawking 2001). In all of this Hawking admits that a consistent theory of quantum gravity is not yet available.

While we note these limitations, what are the theological consequences of such a 'brief history' of time? Few theologians have responded to Hawking's theory of quantum gravity. This is possibly due to the difficulty of non-scientists understanding the scientific concepts, and the difficulty of using appropriate analogies to describe these concepts. This has especially been the case on the question of time. One of the exceptions is Craig who criticizes Hawking for being a 'non-realist' because of his use of imaginary time (Craig and Smith 1995). Craig argues that imaginary time is just a mathematical dodge, and any conclusions drawn from it have no relation to the real Universe. In Craig's view Hawking can say nothing of value about the real origin of the Universe. However, we need to be careful here. It is wrong to write off Hawking as just an idealist or having just an instrumentalist view of his theory. He is using a mathematical technique in order to describe the real Universe. This is admittedly not always clear from his popular writings. He occasionally states that he is just interested in the mathematics, but his over-riding commitment is to describe the Universe itself and its origin. His use of imaginary time allows a description of the Universe that begins as small, finite and expanding in real time. This is a reasonable scientific method, whether or not the theory actually works. Craig misunderstands Hawking's picture. Hawking is suggesting that time is real, not that it is just a useful ordering device imposed by our minds. At the same time, he is suggesting the possibility that as we move closer to the origin of the Universe, the nature of time changes. Indeed, as one goes back the notion of time eventually melts away. The origin of time is separated from the origin of the Universe and the Universe is such that 'once upon a time there was no time' (Barrow 1993).

The theological consequences of this picture are intriguing. First, Hawking's grappling with the nature of time at the beginning of the Universe has showed us even more deeply how mysterious and subtle is the nature of time. As we look forward to new creation, we must be prepared to allow our view of time not to be rigidly fixed by our everyday concepts. It is not that imaginary time will be the way to describe the relationship between creation and new creation. Simply, it is that we need to be careful not to be ruled by the tyranny of common sense. Second, it very clearly it destroys any sense of the cosmological argument in temporal form. Cause/effect arguments for a Creator do not work if time fades away before we get back to the origin. Third, it reinforces the view that time is inextricably linked to the physical Universe. Time appears only because of the expansion of the Universe. We return here to Augustine's understanding that the Universe was created not in time but with time (Augustine 1946: 2.237). Fourth, it is possible to have time without some of the traditional philosophical problems and descriptions that involve the beginning or end of time. Fifth, Hawking's view corresponds to 'creation out of nothing'. Traditionally, theologians have considered this in terms of matter or even space. Here we are faced with a model of a Creator who transcends time and creates it. Sixth, does the use of multi-dimensions of space-time help us in thinking about how God gives the Universe an arrow of time and yet is not confined to it?

Before we take these questions forward, Hawking has illustrated one more important issue, that is, it is extremely difficult to communicate concepts of time. This too has important theological consequences.

With Huygens' invention of the first successful pendulum clock in the 17th Century, the clock became the image of a predictable, mechanistic universe. Time was disentangled from human events and was absolute. Such an image became important for the development of Western theology. The Universe was understandable and predictable. Thus, Paley likens it to a watch in his exposition of the design argument (Paley 1825), an image which surfaces again within the recent intelligent design movement (Broom 2001). This image of the Universe led to a deistic understanding of God. As Leibniz and others pointed out, such a predictable mechanism means that God cannot and would not want to intervene in such a Universe.

The linear view of time, encouraged by the Judaeo-Christian tradition led to a framework for progress. This aided the development of science and technology. However, in this God's purposes had a direction to them, as the history of salvation unfolded from the beginning to end, sustained by the action of God. A major change came when God was replaced by human ability. In fact the 20th Century has been dominated by the 'myth of human progress', an overarching story by which human history was pictured as a march towards Utopia, a state of perfection both for the society and individual. The path to such Utopia became identified with the power of human beings to change the world through science, technology and education (Bauckham and Hart 1999). As we have seen such a dream has not delivered, but that sense of human progress still strongly informs many speculations about the future. It reinforces a view that stresses the continuity between creation and new creation, seeing a gradual and inevitable progress towards the Kingdom of God.

We see here an important issue. The way that time is represented in models and in culture has an important influence on theology. The theological implications of a clockwork Universe or the myth of human progress have left a long legacy, partly because they have not been able to reflect the complexity and subtlety of the nature of time. Science can give some insights, however, it is not enough to represent the whole of our experience of time, both objectively and subjectively. Ricoeur comments, 'speculation on time is an inconclusive rumination to which narrative activity alone can respond' (Ricoeur 1984: 122). He argues that discussion of the nature of time must be in a form which itself is time-dependent, that of narrative. This is shown in the widespread use of fictional stories to speculate about time by philosophers (Quinton 1973; Swinburne 1981; Shoemaker 1984), physicists (Feynman 1964: 42–9) and science fiction writers. This should not be underestimated. The physicist and the theologian must recognize the importance of narrative. Indeed any discussion of the relationship between creation and new creation must involve the use of narrative, which is the way that many of the biblical writers engage with these questions. Do the concepts of modern science allow us to translate those narratives in a way that is fruitful in thinking about new creation?

6.5 Space-time, eternity and God

Theologians and philosophers have tried to understand how an eternal God can relate to a temporal Universe. Augustine's view has been characterized in terms of 'the sharp, metaphysically grounded distinction he draws between time and eternity' (Daley 1991: 131). Time is created as an entity. The Universe expands not in time but with time. Time is the 'place' in which we dwell, the place of change and corruption. Eternity is where God dwells, the place of changelessness and incorruption. The bridge between the two is the life, death and resurrection of Christ. Thus Augustine preserved the immutability of God, as only creation is the realm of change and time. This metaphysical separation of God and the temporal Universe is reflected also in the classic picture of Boethius who saw God as outside time, looking down on all of time. Thus God experiences all time at once and knows every moment of the future as well as the past simultaneously. Some have interpreted general relativity to support this kind of picture (Stannard 1989). The four dimensions of space-time are laid out as a sheet before God and he can both see all that is happening or is going to happen as well as intervening at any point in space or time.

Although such a picture may have some support from general relativity and from some theologians (Garrigou-Lagrange 1934: 1.3–4; Stump and Kretzmann 1987: 219–52), there are some fundamental problems. Many have argued that to say that God is outside of time is to deny that God is a person (Kneale 1960–1: 87–108) and that time is an inevitable concomitant of both communication and consciousness (Lucas 1973: 45, 300). For God to be active in personal relationship he must in some sense be in time. The picture of Boethius also underestimates the difference between space and time, and the difficulties of God's perception of space and time. He suggests that everywhere is present to God in the spatial sense. This depends on whether God's possession of space can all be present to Him spacelessly, that is present in His mind. However, you cannot argue by analogy as Boethius does that this is true of time. As Lucas points out, time is not a point like space. Rather than being an instant, it is in fact an interval and it is difficult to see how intervals can be simultaneously present in God's mind. We also need to be clear that the Boethius picture rests on a view of the world as predictable mechanism. We shall return to quantum theory and chaos in Chapter 7, but at this point we need to note that in our current view of the world the future may not be fully determined. Peacocke sums up the force of this:

> 'God has so made the natural order that it is, in principle, impossible even for God, as it is for us, to predict the precise, future values of certain variables.' (Peacocke 1995: 280)

Therefore there may be a 'self-limited omniscience' on the part of God (Hasker 1989; Owen 1984; Polkinghorne 1988). The space-time map of Boethius may not be all filled in. Such self-limited omniscience is not helped by Aquinas' future potentialities known by God because Aquinas assumed that every effect has a cause, which is not the case in quantum theory.

This issue of God's knowledge of the future and God's relationship to time has provoked controversy among theologians. Some defend God's omniscience and foreknowledge in a classical sense (Craig 1991; Kvanvig 1986; Plantinga 1987: 171–200). However we must disagree with this view. God cannot be totally separated from time, if he is in some form of personal relationship with creatures and the Universe which takes petitionary prayer and human responsibility seriously (Pike 1970: xi; Gale 1991). From biblical studies Cullmann states, 'Primitive Christianity knows nothing of a timeless God' (Cullmann 1951: 63). The personal and living God of biblical theism is a God who changes not in his essential nature, character or purposes but does change in the way he responds to his people. Wolterstorff emphasizes this further:

> 'If God were eternal, he could not be aware, concerning any temporal event, whether it was occurring, nor aware that it will be occurring, nor could he remember that it had occurred, not could he plan to bring it about. But all of such actions are presupposed by and are essential to, the biblical presentation of God as a redeeming God. Hence God as presented by the biblical writers is fundamentally in time.' (Wolterstorff 1975: 200)

Many systematic theologians now argue for God's temporal not timeless eternity and that God must possess time as a personal agent (Davis 1983; Padgett 1992: 23–27). Polkinghorne goes further arguing that if creation is characterized by the God given process where the Universe can explore its own potentiality, then that temporal process should have some continuity with God's continued purposes in new creation (Polkinghorne 2001: 103). Thus some theologians have suggested that God has both eternal and temporal poles to his nature. Others use the Trinity as a way of maintaining both his eternal and temporal aspects. Yet others speculate that God is timeless without creation and temporal subsequent to it (Wolterstorff 2000: 5–10).

Perhaps the solution however is more fundamental. Rather than separating time and eternity, we may need to see time as a fundamental part of eternity. Here a popular analogy that has been used in apologetic writing can be of assistance (Houghton 1995; Middleton 2002; Ross 1999). It is the notion of multiple dimensions. Imagine a 2 dimensional world as first suggested in Abbott's *Flatland* (Abbott 1999). Beings in this world are limited to moving in the 2 dimensions of their sheet-like universe. A being inhabiting 3 spatial dimensions instead of 2, therefore has an interesting relationship with the 2 dimensional world. The being inhabits the same 2 dimensions but is not limited in the same way. They are not bounded by the 2 dimensional world, can interact with any point within that world in ways that could be both describable but inexplicable to the inhabitants, and can give freedom to the 2 dimensional world. Such an analogy has been used widely and indeed partly underlies the Boethius model. However, it is always used with an emphasis on the spatial dimensions. What if the analogy viewed the imaginary world as being characterized by one dimension of time with its own direction of flow? What then if a being existed who inhabited the same dimension of time but is not limited in the same way? He or she is not bounded by the one dimension of time world, can interact with any instant within that world in ways that could be both describable but inexplicable to the inhabitants, and can give freedom to the one dimension of time world.

I am therefore suggesting that our experience of time in the physical Universe is a small and limited part of an ontologically real time that we might call eternity. God in Trinitarian relationship inhabits these higher dimensions of time. We need to be clear about what is being suggested here. Our knowledge of multi-dimensions is being used as an analogy to model God's relationship to the temporal Universe. It is not a claim that these higher dimensions are open to scientific investigation. However, such an analogy receives support from the claims that certain models for quantum gravity require 10 or even 26 dimensions for the physical Universe. Out of these large numbers of dimensions, the 3 dimensions of space and 1 dimension of time of the Universe we experience crystallize out in the early stages of the emergence of the Universe from the Big Bang. We can think of the one dimension of time with its arrow 'crystallizing out' of eternity through God's creative action, providing a world though limited yet possessing a small part of God's eternal time. God thus exists in time but is not limited to the one dimension that limits us.

Others have suggested similar models in terms of eternity as a depth dimension to space-time (Conradie 2002: 288; van den Brom 1993; Conradie 2000). Conradie goes on to claim, 'Higher dimensions would, by definition, be inaccessible to scientific investigation and would therefore transcend any scientific competence' (Conradie 2002: 290). Yet is the possibility of the existence of the higher dimensions implied in quantum gravity and string theory, a pointer to the fact that our everyday experience of this Universe is not all there is? However, if we push for using this multi-dimensionality as more than an analogy, we run the risk of limiting God in the higher dimensions and produce a panentheistic understanding of the relationship between God and the world.

Swinburne offers an alternative to this. In his discussion of space he argues that it is not a logically necessary truth that there is only one space. He then suggests that heaven is regarded as a doctrine about another space:

'Christians have always maintained that in Heaven after the General Resurrection men will be embodied ... Bodies must be located at places. So Heaven must be a place ... If the Christian wishes to maintain the doctrine that Heaven is a place, he does much better to claim that it is a place not spatially related to Earth.' (Swinburne 1981: 40)

However, this raises far more problems than it solves. If we were to use this as a model for time, the problems would be severe. What does Swinburne mean by 'another space' and if this space is not related to Earth then how does God relate? Swinburne does not seem to see that these problems could be overcome by referring to more dimensions of space-time than the ones we experience. In fact, he is stopped from seeing this, by trying to show logically that the Universe must only have 3 dimensions of space (Swinburne 1981: 125). His argument is weak using our experience to be the logical basis of the nature of the Universe. Because we cannot conceive of more than 3 dimensions of space, Swinburne concludes that there cannot be more than 3 dimensions. However, as we have seen, our everyday experience of space-time is not enough. General relativity, Riemannian geometry and 10 or 26 dimensional space-time show us a very different Universe with degrees of good experimental evidence. Swinburne is right to emphasize the importance of space both in this world and the world to come. By thinking about higher dimensions of space-time he would not need to introduce the false notion of 'different spaces'.

Another difficulty with the Boethius view is that it does not take seriously the arrow of time and the distinction between past and future. It could be argued that this is simply due to human psychological understanding, but the issue is highlighted when we look at chaotic systems. Many systems in the Universe are inherently unpredictable, even if their laws are understood. These so-called 'chaotic systems', such as the weather system, can never have their future fully predicted. Does this unpredictability mean that the future itself is still undecided? This is an important insight but we need to be careful about this. Not all systems in the Universe are chaotic, and so it is possible for human beings, never mind God, to be sure about certain things in the future. For example, we can know that the Sun will one day run out of hydrogen fuel and swell up as a red giant. Further our inability to predict a system does not rule out God knowing the future.

As is often the case the reality may be more complex than any simplistic philosophical solution. Within the Judaeo-Christian tradition represented in the Bible, God is seen as both sovereign over the future and able to respond in a real way to the present, for example in answering prayers. God both transcends time but also engages with time, relating in a personal way to his creation. Does our dimensional analogy help us here? God transcending time surely means that he is not limited by our experience of time. Personal relationship means that God has some real relationship with time. Indeed we might invert the order and argue that because God exists in Trinity, time is the result of God's nature. Both these things can be naturally accommodated by the analogy of God existing in (or indeed providing) higher dimensions of time. But does this rule out real openness in terms of the future?

This is difficult to envisage within the analogy. However, the key is distinguishing the difference between God knowing the future and God controlling the future. The openness to the future is a result of an arrow of time in our Universe. Here the parallel with space breaks down. Space does not have any equivalent arrow. However we might note that space is still real without an arrow. Can time be still real without an arrow? Time can be real without an arrow, but growth and relationship seems to presuppose an arrow. Lucas argues that communication is dependent on time having a direction and indeed time is the pre-requisite of change (Lucas 1973: 45; 1973: 102).

Therefore does God experience a flow of time? By the very act of creation of the Universe, to which he relates, God experiences a flow of time. The difference then between our experience of time and God's is twofold. First, he is not constrained by the arrow of time in the way that we are. Imagine the flow of a river. A person who cannot swim is taken along by the flow. However, a strong swimmer experiences the reality of the flow but is not controlled by it. He or she is not limited by the flow. Second, as Brunner has suggested, our experience of the flow of time seems to be inevitably coupled with the experience of decay (Brunner 1951: 1–12). We can identify that either in terms of individual ageing or the increasing entropy of the Universe. It has been suggested, although not worked through in any detail, that time is radically affected by sin (Doyle 2000). Is finitude the impact of sin, so that our experience of death and the end of the Universe are 'the sting of finitude' (Conradie 2002: 283). We need to be careful about this. While it may be right that 'finitude in awareness is anxiety' (Tillich 1951: 1.191–94), there is also the desire for narrative completion of our life stories. Finitude in itself can be both and good depending on its context. Whether the coupling of decay and time is the result of sin, or whether simply part of the 'vale of soul-making' of this creation, the reality of decay and our experience of the flow of time cannot be denied.

God's kenosis is characterised by allowing and sustaining the Universe with an arrow of time, yet he is not constrained by this arrow. He does interact at various points in this time. In fact, the biblical writers see that within that flow of history, time is given meaning by God's acts (Ps 118.24; Mk 1.15; Jn 7.6; 12. 23). This multi-dimensional view of time has something in common with the 'eternalist' position which traces its history back to Plotinus (Braine 1994: 340). In this view, God is not outside of time but is in time, 'temporally omnipresent' in that he has all times in actual presence (Gutenson 2004: 117–132). Some have argued that this position is incoherent or unintelligible. Gutenson defends it by an appeal to special relativity suggesting that if God is travelling around the universe at the speed of light, absolutely no time would pass for him while the entirety of universal history would pass for the rest of the cosmos. While Gutenson is not claiming that God is travelling at the speed of light, he is trying to use special relativity to argue for the passage of time and timelessness to be held together. Unfortunately this does not work. Relativity is about relative time, and we do not have the ability to say that at the speed of light there is timelessness.

In contrast our multi-dimensional model can suggest temporal omnipresence in addition to kenosis. God gives an arrow of time to this creation which operates within the 4 dimensions of space-time. His faithful upholding of the physical laws sustain the movement of time as we experience it. Further if he does exercise his own temporal freedom in unusual actions of grace, these need to be minor departures from the overall flow of the creative process. If we are locating the arrow of time in the act of creation then we may tentatively make the theological prediction that the arrow of time is not simply psychological but should emerge as a natural consequence of the laws of the physics, in a similar way to Rees' hope that the arrow of time would emerge from any theory of quantum gravity. Indeed we might also make the theological prediction that higher dimensions of space-time will be necessary to understand the nature of the Universe. In this we have responded to Russell's challenge that in a fruitful dialogue theology might be able to contribute towards scientific research programmes. At the very least, any future theory of quantum gravity would possibly invalidate the above model or keep the door open to it.

How might we envisage God in this kind of model? The differentiation in unity of the Trinity has been a classic way of describing God as transcendent and immanent. In this the mediating work of the Spirit becomes important. Pinnock, following Augustine, has suggested that the Spirit can be thought of as the bond of love between the Father and the Son (Pinnock 1996). While in danger of depersonalising the Spirit, we agree with Pinnock of the Spirit as key in relations. Pannenberg wants to talk about the Spirit in terms of a field, but would there be some help in talking of the Spirit as the ground of the multi-dimensional space-time? Again there are problems of physicalisation and depersonalisation with such an image, but the Spirit as the activity of God in relating different dimensions of space-time might be worth further thought. The Spirit as the dynamic connection between dimensions reflects both the creating and redeeming aspects of God's work.

6.6 The nature of space-time in the new creation

How might this relate to new creation? Biblical eschatologies stress both the present and future natures of new creation. We live in the 'in-between times', following the death and resurrection of Jesus which inaugurates the last days of this creation and the beginning of new creation. Thus, Christian discipleship and community exists in the tension and worship is the focal instance of the tension between present and future.

We have suggested that higher dimensions may be a model to help us in thinking about God's relationship with time without being limited by it. Torrance makes a similar point on the basis of the incarnation:

'while the Incarnation does not mean that God is limited by space and time, it asserts the reality of space and time for God in the actuality of His relations with us, and at the same time binds us to space and time in all our relations with Him.' (Torrance 1969: 67)

If space and time are important in relationship with God, then is this true of new creation also?

Torrance goes on to argue that the relation between God and space is not a spatial but creative relationship, and in that both God's transcendence of and immanence in space and time can be understood. He traces the Greek view as characterized by the Aristotelian definition of space as a receptacle. This view surfaced again with Lutheran theology, space being a receptacle containing within its limits that which occupies it. Torrance argues that this view also underlies Kant and Newton's absolute space and was often coupled with dualism, in seeing space and time as ontologically independent from God. In contrast, the view of 'Nicene theology' as represented by the Patristic period and Reformed theology, saw God as containing the entire Universe not in the manner of a receptacle but by his divine power. Space and time have to be thought of dynamically, that is in their relation to the power of God. Patristic and Reformed theology work with a relational view of time differentially or variationally related to God and to human beings (Torrance 1974: 43–70). Thus:

'time and space are functions of events in the Universe and forms of their orderly sequence and structures. Space and time are relational and variational concepts defined in accordance with the nature of the force that gives them their field of determination.' (Torrance 1976: 130)

Space and time are therefore inherent in the contingent processes of nature.

What then of the resurrection which, as we have constantly argued, is the key to understanding the continuity and discontinuity? Torrance quotes with approval Barth's comment on space and time, 'Mark well, bodily resurrection' (Torrance 1976: xi). However, if the resurrection implies the importance of space and time to the new creation, we need to be cautious. Cyril of Alexandria argued on the basis of John 20.19f that there is a fundamental problem in fully understanding the resurrection (S. Cyril 1874–1885: 12.1). Torrance follows this line not being able to apprehend the resurrected order from within the frame of the old order. If we could, then there would be no difference between creation and new creation. However, as resurrection is the eruption of the new creation in the midst of the old, it 'brings with it the capacity to create in us new conceptions and new categories of thought with which to apprehend and speak appropriately and therefore objectively about it' (Torrance 1976: 177). Resurrection stresses the discontinuity of creation and new creation, but also brings with it the capacity (however limited) to understand the nature of new creation. Further, as Barth stressed, resurrection of the body goes against the view that human existence in time and space is unreal and asserts the being and action of God himself in space and time (Barth 1936–62: I. 2.130f).

Pannenberg of course has continually stressed that the resurrection is the 'unique break-in of the reality of the end-time'. He goes on to comment on the way this relates to the scientific picture:

> 'One often hears the objection that a historian who reckoned with possibilities of this kind would come into conflict with the natural sciences. Curiously enough this objection is seldom raised by scientists nowadays, and least of all physicists; it is most often heard on the lips of theologians, or even historians. In these quarters a dogmatic view of the natural sciences is evidently still widespread which is no longer held by the sciences themselves'. (Pannenberg 1972: 110)

In terms of our understanding of space and time, Pannenberg has a point. We have seen the modern scientific picture is a long way from the world of absolute space and time and the mechanistic Newtonian worldview. However, we do need a model of space and time in the new creation and the resurrection gives us that. Barth has stressed that Jesus is the point of supreme focus for the whole universe of space and time, by reference to which all its meaning and destiny are finally to be discerned (Barth 1936–62: III. 1.437–511).

As we saw earlier, Brunner characterized our experience of time as the experience of decay. Torrance sees the resurrection however, as a 'new kind of historical happening ... historical event emancipated from decay' (Torrance 1976: 88–89). Can this be model of new creation? The new creation will have history that is a real experience of time but will be emancipated from decay. It is interesting that we also saw this kind of concept emerging from the biblical literature concerning resurrection.

Certainly if the resurrection is the model for new creation, then time has to be real in the new creation. As Künneth states, 'time is embraced in the new creation, in the reality of the resurrection' (Künneth 1965: 188). Yet how is space-time different? Torrance uses the language of redemption, healing and restoration (Torrance 1976: 90). For someone who specifically states that he wants to explore this issue in both theological and scientific terms, Torrance is then disappointing in actually describing what it means for space-time to be healed and restored. A parallel with our own experience of healing and restoration is difficult to see. Some of the biblical images stress that the resurrection leads to human beings having the image of God renewed (Col 1–3). Other biblical images perhaps more helpfully in this context stress the resurrection leading to a new existence where there is no decay, that is, an individual life free of suffering, tears and death. This may be a helpful way forward. The continuity stresses the reality of time in new creation. The discontinuity stresses the way time is now decoupled from decay.

Maximus the Confessor defined eternity as time in the absence of change:

> 'For time is eternity, whenever it stands apart from change, and eternity is time whenever it is measured by being the vehicle of change'. (St. Maximus Confessor 1862: XCI. 1164B14–C3)

However, as we have seen, change is important to relationships and growth. I suggest that change will be part of new creation but that change will be positive. The resurrection is a historical happening that points not to decay, but points forward to the end time of restoration and renewal. Polkinghorne uses the helpful illustration of music, which gives an image of change without repetition or loss (Polkinghorne 2002b: 120).

The experience of decay will no longer be part of the flow of time. Lucas characterises eternity:

> 'We should not think of it as timeless or changeless, but as free from all those imperfections which make the passage of time for us a matter of regret … All our feelings about time are coloured by our own imperfec-tions: our limited lives, the impermanence of what we love and value, the weakness and fallibility of our judgement, our failures of will, our inability to cope with circumstances or to control the course of events, our undera-chievements and our straight sins.' (Lucas 1973: 307)

In addition, to this decoupling of the flow of time and decay, the resurrection suggests that time will not limit us in the same way that we are limited by it now. As we saw in a previous chapter, the New Testament writers see the risen Jesus in time, in that he communicates and relates to the disciples, but at the same time he does not seem limited in the same way. It is interesting to note that we have been led to the suggestions that time is decoupled from decay and the experience of time does not involve limitation from a consideration of the resur-rection. Lucas arrives at the same conclusion by a philosophical investigation on the nature of time.

Such a view of continuity and discontinuity in space-time means that the new creation will be an existence of growth and flourishing. In the words of Polkinghorne, the continuity between this and new creation is 'a history characterized by persisting fulfillment rather than transient coming-to-be' (Polkinghorne 2002b: 16). Jackelén has recently characterized time as not marching but dancing, a metaphor which highlights the dynamic nature and relatedness of time and eternity (Jackelén 2002).

Interestingly enough, such a temporal eschatology is seen in the theology of Wesley. Bence has pointed out that not just did Wesley believe eschatological salvation had a present dimension, but that he emphasized how this dimension is subject to ongoing realization (Bence 1979: 45–59; Bence 1981). In contrast to Augustine he did not see the final goal as a restoration of a static state of a restored Garden of Eden, nor did he think that our imperfect moral character is instan-taneously transformed at death into the perfect character required in eternity. Wesley was always committed to further growth and transformation, and so life in the new heaven and earth will be a greater existence than that of Adam and Eve (Wesley 1978: 11.426; 1988: 2.411–12; 1931: III. 334). This dynamic view of creation and new creation certainly reinforced Wesley's emphasis on holiness and his optimism of grace. Key for Wesley was also the doctrine of the Spirit in terms of prevenient grace. It was the Spirit going ahead and making any choice for good possible that gave both evangelism and the holy life their energy.

We therefore come back to the importance of the Spirit in exploring the relationship between creation and new creation. A Trinitarian view reinforces a dynamic and complex view of creation and new creation. This needs to be developed further following this present work. The Trinity itself guards us from too static a view of God and God's relationship to creation and time. It further reminds us of the complexity of such a relationship. The triune pattern is the way God relates to all things but is also the pattern of our knowledge of that relation. To the extent that we can understand how God is related to what goes on, we understand it 'through Jesus Christ' and 'in the Holy Spirit.' So it is with our perception of creation and new creation.

Russell has suggested there are five themes to contemporary thought on eternity. First, the co-presence of all events without destroying their distinctiveness; second, flowing time; third, duration; fourth, prolepsis where the future is already present and active in the present; and fifth, a single global future for all creation so that all creatures can be in community (Russell 2002a: 27). It may be beyond any one model to hold all these things together. Of the five the most difficult to envisage is co-presence while maintaining distinctiveness. Having said that, our picture of new creation is not too different from the other elements.

We are suggesting that time is real in new creation. Yet new creation does not simply begin after the ending of the old. While ontologically present in more dimensions of time, it can only be seen in this creation with an epistemological limitation, that is, we see just glimpses of it without being able to fully explain it. If the model of higher dimensions is used to help us picture this, then we need to be careful to distinguish between God and new creation, or in other words we need to hold God's transcendence as something always greater than the created order of both creation and new creation. It may be here that we can employ the traditional language of 'heaven' (Conradie 2002: 277–296). If heaven represents the higher dimensions of creation, then heaven can be God's dwelling place, even though the highest heavens cannot contain God. Heaven is the relative transcendence of the Earth, while the Earth is the relative immanence of heaven. Thus, heaven is a dimension that transcends but also includes the Universe, but heaven cannot be equated with God. Here the biblical pictures of new creation where heaven and Earth come together and God comes down to his people (Rev 21) are helpful, not least in the way that they give central importance to the Christian hope of new creation rather than being 'taken off to heaven'. An alternative way to use our multi-dimensional model to picture Christian hope would be to relate it to the perishable being clothed with the imperishable (1 Cor 15.53). If new creation is the expanding the dimensions of this creation, then we are no longer limited by decay and we experience eternal life in all its 'fullness'.

6.7 Continuity and discontinuity in the space-time of new creation

Reviewing the wide range of insights into space and time, from contemporary culture, science, philosophy and theology, we see the importance of narrative. As Crites comments:

'the formal quality of experience through time is inherently narrative ... The self in its concreteness is indivisible, temporal and whole, as it is revealed to be in the narrative quality of its experience. Neither disembodied minds nor mindless activity can appear in stories. There the self is given whole, as an activity in time.' (Crites 1971: 291, 309)

This is another illustration of direct dialogue with the biblical accounts. They especially question an over reliance in systematic theology on Greek philosophical concepts of time and eternity.

Our emphasis on resurrection and new creation suggests that the continuity/discontinuity between creation and new creation can be explored through maintaining the following:

- Time is real in both creation and new creation
- There is a decoupling of time and decay in new creation
- Time is not limiting in new creation, in the same way that it is limiting in this creation.

This is in contrast to those who see eternity as timeless such as Pannenberg for whom fulfilment is impossible 'without an end of time' (Pannenberg 1998: 561). Van den Brom rightly suggests that Moltmann and Pannenberg reject an ultimate role for temporality (van den Brom 2000: 165). In trying to redeem history they neglect the value of history. Holding continuity and discontinuity sees the value of temporality and history.

Further, we have suggested a model which sees God's experience of time as in more dimensions of space-time than the one dimension of time which we experience. In that model God experiences time as real, but is not limited by our one dimension. This multi-dimensional view, which receives support from cosmological work on the early Universe, provides a new model with some clear advantages in thinking about God's relationship with time and time in new creation. Could this be pushed further to claim the making of a scientific prediction from the theological understanding of the Universe? We have tentatively suggested that theological considerations might point us towards the arrow of time being a consequence of the fundamental laws of the Universe and that there are more dimensions to time. Russell sees the ability of theology to make such scientific predictions as part of the true integration of science and religion, and indeed necessary if theology is going to be taken seriously by scientists (Russell 2008). While sharing that conviction if dialogue is real, we must acknowledge that such theological 'predictions' are not of the same status as scientific predictions which are made on the basis of scientific models in order to explore their realism and coherence. Russell goes too far in implicitly suggesting that theological predictions can be brought to the same table. This would require a methodological openness which is not typical within scientific communities.

Even with that, we must however exercise caution on such theological predictions. As we stated such a model is conceptually reinforced by some models of quantum gravity that see the Universe as having more than 4 dimensions. Such a consideration of other dimensions has a long history with Kant asking, 'Why does space have three dimensions?' (Handyside 1929). In fact, much more work needs to be done. Initial work on the nature of universes with different dimensions of both space and time suggests that three dimensions of space and one of time is important for stable life to exist (Barrow 1983a: 24; Barrow 1983b: 337; Tegmark 1998: 1; Whitrow 1955: 13, 1959). Barrow sums this up:

> 'Worlds with more than one time are hard to imagine and appear to offer many more possibilities. Alas, they seem to offer so many possibilities for happenings that the elementary particles of matter are far less stable than in worlds with a single time dimension ... Worlds with more than one time dimension do not allow the future to be predicted from the present.' (Barrow 2002c: 4.13)

So there is a problem with the physics of multi-time dimensional worlds. However Barrow points out the link with matter. If one were to postulate a continuity/discontinuity with space-time then that would be related to a continuity/discontinuity in matter. To this we turn in the next chapter. We are not worried by the fact that worlds with more than one time dimension do not allow the future to be predicted from the present. So while this is an important corrective it does not rule out multi-dimensional time. Indeed there is a suggestion that in certain circumstances, such as low temperatures, complex structures can be stable in such Universes (Yndurain 1991: 15). Now this does not mean that the new heaven and the new earth are going to be a cold place! We are simply noting that this is an active area of scientific research where theologians can take a keen interest and indeed may be useful conversation partners.

Current scientific thinking does provide some difficulties for the model we are suggesting. However, more work needs to be done on this and indeed there may be observational tests of such possibilities. Barrow argues that if the constants of nature are really framed in more dimensions than three, then the dimensions would change their size with the expansion of the Universe which would then be revealed by a change in our 'constants' of Nature (Barrow 2002b). Current observations testing the fine structure constant in the absorption spectra of distant quasars may find some evidence of change (Webb et al. 2001: 1208). Not only would changes in the constants of Nature signify the possibilities of more dimensions but would also mean that 'life could be on a one-way slide to extinction' (Barrow 2002c: 4.15). It is possible that they would slip out of range that allows life to exist, although recent research suggests that the vacuum energy may limit any change in the fine structure constant (Barrow, Magueijo and Sandvik 2002c: 043515; Barrow, Magueijo and Sandvik 2002b: 201–210; Barrow Magueijo and Sandvik 2002a: 284–289).

It is clear that the other area that needs to be explored, in addition to space-time, is the question of the nature of matter in both creation and new creation. If persons are going to exist in new creation, then we have seen that space and time seem to be necessary to maintain personal relationship. However, the only persons we know are embodied beings. How do we represent the continuity/discontinuity tension in terms of the matter in creation and new creation? This is especially important for the Christian tradition in terms of its doctrine of creation and indeed its sacramental view. To this we turn next.

Chapter 7

The Future of Matter

What will be the nature of matter in the new creation? In an oft-quoted remark, Bede once asked 'When the risen Jesus ate fish, what happened to the fish?' It is interesting that the emphasis on the occurrences of the risen Jesus eating in the gospels cannot totally be explained by a Eucharistic interpretation (Lk 24.28–43; Acts 10.41; Jn 21.13). The resurrected Jesus implies some form of physical embodiment that has the continuity with this creation of eating fish and seeing the marks of the nails. However, the risen Jesus does not need to eat fish to survive, and the marks of crucifixion are marks of glory rather than suffering. Physical matter has been transformed. But can we say anything at all about such a transformation?

In order to explore how the continuity and discontinuity in transformation apply to matter, we find ourselves once again at an exciting time in both science and theology. Insights from the physical and biological sciences and biblical, feminist and sacramental theology give us fascinating insights and challenges.

7.1 Matter in this creation: scientific insights

Polkinghorne comments that in eschatology science poses questions to theology but the answers:

> 'will have to bear a sufficiently consonant relation to the process of this present Universe so as to be persuasive that, amid the redemptive trans-formation of the old through God's gracious action, there is enough continuity to make sense of the conviction that it is indeed Abraham, Isaac and Jacob who live everlastingly in the divine presence'. (Polkinghorne 2000: 41)

So what are the questions and the 'consonant relations' in terms of matter? In the last century insights from relativity, quantum theory, chaos and complexity theory have been important in how we understand matter.

7.1.1 Relativity and the conception of mass

A popular conception of matter is that it is 'stuff' which is a non-varying entity in the Universe. Yet $E = mc^2$ reminds us that mass can be converted to energy and energy to mass. The prime example of this mass-energy equivalence is provided by stellar thermonuclear reactions. But the equivalence also applies to changes. Any change in the energy of a body implies a change in the body's inertial mass. Einstein commented that the 'most important result of a general character to which the special theory has led is concerned with the conception of mass' (Einstein 1920: 46).

He saw it as a fundamental link between the laws of the conservation of energy and the conservation of mass. But theologically it is important also. Many will see a body in terms of what Newton called, 'solid, massy, hard, impenetrable, moveable Particles' (Newton 1952). Yet the atoms themselves have a mass containing both the kinetic energies of its constituent particles and the potential energies of their electrical and nuclear interactions. In addition, any change in the internal state of the atom is accompanied by a flow of energy into or out of it, with an associated increase or decrease in mass. This is a dynamical, not static context.

Special relativity has even more to say. The inertial mass of a body varies with its movement. We need to distinguish between a body's rest mass and its mass depending on the velocity at which it is travelling. Between 1909 and 1915 this effect was shown experimentally in series of experiments (Shankland 1961). At the very least these insights question any theological or philosophical pictures of our bodies as simply a static collection of unchanging particles. To characterize matter we need to be aware of its energy equivalent and indeed the context it finds itself in, at its simplest whether it is moving or not.

7.1.2 *Quantum and chaotic relationality*

Contemporary science further demonstrates the relationality of the world. The special and general theories of relativity mean that we must take seriously the relationship of space, time, matter and motion. Indeed, fundamental to relativity is also the role of the observer. The time interval that the observer measures depends on where the observer is and how they are moving.

Quantum theory also stresses this aspect of the world. This immensely successful theory reveals a world quite different from the everyday world described by Newton. Instead of things being determined, they are uncertain, uncaused and unpicturable. This uncertainty of position and momentum, and energy and time, dissolves our classical picture and indeed many of the solid foundations of 'common sense'.

However, the implications go further, although admittedly it is in dispute in just which direction. A fundamental problem remains with quantum theory and that is how the quantum uncertainty of atoms becomes the definite world of the everyday (Milburn 1998). The traditional answer given by Bohr is that the intervention of macro world measuring instruments 'collapse' the probability of the quantum world into definite answers. Yet those very measuring instruments are themselves composed of atoms that have quantum behaviour. What makes them different to the atoms or electrons in them? To avoid this difficulty, an alternative is that the intervention of a conscious observer leads to a measurement. It is not until mind becomes involved that an answer becomes definite. This has the same problem as before, the brain being composed of atoms, but it might be argued that we still do not fully understand the relationship between mind and brain. Wheeler extended this interpretation to suggest that mind has brought the Universe into being.

There is however one more suggestion. Everett's many worlds interpretation states that in every act of measurement, each possibility available is realized and at that point the Universe splits into separate universes corresponding to the realized possibilities. Every possibility is realized in different universes. The number of universes that this produces is unimaginable and it sees to be the antithesis of the quest of physics to look for the simplest explanation. However, it has become popular with cosmologists, particularly those who want to apply quantum theory to the beginning of the Universe.

While some of the philosophical questions remain unanswered, quantum theory demonstrates yet more relationality in the nature of the physical world. In 1935, Einstein, Podolsky and Rosen highlighted what they believed was an unacceptable consequence of quantum theory. In this EPR paradox, they pointed out that two quantum particles such as electrons, once they have interacted with each other, retain the ability to influence each other even though extremely large distances separate them. Einstein felt this showed that quantum theory was incomplete. Yet observations have confirmed that this really happens. What the experiment demonstrates is that at the quantum level, there is in Polkinghorne's phrase 'togetherness in separation'. Quantum theory highlights the relationality of quantities, measurements and observers. Matter cannot be isolated from this complex web of relationships.

Alongside, relativity and quantum theory the emerging field of chaos and complexity theory are a strong reminder that entities cannot be treated in isolation from their environments. Many systems in the world are simply too complex to admit long-range predictability (Lorenz 1963: 130–41; Lichtenberg and Lieberman 1983; Crutchfield et. al. 1986: 38; Gleick 1993; Stewart 1989; Houghton 1989: 41–51; Kim and Stringer 1992). These systems exhibit a great sensitivity to initial conditions, very different outcomes arising from infinitesimally different starting points. Lorenz named the phenomenon 'the butterfly effect', that is systems like the weather system are so sensitive that the flapping of a butterfly's wing in Rio could lead to a hurricane in New York. Thus the reductionism so central to Dawkins' view of the world (Dawkins 1995; Dawkins 2003) is not a good model for understanding the complexity of the natural world.

7.1.3 Complexity, pattern and information

Complexity theory portrays a picture that to understand the physicality of the Universe you need not only to understand the constituents of nature but also how they relate. Many systems are not simply reducible to their constituent parts, but new levels of organization arise out of complexity. Page highlights the fact that the world contains both order and chaotic systems, continually in state of change (Page 1985; Page 1996). We need to understand the changing and developing character of the natural order and in that explore the processes behind the patterns as well as the protons.

Gregersen and others have reviewed the development of complexity theory and conclude that not only does it break the dominance of reductionism but that it also raises the importance of pattern and information (Gregersen 2003). It has been applied to landscapes, ecological systems, brains and even the economy (Yang and Shan 2008; Guastello, Koopmans and Pincus 2009). It demonstrates that systems can be very simple at one level and also very complex on another. Patterns emerge in complex systems that are not reducible to their constituent parts. Further these patterns can be understood by taking into account information transfer within the system and with the environment.

When applied to biological systems several authors have stressed the informational aspects of life (Loewenstein 1998; Küppers 1985; Yockey 1992; Davies 1998; Küppers 1990). Molecules like DNA and RNA can be considered as a genetic databank where life is an information processing and propagating system. Thus the traditional emphasis on trying to explain life in terms of physics and chemistry is never going to yield results. In the words of Peacocke it confuses the medium with the message (Peacocke 2001). Information theory is still in its infancy (Chaitin 1990), and has been used by some to argue for a renewed design argument with God as the one needed to insert the information (Dembski 2002a; 2002b). While this may not be a wise apologetic strategy, nevertheless it is clear that information depends on context and links the local and global properties of a system (Küppers 1995). Further, information is never absolute but only relative and that indeed information can only have a meaning with respect to some other information. The meaning of information always depends on the context of understanding between sender and receiver, so that meaning is determined by the interpretation of the information through the receiver that also links to history as well.

Thus, as Kauffman argues, the behaviour of complex systems can only be understood by both a reductionist account of its constituents but also a holistic account of the overall pattern (Kauffman 1995). All of this demotes the 'stuff' of matter from its central role in our understanding of the world. We see from the above that in exploring the continuity/discontinuity in the transformation of the physical Universe we must hold together mass-energy-pattern-information. Gregersen is helpful in saying that complexity theory is a reminder that God is the 'richness of everyday phenomenon'. God's action in the world has to be seen in the context of mass-energy-pattern-information.

7.2 Transforming water into wine

Alongside these scientific insights, we see some theological developments, such as renewed recognition that the biblical documents demonstrate the importance of the material. Brueggemann suggests that an important role of Old Testament theology is to remind the church of the elusiveness, materiality and concreteness of Yahweh's dealing with Israel, against Hellenizing trends which would downplay it (Brueggemann 1997).

Yet in terms of the transformation of matter in new creation we have very little apart from the resurrection narratives. The turning of between 120 to 180 gallons of H_2O into alcohol at the wedding feast at Cana is one example, yet most commentators are silent on the physical transformation. This is particularly interesting when Beasley Murray claims that the sign of John 2 denotes 'events that herald things to come, especially in relation to eschatological future' (Beasley Murray 1999: 33). While the centrality of Christology is noted by a number of commentators they do not see any issue in the transformation of matter (Brown 1983: i–xii; Barrett 1978; Slovan 1988; Carson 1991; Morris 1971). The nature of the miracle has even been called 'profane' (Hengel 1987: 83–112). Indeed Lindars states, 'we have a miracle-story in which the miracle itself is unimportant' (Lindars 1987: 123). Lindars is too quick to dismiss its historicity, but even if it is myth the transformation of matter is central to the miracle story. It is difficult to find any commentators who have engaged with this issue (Green 2002b; Padgett 2002b). The surprising exception is Grayston, who with a high degree of scepticism over historicity, nevertheless raises the question of whether the water was turned into wine (Grayston 1990: 31). He suggests two possibilities, either the guests were given appropriate mental stimulus to perceive water as wine or that the water underwent atomic transformation from a compound of hydrogen and oxygen to a compound of carbon, hydrogen and oxygen. This he concludes would have been 'remarkable' but then does not pursue it further. It is remarkable that virtually none of the commentators see in the sign a very clear demonstration (whether historical or in story) of the capacity that God possesses for the transformation of matter. This could be in a fundamental changing of the substance of matter, or it could be the way that we perceive matter. Of course biblical scholars would pass the issue of how such a miracle might have happened over to the philosophical theologians. Yet it is striking that so few actually recognize it as an issue in the story.

7.3 The matter of the soul

If systematic theology has been controlled more by the legacy of Greek philosophy than by the biblical narratives, then nowhere is this able to be more demonstrated than in the debate over the existence and nature of the soul. The dominance of philosophical theology at the expense of biblical studies has controlled many systematic approaches in this area. While the miracle stories of transformed matter have had little attention, there has been a revived debate concerning the existence or non-existence of the soul and its relation to the body. This has been part of a larger contemporary debate as to what is the human person (Gregersen, Drees and Görman, 2000; McMullin 2000: 367–393; Myers and Jeeves 2002; Barbour 2003; Shults 2003; Green 2004a). Of course this is a debate with a long history. Augustine saw soul and body, after the fashion of Plato, as two separate substances held together in an uneasy union. Aquinas reflected a weaker form of dualism inspired by Aristotle. Soul was seen as the substantial form of the matter-form composite and therefore not a complete substance in its own right. In terms of the modern debate we can distinguish a number of features.

7.3.1 *Modern defences of duality*

Barr has long argued that body/soul duality is embedded in the Bible on the basis that for the believer 'the relation of his or her soul to God was central' (Barr 1992: 103). Indeed, some have argued that Paul had a view of resurrection of the dead in 1 Corinthians 15 but moved to immortality of the soul in 2 Corinthians 4.7–5.10 (Boismard 1999). Yet these are minority voices within those who work with the biblical material.

Belief in the soul has been defended by primarily Christian philosophers who want to solve what they think is a problem of disembodied personal existence after death (Cooper 1989; Hasker 1999: 206–7; Moreland and Rae 2000: 23–40; Cooper 2001: 218–28; Swinburne 1986). While accepting that resurrection is the eventual outcome after human death, they see this as not happening until the day of resurrection. How then is personal identity or continuity held between the death of the believer and the time of resurrection? (Harris 1983: 133) This then influences some biblical commentators. For example, Martin argues that Paul in 2 Corinthians 5.1–10 is discussing such an interim state (Martin 1986: 101–108). In large part this is simply due to a difficulty in too linear view of time. With a multi-dimensional view of time, a believer is liberated from the linear flow of this creation's time. Thus resurrection for the believer can be instantaneous while for those still alive in this creation it is still in the future (Cassidy 1971: 210–217; Best 1987: 48). The Pauline image of going to sleep is helpful. For the bedside clock hours pass, while for the sleeper morning comes instantaneously.

There also seems to be a pastoral reason why the doctrine of the soul has maintained its appeal. Fergusson points out that the soul maintains the hope of release from physical suffering (Fergusson 2000: 4). It has been embedded in Christian spirituality for many centuries and is not easy to move beyond. We also notice the strong influence in this of an individualistic focus on life after death. If the focus is actually on new creation of which individual resurrection is a part, then the pastoral needs are put into the much healthier context which values community and the structures of this creation.

The problems with the soul are well known. Such a view tends to devalue the body and by implication matter. It pushes discontinuity too far in eschatology and denies the sovereignty of God. If the soul is absolute, is it uncreated? And does an immortal soul devalue the action of God in resurrection and new creation. Of course those who defend the soul often see immortality to be a gift from God, and a number of revised forms of dualism have been suggested such as 'integrative' (Taliaferro 1994) or 'emergent' (Hasker 1999: 206–7) Yet it does not do justice to either the biblical sources or contemporary scientific insights.

7.3.2 *Psychosomatic unity in science*

The study of the human person and the nature of mind/brain have faced a number of scientific challenges in recent years. The growth of neural networks and artificial intelligence provokes the question of whether a machine will become conscious (Foerst 1997: 6; Herzfield 2002b; Ashbrook and Albright 1997). The success of the Human Genome Project and the development of modern medical techniques raises the question of whether we are more than our genes. Psychology has developed in seeing the complexity of the mind/brain relationship (Jeeves 1997; Feinberg 2001: 150–152) and philosophers have begun to examine the nature of consciousness (Dennett 1993; Dennett 1996; Chalmers 1996).

There have been reductionist voices saying that human beings are simply 'gene survival machines' (Dawkins 1989). However the weight of evidence points to a rediscovery of the psychosomatic unity of the human person, speaking of an intrinsic interdependence of mind and brain (Kendall 2001: 490–493; Jeeves 2002: 3–32; Jones 2004: 31–46; Jeeves 2004: 13–30). Murphy suggests that the tightening of the mind/brain link in neurobiology makes it more improbable for such an ontologically separate entity as the soul to exist and this has become increasingly popular in much contemporary theology (Miller 1994: 507–19; Murphy 2000: 99–131; Pannenberg 1991–98: 182; Booth 1998: 145–62; Miller 2004: 63–74).

7.3.3 Psychosomatic unity in the Bible

In addition, there has been a significant movement in biblical theology in seeing the human person as a psychosomatic unity (Edgar 2000: 151–64; Berger 2003). The Greek tradition of an immortal soul, it is claimed, has been imposed onto the biblical texts. Indeed dualism rather than monism is the minority opinion amongst biblical scholars over the past century (Chamberlain 1993: 765–74). The Hebrew tradition does indeed have a view of the psychosomatic unity of the person (Mason 2000: 67–82), yet is silent about the fate of the dead (Johnston 2002). Bauckham points out that the Old Testament has no interest in parts of human being surviving after death. However, relationship with God is the important thing and at death this is severed and therefore life comes to an end. Thus, no soul or spirit survives death (Bauckham 1998c: 80–95).

In terms of the New Testament, Green has made an extensive study of the data (Green 1999a: 3–22; 1999b: 51–64; 2002: 33–50). He reviews the evidence used by those who hold anthropological dualism and sees it based on the belief that biblical eschatology holds to a disembodied intermediate state. The concept of Sheol, the parable of the rich man and Lazarus (Lk 16.19–31), the words of Jesus to the criminal on the cross (Lk 23.39–43), and Paul's discussion in 2 Corinthians 5.1–10, which have all been used to argue for such a disembodied intermediate state do not justify such a conclusion. Green shows that this belief is an extra-biblical construct. Therefore the overall biblical picture presents 'the human person fundamentally in relational terms'. If the language of the soul is to be used it needs to be recast in relational terms.

It is no surprise to see Barr as one of the few dissident voices on this. He questions the recent swing from discontinuity to continuity as shown by holistic views of the human person, arguing that it has obscured the extent to which traditional Christianity committed itself to Greek philosophical concepts (Barr 1992: 99). He argues that belief in the soul exists alongside resurrection in the

New Testament and he shows how immortality of the soul is clearly present in the Westminster Confession. Barr is certainly correct in identifying the swing from discontinuity to continuity. The New Testament is more complex in its views of immortality and resurrection than is often represented. At the same time, Barr's view needs to be resisted. The New Testament is not as dualistic as some traditions of Christian theology have led us to think. The dominant view of the human person is that of ontological monism, and this 'emphasis on anthropological monism in the New Testament underscores the cosmic repercussions of reconciliation, highlighting the notion that the fate of the human family cannot be dissociated from that of the cosmos' (Green 1998: 127).

In one of the most recent volumes on the soul, the biblical scholars and scientists find common ground (Green 2004b). It is only the philosophical theologians who are still trying to defend dualism. Bynum observes that the concern for material and structural continuity was so important to traditional Christian understanding of the resurrection and new creation that it had to be maintained against philosophical incoherence, theological equivocation and aesthetic offensiveness (Bynum 1995). Systematic theology today has a tendency to object to philosophical incoherence at the expense of the biblical material and scientific insights.

7.3.4 The revival of the soul?

Therefore it is difficult to imagine any future for the concept of the soul. Surprisingly however Polkinghorne is one who wants to retain it. He wonders whether the consequence of anti-dualism is that we do not speak of soul and therefore lose a meaningful way of talking about continuity between this life and death. He finds the term 'soul' helpful in describing the 'real me' which links the boy of early childhood to the ageing academic of later life. He rightly points out that there is no evidence for the soul as an independent spiritual component. Further he suggests that the 'real me' cannot be described in material terms, as the atoms within the human body are continually being replaced with a cycle of a few years. Thus the carrier of continuity is:

> 'the immensely complex "information-bearing pattern" in which matter is organized. This pattern is not static; it is modified as we acquire new experiences, insights and memories, in accordance with the dynamics of our living history. It is this information-bearing pattern that is the soul.' (Polkinghorne 2002b: 105–6)

In locating the continuity in pattern, Polkinghorne sees in this a revival of the Aristotelian idea of matter and form, in terms of matter/energy and pattern-forming information. He follows this with suggesting the revival of the Thomist notion of the soul as the form of the body. Not only does this provide continuity in this life but also links the person who has died with the person in new creation. Souls are held in the mind of God before resurrection in the matter of the world to come.

It is right to see the body as more than matter and that continuity cannot be maintained in just the body or indeed in a dualist spiritual entity, but it is seems an unwise and unnecessary move to reintroduce language of the soul. It complicates the picture due to the long intellectual history connected to 'soul', which continually raises the dualist view. Wright has commented that 'the language of soul is telling us a story; the trouble with shorthand is that they can become absolutised' (Wright 2000: 31–51). The consequence of this has often been neglect in seeing any continuity in the material at all. McMullin points out that the value of stressing continuity in non reductive physicalism means that resurrection or eternal life 'would be a consequence of grace, not of nature' (McMullin 2000: 170). The danger is that it locates the continuity in nature not grace.

Then the soul is too static a concept to convey the 'real me'. Jarvis suggests that the 'self' is itself the integrative process, a process that is never finished and which may be affected by the physical body (by age, illness, tiredness) but transcends it. So a person, a self, has traits and characteristics that are formed but not unchanging (Jarvis 1995: 44). Further it does not do justice to modern biblical scholarship in either language or concept (Shults 2003). If one does want to talk about the pattern providing continuity then there is no reason why this cannot be held in the divine memory and/or the resurrection being immediate in the time frame of the believer and God (1 Cor 15.52–53; Lk 23.43).

The reintroduction of the language of soul also has the danger of individualism and the neglect of relational aspects. We have argued that continuity/discontinuity must be held in matter-energy-pattern-information, but we need to be clear that this is a combination which is both dynamic and has to be seen in context. A pattern is not intrinsic to entity, in the sense that a pattern only makes sense in the interpretation of an observer. That is, it is a relational quality. The pattern that is 'me' must include the human relationships and relationship with God, and indeed we may also add history and potentiality.

The importance of context is also shown in a very different arena, that is, in recent work in learning organizations. Senge starts from the basic premise that contrary to the integrative process of the development of the self, people are taught to break apart problems and complex tasks into smaller component parts because these are seen to be more manageable (Senge 1992). But problems usually are complex and the result of this fragmentation is that we tend to lose the connectedness of the wider whole; we no longer see the wider picture. Senge destroys the illusion that the world (or an organization) is created of separate, unrelated forces and stresses the importance of context, relationships and the way that development is a communal activity rather than an individualistic concept. These are important correctives to the individualism of the soul.

Polkinghorne is aware of some of these dangers but in using the language of the soul neglects the communal aspect that is so central to New Testament eschatology. By not taking seriously enough the context of the information pattern, the soul reduces back to an information entity, rather than the 'real me' being seen in relation to other people and in relation to God. Indeed Polkinghorne at times borders on the Platonic idea of these souls being held in the everlasting realm of mathematical entities. This gives them if not uncreated status, then at least a static eternal concept. There is little room for growth of the 'real me' in new creation.

For these reasons it seems unwise to reintroduce the language of soul. It is better to speak about matter-energy-pattern-information, and indeed to add context. We then need to see continuity and discontinuity within that. Green suggests that life after death should be described as 'relationally shaped and embodied', 'gift' and sharing in the transformation of the cosmos (Green 2004a: 85–100). This does more justice to the biblical and scientific insights than does reviving the language of the soul.

Yet how do we speak about the future of human life? Rahner states that 'eschatological fulfilment is the surpassment of life but not the denial of creatureliness' (Rahner 1974: 323–346). However, is there more to say on the surpassment of life, in particular about re-embodiment? What will be the continuity in resurrection of a baby who dies in childbirth or an older person who dies with Alzheimer's disease? Does divine grace redeem, restore what was lost, and will the good that was never bestowed be regained? The issue of ageing or the decay of this body is especially important, not least in the way we view disability. While there is a sense in which a person who has been confined to a wheelchair all of their adult life might gaze forward to the hope of being able to run in the new creation, there is also a sense in which their disability is part of who they are. To move too quickly to the suggestion of a 'repaired' body in new creation, has the danger of suggesting that they are somehow sub-human in this creation and of adding to the discrimination they experience within society. Is there any way of thinking of the transformation of the body in terms of continuity and discontinuity which values this insight? Indeed, the context here is important. The decay of this creation's physical body can affect both our relationship to others and to God either in positive or negative ways.

Further, does a transition state such as a disembodied soul help with the problem of change between this life and the next? It has been argued that if the new creation is characterised by new community, then how will this be possible with such diversity between people of today and people of 1st Century Palestine? Will we all need to be cleansed from sin and given some kind of common ground before community is possible? In addition, some have asked whether babies who died before childhood are transformed into adults before new creation? These are difficult questions. Yet an intermediate state does not necessarily help, unless you view new creation as timeless with no space for change, growth or development. In creating new community with common ground perhaps one of the biblical themes which needs to be developed is that of the process and event of judgement. Does God in this clear away all that which would inhibit the new community?

Before we attempt an answer to such questions we need to explore the relationship between body and context with insights from feminist and sacramental theology.

7.4 Feminist theology and the importance of the body

If the defence of the soul emphasizes the neglect of the material body and the danger of individualism, feminist theology has been an important movement that provides a corrective. It is a complex movement with a complex history. Yet of particular interest for our present subject is the way it develops the interrelation of creation, redemption and sacramentality (Radford Ruether 1992: 240; Johnson 1993). In reaction to some theologies that have at times demonized the physical, it has emphasized a reverence for the Earth and the body with regard to goodness and revelatory power (Moulaison 2007: 341–359). This link to the natural world has led to an involvement in ecology (McFague 1993) which stresses the interconnectedness of human beings with the natural world, opposing a theological tradition that has made the human condition the centrepiece of its reflection (Gaard 1993).

This anthropocentric theological tradition has 'treated nature as a timeless and static backdrop' (Clifford 1995: 177). In eschatology the human condition has been the centrepiece of reflection and the Universe has become a timeless and static backdrop, as we have seen even for someone such as Moltmann. In his picture the Earth is transformed but the Universe remains an unchanging backdrop.

Feminist theologians/thealogians also point out the importance of the body and how it has been devalued. There has been the linking of sexuality to sin, part of the broader understanding that the soul is good but the flesh is evil (Brown, P. 1993). A rediscovery of the goodness of sexuality and the body has been a valuable contribution (Cooey, Farmer and Ross 1987; Gudorf 1994; Parsons 1996). In addition to the influence of dualism, the nature of theology in the Western tradition has devalued the body. Cunningham challenges the intellectualizing logic that has divorced theology from reality and calls for a new Trinitarian theology of human embodiment (Cunningham 1988: 301).

Feminist theologians emphasize embodiment for related reasons, that is, they perceive that intellectualized theology dehumanizes women and robs them of the significance, reality, locus and status of their bodies.

Ross has pointed out that feminist understandings of embodiment go further than just the goodness of physicality (Ross 1998; Ross 1993: 93–100). The body needs to be seen in its social/relational context. Ross sees this as primarily the family, but the insight can be extended to the relational, socio-political and indeed cosmic structures in which we live and interact. We see here resonances to our emphasis that in trying to understand the body and any resurrection then the social/relational context is important.

This emphasis on the body as well as relationships has brought some feminist theology into conflict with certain post-modern views of the body which emphasize the endless play of possibilities, and its lack of stability. Bordo sees this post-modern view as dangerous, asking what kind of body is it that:

'is free to change its shape and location at will, that can become anyone and travel anywhere? If the body is a metaphor for our locatedness in space and time and thus for the finitude of human perception and knowledge, then the postmodern body is no body at all.' (Bordo 1993: 229)

Thus feminist insights reinforce the value of matter, context and relationships in any talk of eschatology (Jones 2007).

We may ask however whether feminist theologians have explored any sense of continuity/discontinuity in the eschatological transformation of matter itself. In fact one finds little consideration of the transformation of matter or indeed eschatology in general. One of the exceptions in eschatology has been Radford Ruether (Radford Ruether 1983; Radford Ruether 1990: 111–124). Phan comments that the movement in Western theology to individualistic otherworldly eschatology:

> 'introduced a sharp separation between body and soul, between self and the cosmos, between the immortality of the soul and the resurrection of the flesh, between earthly realities and the world beyond, between time and eternity. This dualism destroyed the ontological unity of the human person, bifurcated the destiny of history into natural and supernatural, and drove a wedge between nature and grace.' (Phan 1995: 208)

Radford Ruether responds to such a movement by pointing out the denigration of the body and especially female physicality. She emphasizes collective eschatology that is focused on the human person, the present and the struggle for justice as a never-ending task. Thus with no stress on discontinuity she sees the future as:

> 'Our existence as an individual organism ceases and dissolves back into the cosmic Matrix of matter-energy out of which new centres of individual beings arise. It is this Matrix, and not the individuated centers of being, which is everlasting'. (Radford Ruether 1990: 122)

The body is given to the earth so that it becomes food for new beings to emerge. Here she develops the theme of the importance of birth. The 'cosmic Matrix' means the God/ess, the mother-matter-matrix. The stress on continuity gives little hope for transformation and resurrection. She believes however that her picture sees the primary importance of ecology (Radford Ruether 1992: 240). However in discounting discontinuity completely the eschatology offers little hope for the future for the individual or indeed the Universe whose death will not lead to a recycling of a new Universe. No new birth follows heat death. Even the importance of ecology may not be as easy as she suggests. As we will explore in the next chapter, environmental ethics depends not just on an affirmation of the present but also on a vision for a transformed future.

Radford Ruether is helpful on embodiment and the value of this creation, but her eschatology is weak. It is an example of an over-emphasis on continuity at the expense of discontinuity. Such eschatology is also weak in the area of disability. Stuart comments:

> 'The disabled body queers a great deal of the pitch upon which the theologies of sexuality and gender have built themselves ... the disabled body casts a shadow over the efforts of these theologies to claim embodiment as good.' (Stuart 2000: 166)

While raised in the context of feminist theology, Stuart's point links with our previous discussion, where we raised the question of how to speak of the resurrection in the transformation of the disabled body. Too much stress on discontinuity in terms of complete 'healing' can often be interpreted by those who are disabled themselves as implying and reinforcing their feeling of the oppression of being told by society that they are sub-human. However, too much stress on continuity does not take seriously the pain, decay and hope for future transformation which is part of human embodiment. Again this is where a tension needs to be held in continuity and discontinuity. We have stressed the importance of the tension in systematic theology but the tension is extremely important also in pastoral theology. It is significant that the risen Jesus still had the marks of the crucifixion. Those marks are part of his identity, but they become symbols of glorification and transformation rather than pain and death.

7.5 Sacrament, body and world

The importance of the body is also central to sacramental theology. Ross comments that 'the corporeal dimension of human life is the basis for all sacramental activity' (Ross 1998: 97). Indeed, feminist insights into the goodness of the body and its physicality have fed into a renewal of sacramental theology. However, we might expect that sacramental theology will help us more in discussing the transformation between creation and new creation in terms of matter. Recent reflection on the liturgy has helped in the areas of anthropology, Christology and ecclesiology (Vaillancourt 1979), so why not in eschatology? Sacramental theology itself has stressed the importance of the body and incorporated insights from anthropology and social scientists (Worgul 1980; Duffy 1982). Will it therefore provide a fruitful dialogue with cosmology also?

7.5.1 *Doors to the sacred*

Certainly its emphasis on the nature of the sacred in the Universe should open the door to such a dialogue. Matter is seen as the medium of the divine, 'The world was created as the "matter", the material of one all embracing Eucharist' (Schmemann 1965: 16). Following Temple, Baillie suggested that natural objects can become sacramental only because we live in a 'sacramental universe' (Baillie 1958: 47; Temple 1934). This means that the world is charged with the grandeur of God, a concept used by Irenaeus, Aquinas, Bonaventure, Hildegard of Bingen, Gerald Manley Hopkins and more recently by Tracey (Tracey 1982). Thus the matter of this creation gives the possibility of 'doors to the sacred' (Martos 1991), as 'God's mysterious and surprising presence is shot through the world' (Ross 1998: 92). This comes from the doctrine of creation and indeed from the Lordship of Christ in creation. There is ambiguity in that the created reality both reveals and conceals the presence of God, but this does not detract from the conclusion that the physical reality is inherently good and a source of God's revelation.

This understanding of the inherent goodness of the physical reality has been one of the important elements of post Vatican II sacramental theology (Cooke 1983: 7). While this has been a growth area in theology, it is interesting that with such a basis there has been little consideration of the eschatological transformation of this physical reality (Rahner 1963; Downey and Fragomeni 1992). Schillebeeckx describes the sacraments as 'manifested signification' (Schillebeeckx 1963: 96) and develops this to see the sacraments are anticipatory, mediating signs of salvation (Schillebeeckx 1980). But if the sacraments are anticipatory signs, what kind of signs do they give us about the future of matter? Initially we might say the importance of continuity. But at the same time we also see the importance of discontinuity. They both affirm the present creation but point forward to a new creation.

Habgood sees the sacraments as helping us to perceive a deeper meaning in the natural world through the transforming presence of Christ. At the same time they are also a conveyance of grace, which is the active work of God transforming human beings. He comments that 'sacramental thinking points to a world which has to be redeemed before it can truly reveal the face of God' (Habgood 1995: 28). Brown and Loades comment on this in relation to time and space:

'time speaks of the inevitable decay of the world, space of finitude, that we are bound to one place rather than another ... one may argue that this is how time and space themselves operate sacramentally: not by endorsing the present universe's temporal and spatial co-ordinates nor by pulling us out into a world without either, but rather through faith generating it own distinctive medium, its own set of spatial and temporal co-ordinates.' (Brown and Loades 1995: 2–3)

We made a similar point in relation to the biblical material and in the previous chapter on the transformation of space-time. There must be an element of discontinuity alongside the continuity. Yet it raises the important question as to how much of God's sacramental involvement is in this creation such as this time and place and how much is it movement through transformations.

7.5.2 The feast in new creation

Eucharistic theology has often emphasized questions of the ontological presence of Christ, the role of sacrifice and the response of the individual rather than the proclamation of the 'Lord's death until he comes' (1 Cor 11.26). In contrast, Wainwright points out that eschatology is embedded in the biblical images of Eucharist such as messianic feast, the advent of Christ, and first fruits of the Kingdom. The Eucharist is already the meal of the Kingdom but the final fulfilment is still awaited (Wainwright 1971: 92). In this tension of the already and not yet, the Eucharist expresses the positive value of the material creation and the physical, a point noted by Irenaeus (Irenaeus 1992: IV, 18, 5, 1027–29). Wainwright could have followed this naturally through to the positive value of the material in new creation, and indeed that the imagery of a feast implying a communal aspect.

Nevertheless we are faced with the question of the relation of Christ's presence at the Eucharistic feast and His final coming? If Christ is present now

(Mt 18.20), how can his coming be spoken of in future terms? Wainwright sees the link through remembrance, and because of God's sovereignty over time the Eucharist becomes the temporal projection of Christ's final advent into the present. In this way it can be seen as first fruits of the Kingdom, seeing Jesus as speaking the re-creative word which transforms the old creation into the new. The new creation will be characterized by divine glory:

> 'Not only will all God's saints bless Him, but all his works will give Him thanks ... and in this way the whole creation will share in the liberty of the glory of the children of God ... a glory that is derived from God and rendered to Him in that service which is perfect freedom. It is on account of this circulation of divine glory that it may be said that "God will be all in all" in a sense that maintains the distinctness of the transcendent God from His creation and yet will allow the whole of that creation to enjoy the divine life in so far as it is communicable.' (Wainwright 1971: 103)

This picture sees the renewed creation so entirely submitted to the divine lordship that it would enjoy total penetration by the divine glory, while remaining distinct from the transcendent God it worships.

What then is the relation of consecrated elements and the transformed creation? If the elements are seen as first fruits of the Kingdom, how are they also the body and blood of Christ? In addition, for those who view the bread and wine as anticipatory feeding with Christ on the fruits of new creation, how do they understand the image of 'feeding on Christ' (Jn 6.53–58)? Wainwright wants to avoid either extreme. He suggests that the final Kingdom is life in Christ, with Christ and Christ living in us. Thus it is about:

> 'feasting in fellowship with Christ ... on the fruits of the creation which has been transfigured through His agency as the mighty Word; for this suggests both the transcendence of the giver on whom all life depends and also an intimate communion with the Godhead ... which yet respects the distinction between Creator and creature.' (Wainwright 1971: 107)

Christ is not just the host but also the food. This is a reminder of the mystery involved but are some guidelines needed to limit just how far the mystery goes? Wainwright suggests a number of such guidelines. First, following Mascall, he suggests that transcendence is theologically prior to immanence for God is prior to creation (Mascall 1943). Therefore we must take seriously images which safeguard transcendence, such as Christ as the giver. Second, a greater emphasis on the role of the Holy Spirit means that there is less danger of confining Christ's presence to the elements. Further the gift of the Holy Spirit expresses the relationship of 'already' and 'not yet'. Third, it is important to see the Eucharist in its communal setting. One of the dangers of the development of the individualistic view of Eucharist in the West is an 'atomistic eschatology' (Wainwright 1971: 148) In all of this Wainwright resonates with some of the themes that we have been suggesting. Once again we see the key theme of the role of the Holy Spirit in relationship. Further, the Eucharist says that the physical is important, transformation must have both continuity and discontinuity, and that transformation is not just about the matter but the context of relationships in which the matter is located. He comments:

> 'No schema of general eschatology is acceptable which fails to take into account the constitutive relation between the "now" and the "then", the "here" and the "there", and within that relation the polarities of hiddenness and visibility (contestability and incontestability), interruption and permanence, limited extension and universal scope.' (Wainwright 1971: 147)

Farrow also explores Eucharist and eschatology and concludes that the Eucharist conveys 'presence testifying to absence' (Farrow 2000: 203). He sees the ascension as one of the strongest affirmations of physicality as the transformed resurrection body of Jesus is taken up into heaven (Farrow 1999). In this picture, the church exists in the tension of the presence and absence of Christ. The Spirit resolves this tension in the Eucharist where we are both reminded of the absence and raised to the presence of Christ in a similar way to the view of Calvin. Yet it does not solve adequately, the question of where and in what form is the risen body of Christ now? We have encountered this a number of times without gaining a clear answer. Is the risen body of Jesus now hidden in the future new creation, his presence mediated by the Holy Spirit?

Certainly the Eucharist is a reminder both of the transforming work of the Spirit now and the 'not yet' or 'absence' of the new heaven and earth. The resurrection body of Jesus liberated from the constraints of space-time may now inhabit the new heaven and new earth, able through the Spirit to work in the space-time of this creation. The matter of this creation is good and part of God's future possibilities, but also points forward to something better. Under all of this is the constant activity of God. Schwöbel comments:

> 'The continuity of divine action and the discontinuity of created matter together provide the basis for a hope which trusts in a real transformation in the eschaton, because we can already hear it, feel it and taste it in the promise of the gospel and the celebration of the sacraments.' (Schwöbel 2000: 240)

7.6 'Radically different'? Polkinghorne and the future of matter

Polkinghorne has been one of the few to explore how matter might be transformed in new creation. Key to his view is the empty tomb and resurrection because it means that the Lord's risen body is the transmutation and glorification of his dead body. This gives hope for matter which 'participates in the resurrection transformation, enjoying thereby the foretaste of its own redemption from decay' (Polkinghorne 2002b: 113).

In terms of redemption, he sees different dimensions of the totality of divinely sustained reality, with 'resurrection involving an information-bearing mapping between the two, and the redemption of matter as involving a projection from the old onto the new' (Polkinghorne 2002b: 121). It is this model that he applies to the future of human beings after death. Identifying the soul as the 'information-bearing pattern' of the body/brain, he suggests that this pattern is remembered by God and then resurrected in a new way (Polkinghorne 1996a: 100).

When it comes to attempting to describe the transformation of matter-energy he stresses discontinuity:

> 'The matter-energy of the world to come will certainly have to be radically different in its physical properties to the matter energy of this present creation … The matter of this universe is perfectly adapted to its role of sustaining that evolutionary exploration of potentiality which is theologically to be understood as the old creation being allowed to "make itself". In an evolving world of this kind, death is the necessary cost of life; transience is inevitably built into its physical fabric … The entities arising in this way are sufficiently structured to endure for a while and sufficiently flexible to develop and grow, but they can only sustain their dynamic patterns for limited periods. In our world, the cost of the evolution of novelty is the certainty of its impermanence. If the world to come is to be free from death and suffering, its matter-energy will have to be given a different character.' (Polkinghorne 2000: 39)

He justifies this discontinuity by quoting 1 Corinthians 15.50, but gives it no detailed consideration. He sees it in a literal sense rather than in the sense of Jeremias' idiom referring to living, but frail and sinful human beings. We saw in Chapters 5 and 6 that one of the characteristics of this creation is that the flow of time is coupled with decay. In the above passage, Polkinghorne sees this as part of the creative process within the Universe and that this is built into the physical fabric of the Universe. In an apologetic context, these suggestions are often presented in a model which uses computer software and hardware. The 'software' of our information pattern could be re-embodied on new 'hardware' of our resurrection body.

On should not underestimate this unique exploration of a key question or indeed how valuable these suggestions are. However, a number of questions need to be raised in order to help the exploration go further. First, does the language of 'radically different' overstress the aspect of discontinuity? It is an easy distinction to locate the continuity in our information pattern and the discontinuity in the nature of matter, but the overwhelming evidence of our exploration of biblical and scientific material has been to emphasise the interconnectedness of information-pattern-matter-context. The tension of continuity/discontinuity has to affect all of these elements together. It is interesting to note that such questions have a long history. Origen viewed the body like a river in that the actual matter does not remain the same but the entity is the same. A similar view was championed by C. S. Lewis who argued for a continuity of form in terms of a curve in a waterfall, that is the form stays the same but the matter in it changes (Lewis 1967: 155). Origen was then challenged by Methodius in the third century and by the Second Council of Constantinople in the sixth century on the basis of whether this gave enough continuity of the body between this life and resurrection, or whether he had overstressed transformation (Bynum 1995: 67–9).

Second, while Polkinghorne characterises matter in new creation as 'radically different' he does not go on to explore what that difference will be. Talk of different kinds of atoms or physical laws is not terribly illuminating. In fact, can we say anything meaningful on this? Yet if there is some continuity with this creation and the resurrection body of Jesus interacts with this creation then perhaps we should be able to speculate a little.

Third, the analogy of information pattern put onto another piece of hardware suffers from the assumption that the thoughts, memories and feelings define the human person. This raises the immediate apologetic problem that if this is the soul why cannot such a piece of different hardware be created by human beings? In fact, this has been the dream of 'cybernetic immortality' (Herzfeld 2002a: 196). Some have even seen human beings having the ability to produce artificial intelligence as part of the evolutionary progress in such a way that 'the cosmic function of Humanity is to act as the evolutionary interface between Life and Intelligence' (Stonier 1992: 214). Another way of achieving immortality would be to use virtual reality where one's mental self might only exist within cyber-space (Stenger 1991: 52, 58). Thus Polkinghorne opens the door to those who want to recreate the myth of human progress in terms of immortality.

Fourth, does this picture still stray too much towards dualism and undervalue the human body? Polkinghorne of course stresses the importance of the human body but has a tendency to see the essence of the human person as non bodily. The same problem occurred theologically in the different attempts to define the image of God as reason, morality or free will. Even in my own preference to see the image of God as responsible relationship in community (Wilkinson 2002: 31–45), there is the weakness of downgrading the physical. Goldingay suggests that has been due to the imposition of Greek philosophical categories onto the narrative structure of the earlier chapters of Genesis (Goldingay 2000: 141). Is a similar thing true in eschatology?

Fifth, does Polkinghorne's view of a resurrection body which has radically different matter take time seriously? The nature of matter in more than one temporal dimension can be very different. Is this the source of discontinuity rather than a discontinuity characterised by radically different matter? Further, is there enough stress on the way that personal identity evolves? Indeed personal identity is not just determined by my past history and present experience but also by my future potential. This is especially true when we come to consider the resurrection of those who have died before they have matured physically, psycho-logically or spiritually. We often make the assumption that babies who have died in infancy will not be resurrected as infants, but can we think more about this assumption? There is a potential in the material development of the human body in this creation. How can we think about this in new creation?

Sixth, underlying Polkinghorne's approach is a strong individualism that focuses on the future for the individual human person. He is ready to acknowledge this as a weakness. Although focused in his discussion of the soul, does it also have implications for his discussion of the future of matter? We have argued that context and relationships are crucially important. Personal identity cannot be understood as an information pattern without seeing that information pattern in its context of a web of relationships with others, the natural world and indeed God. The insights of feminist and sacramental theology stress this and the biblical insights of the corporate nature of new creation critique any eschatological individualism. Murphy strongly defends physical monism and acknowledges that personal identity involves 'self recognition, continuity of moral character and personal relations, both with God and with others' (Murphy 2002: 208). However, she does not give enough stress to the relational aspects. We readily accept that the nature of relationships between human beings and God will be different in new creation. Do we also need to ask about whether the relationships in the physical world will be different? If our horizon is simply the perspective that matter is made up of discrete atoms, we are therefore limited to asking questions about whether the 'atoms' will be different in new creation. If however our perspective recognises that we need to speak of matter not just in terms of atoms but also their relationships to each other, observers, macro-systems and ultimately the sustaining power of God, then the character of new creation may be in fundamental change in those relationships. For example, even in this creation we see a limited effect of the changing of relationships. Carbon atoms are the same particles in graphite and diamond. But the way they are configured, used or perceived in a pencil lead or in a diamond ring involves a whole number of relational aspects, both impersonal and personal. A resurrection body may still conceivably be composed of carbon and the other elements known to us in creation but the nature of relationships may change. Polkinghorne is right in suggesting that matter-energy will have a different character but we need to be cautious about postulating that matter will be radically different.

Having said all of this, we need to note also how Polkinghorne develops his picture. He does not accept panentheism (the idea that the creation is in God, though God exceeds creation) as a present reality but believes that it will become the eschatological reality in the new creation (Polkinghorne 1994b). The new creation will be wholly sacramental for God will be all in all. He quotes 1 Corinthians 15.28 which is also a key verse for Moltmann. Thus the world will be integrated in a new and intimate way with the divine life. Polkinghorne suggests that the laws of nature will be perfectly adapted to no more death, crying or pain just as the present laws of physics are adapted to the freely evolving process. So God is involved in a 2-step plan, the first creation is about kenotic space, but the second is about intimate relationship.

It is a provocative proposal and raises a number of questions. First, is there more to learn from the sacramental view of this world? Polkinghorne comments on the Eucharist, 'The bread and wine that are elements of this creation are also the body and blood of Christ, elements of the new creation' (Polkinghorne 2002b: 101). Yet there is little engagement with the presence of Christ, the work of the Spirit or the ascension. Each of these is rich in theological resources which may add to a panentheistic picture of new creation, but also would question such a picture. For example what is the role of the Spirit in new creation?

Second, does 1 Corinthians 15.28 really justify such a panentheistic picture? Chrysostom viewed 'that God may be all in all' as meaning that all things are dependent on him (St. Chrysostom 1989: 39.8). This is true as much of God's action in this creation as in new creation. Moffatt and Collins translate 'so that God may be everything to everyone' (Moffatt 1938: 249; Collins 1999: 547). However, de Boer sees 'all things' as referring to this Universe (De Boer 1988: 125–6). Morris sees it simply as a strong expression for the complete supremacy of the Lord (Morris 1985: 213), while Calvin saw the meaning in reconciliation, that is 'all things will be brought back to God, as their alone beginning and end, that they may be closely bound to him' (Calvin 1996: 328). This certainly would fit with Colossians 1 which we looked at in chapter 5. We need also to remember Wainwright's use of glory to escape a panentheistic picture. Polkinghorne and Moltmann have moved too quickly from the biblical text. There is little to justify panentheism in 1 Corinthians 15.28. Indeed it is difficult to maintain that it differentiates between this creation and the new creation. For even in this creation 'in him we live and move and have our being' (Acts 17.28).

Third, why reject panentheism in this creation and opt for it in new creation. Polkinghorne rejects panentheism as a model to describe God's action in this creation. It is not clear what makes it suitable for the new creation. We can go further with this criticism. On such a view what enables us to distinguish between God's existence and our own existence in new creation? What differentiates us from the life of the Trinity?

For these reasons we do not fully accept Polkinghorne's 'radically different' view of the transformation of matter. There is too much discontinuity in terms of the physical, while not enough consideration of transformation of the context and relationships in which the physical exists. An eschatological panentheism is an attempt to express that context but it does not quite work.

7.7 Is that the end of the matter?

We have attempted to explore the possible transformation of matter in new creation. Continuity without discontinuity is a problem. This is illustrated in the medieval period, when the resurrection of the body was affirmed, but this was typically portrayed as reclaiming the very body placed in the grave, or its regathered parts when necessary (Bynum 1995). At the same time discontinuity at the expense of continuity leads to problems also, not least in the danger of dualism.

However, the resurrection encourages a picture of transformation that holds together continuity and discontinuity. Further, we have argued that matter cannot be isolated in this discussion from space-time or from its context and web of relationships around it. Scientific and theological insights into embodiment and the psychosomatic unity of the human person mean that matter is important in new creation, a conclusion we also came to in exploring the resurrection. Insights from feminist and sacramental theology encourage a consideration of transformed relationships as the key to new creation, but these relationships are not merely between human beings and God but between personal and communal identity and the nature of matter. Noting that the actual atoms in our bodies will change during a person's life, Green suggests that our identity is formed and found in 'self conscious relationality with its neural correlates and embodied narrativity or formative histories' (Green 2004a: 100). We cannot understand the future of human life in new creation without understanding our present embodiment and indeed the future of the cosmos.

These scientific and theological insights on the importance of relationships have interesting resonances with the biblical material. When Paul speaks of life to come, he does not discuss it in terms of soul or substance but in terms of relationship 'with Christ' (Phil 1.23) or 'in Christ' (1 Thess 4.16) (Lampe 2002: 103–14; Green 2004a: 85–100). Work remains to be done on the development of this theme with regard to the doctrines of Spirit, ascension and the nature of new creation.

Nevertheless we can state some tentative conclusions. First, the resurrection means that matter will be transformed. Therefore, there is a future to the physical Universe of atoms, photons and macro-structures. While the circumstances and laws of this creation point to an end of futility, the resurrection points to a different conclusion. Wright suggests the word 'transphysical' as a useful label of the kind of embodiment seen in the resurrection of Jesus (Wright 2003: 477). The 'trans' is intended as a shortening of transformed and certainly it may be a good image of the kind of new creation we have been attempting to describe. It may not be the atoms themselves that are transformed into a different kind of matter with different kinds of fundamental particles. It may be that the atoms find themselves in a different context and web of relationships. The suggestion of a different form of the laws of nature may be the way forward. Or our present laws of nature may admit the possibility of other dimensions of time and this may be key to the transformation of matter.

Second, just as continuity and discontinuity must be maintained there also needs to be an emphasis on holding together pattern and matter in relationship to God. The pattern could be represented in a different kind of matter that may have the property of not experiencing decay. Yet we suggest that there is continuity and discontinuity in the transformation of the pattern. The human being experiences transformation not just in terms of the body but also in terms of past/present/potential experience. It is the relationship to God that allows the pattern and the matter to be configured in way that represents continuity and discontinuity.

Third, the matter of new creation will continue to be located in space and time. Thus the new heaven and new earth will have an everlasting destiny rather than a timeless experience of eternity (Volf 2000: 256–278; Weder 2000: 184–204). Polkinghorne is right to stress that in this creation space, time and matter are all linked and so they will be in new creation. It will be a 'temporal world whose character is everlasting' (Polkinghorne 2002b: 117), 'not an atemporal experience of illumination but the unceasing exploration of the riches of divine nature' (Polkinghorne 2000: 40). This does not necessarily lead to a reformulated concept of purgatory which is popular with both Polkinghorne and Moltmann, as part of the transformation process that fits human beings for everlasting encounter with God (Moltmann 2000: 238–255).

Fourth we have suggested that panentheism is not necessary to new creation. In this we differ from Polkinghorne. Indeed, we have also raised questions concerning Polkinghorne's use of the terminology of soul and his characterisation of matter as radically different in new creation. While some of these differences may be due to the different weight given to the biblical material, there is still much common ground with Polkinghorne. We agree that the resurrection is of central importance to the future of matter and that the promise of new life in new creation is gift.

We hope that we have mapped out some important considerations in the transformation of matter. It is area which will develop with scientific and theological insights working together. While this work which has been focused on the future of the physical Universe is still at an early stage, it still allows us to draw out some general issues beyond that focus. In particular we can move to asking what our conclusions mean for the future of the biological world, the doctrine of providence, the doctrine of hope as it works out in ethics and apologetics, and finally the relationship between science and religion. It is to these topics that we turn next.

Chapter 8

Fruitful Interaction: Working Out the Relationship of Creation and New Creation

We have been exploring the nature of transformation for the physical Universe in the action of God from creation to new creation. We have suggested the importance of continuity and discontinuity based on the resurrection, and suggested models for the transformation of space-time and matter. While these things have been focused on the futility implied by scientific models of the end of the Universe, the question is whether they have wider application. In this chapter we therefore consider new creation in terms of the biological world, the importance of eschatology for models of providence, the relationship of hope in the areas of ethics and Christian apologetics, and finally the dialogue between science and religion.

8.1 New creation and the biological world

Issues within the biological world have been increasingly important in recent years both within theology and within society, in concerns about ecology, the nature of humanity and the nature of animals. However, once again we find very little theological reflection on eschatology and the biological world. For example, 'An Evangelical Declaration on the Care of Creation' states:

> 'We encourage deeper reflection on the substantial biblical and theological teaching which speaks of God's work of redemption in terms of the renewal and completion of God's purpose in creation'. (Berry 2000: 17)

However, in the commentary and exposition of the statement by authors including Moltmann, very little is said on the subject of eschatology (Elsdon 2000). In particular, little work has been done on the nature and purpose of the animal world and how that relates to Christian eschatology. Can we use some of the principles from the context of the end of the Universe to begin to address these kinds of questions?

8.1.1 Animals in creation

The place of animals within creation has until recently had little theological examination (Deane-Drummond and Clough 2009). Birch and Vischer suggest that the Genesis account of creation sees animals as forming a 'limited community' with human beings (Birch and Vischer 1997: 3). Animals are part of the human environment in creation and human beings have a close relationship with the animals. This is illustrated by animals and humans being formed on the same day. The fact that humans then name the animals shows a special relationship with animals, but also that the relationship is limited by differences in status. We can add to Birch and Vischer's 'limited community' by noting that animals though subject to human beings are seen as companions (Gen 2.18–20) and that the story of Noah shows the importance of preserving a community of humans and animals from being destroyed (Gen 6.20; 7.3).

God's care for the animal world is reinforced in the New Testament (e.g. Mt 6.26). This however raises some interesting questions. As Farrer observed, 'It must never be forgotten that God is the God of hawks no less than of sparrows' (Farrer 1962: 104–5). Is the predator nature of the animal world part of God's purpose in creation? Within that context it is important to note Job 38.39–40 where the writer clearly understands that God's providential care is expressed in the provision of prey for the lion and raven. Birch and Vischer interpret this passage to mean, 'It is clearly part of God's creation that life can exist only at the cost of other life' (Birch and Vischer 1997: 3). This a key question. Does the reality of the animal world as we see it now reflect God's purpose in creation or will it be changed in new creation? It is interesting that Birch and Vischer, a partnership of theologian and professional biologist, see the cycle of life and death in the animal world as part of creation rather than fall. They conclude that death is inevitable and that in death animals serve other animals. How one sees creation affects the way that new creation is imaged.

Scientists reflecting theologically tend to stress the importance of creation as a way of understanding the purposes of God. For example in his Bridgewater Treatise of 1837, William Buckland faced with the evidence for a long Earth history distinguished between animal and human death, the former being part of the Creator's provision for creation, the latter being due to Adam's disobedience. Buckland was reflecting the dominance of the design argument which proved the nature and existence of God through nature. A 'fallen' natural world was of no great help to this kind of argument. In addition the status of science as 'thinking God's thoughts after him' would be undermined if the object of science's study was not God's purpose.

A broader yet as important question is then what is the purpose of the biological world and in particular animals? A traditional answer in Aristotle, Augustine and Aquinas and then in both Protestant and Roman Catholic thought is that animals simply serve human beings (Aristotle 1985: 79; Calvin 1965: 96; Hormann 1961: 274; Augustine 1993: I. 20). This has been interpreted to mean that animals serve humans through work, food, or companionship. The argument can be reformed in terms of evolution. That is, animals exist simply as part of the evolutionary process that gives birth to human beings (Elphinstone 1976). On the basis of such arguments the question may be posed as to whether Christianity is irredeemably speciesist? (Linzey 1998: xi)

The difficulty of such arguments is the scale of the animal world. Many animals exist which are not useful to humans, and indeed over the long period of

Earth history there have been millions of animals existing with no human being around. Even in evolution there seem to be many pathways that have no direct connection to the pathway to human beings. Of course, one may argue that it is the nature of the biological world as a whole which gives rise to human beings. This is a fair point in that the evolutionary process holds together novelty with diversity. Without such diversity there would be no process toward intelligence and self-consciousness.

Yet that is not enough to explain the place of the animals in creation. A theocentric approach is much more fruitful. Hick suggests that the 'sub-human animals exist because their existence is accordingly necessary to the fulness of the created world' (Hick 1968: 350). It seems to me that this is beginning to go in the right direction but needs to be developed. Yamamoto suggests that humans cannot be human without the limited community with the animal world (Yamamoto 1998: 89). Hick would agree but would see animals as the setting for the making of human souls. However, the existence of animals is necessary to the fullness of the created world not only in providing the nature of the biological and human world, but also in demonstrating the extravagance of the Creator God. If, in the words of von Balthasar, 'the whole point of creation is for us to know that we are not Creator', then the diversity of the animal world, like the vastness of the physical Universe, is a reminder of our own limited nature as creatures and at the same time the glory of the Creator.

If the animal world is an expression of the extravagance of creation, and God's faithful care includes not just humans, does God's redemptive action extend to animals? Wildmann in his poem *The Holy One and Animals* (1905) imagines Jesus when faced with animal suffering asking whether there is a peaceful retreat where animals can take refuge after suffering. Is there a place for animals in new creation?

8.1.2 *Animals in new creation*

This may seem a trivial question but it has a long theological tradition, possibly due to the need to relate eschatology with the non-human world and the place of physicality. Augustine thought that humans would have some kind of bodies after death, but he viewed this afterlife as timeless, and could see no place for animals, plants, or physical matter in such a setting. Thus he argued that the groaning for redemption in Romans 8 is actually the unregenerate nature of human beings. However this does not do justice to the text. Nevertheless, he saw human beings as microcosms of creation, comprising the physical, the living, the animal, and the rational. While Aquinas followed him, Luther influenced by a literal reading of Isaiah and Romans was drawn to animal salvation. Calvin thought that there would be a renewed Earth, but resurrected humans would only look on it from their heavenly setting. Later dualism triumphed over the biblical passages and animals were reduced to machines.

However, as we have seen, Wesley became one of the strongest proponents of animal salvation. Influenced probably by the Swiss naturalist Charles Bonnet,

Wesley proposed in his sermon *The General Deliverance* that animals would be 'delivered from the bondage of corruption; into glorious liberty ... they shall enjoy happiness suited to their state, without alloy, without interruption, and without end' (Wesley 1988: 2.437–50). As compensation for the evil they experienced in this life God would move various animals higher up 'the Chain of Being' in the next life. This would give them greater abilities, including perhaps even the ability to relate to God as humans do.

As Maddox points out, the most significant aspect of Wesley's reflection on the cosmic dimension of the new creation is his sense of its relevance for present Christian life (Maddox 2004: 21–52). He assumed that 'final things' are also 'ultimate things'; that is, our convictions about God's purpose provides guidance for what we value in the present. Thus, he defended his speculation about God's future blessings of animals on the grounds that it might provide encouragement for us to imitate God whose 'mercy is over all his works' (Wesley 1988: 2.449), and he frequently preached against the abusive treatment of animals (Runyon 1998: 202–5).

Wesley was not only influenced by the science of his day but also by the biblical passages that had influenced Luther and Calvin. As we have seen Paul sees the redemption of human beings very closely associated with the redemption of creation as a whole. But does this include animals? Jesus in his preparation time in the wilderness 'was with the wild beasts' (Mk 1.13). Bauckham suggests that Mark by locating Jesus' ministry within the context of wild animals is expressing continuity to the Isaianic tradition which sees the Messiah bringing about reconciliation between nature and humanity (Bauckham 1994: 3–21). Other commentators suggest that this is a reference to the community of the sixth day being restored in the messianic age.

Certainly there is an element of Christian tradition that has seen such a reconciliation or new community between the human and animal kingdom. A non-canonical strand of tradition from the second to the twelfth centuries associated Jesus and the apostles with peaceable co-operative relationships with animals (Linzey and Sherbock 1997). In addition, many of the saints seem to model a new relationship or community which is without fear and where violence is reduced in nature (Butler 1946; Waddell 1934). These include Kieran of Saighir, St Guthlac of Croyland, St Godric, and even St. Cuthbert who demonstrated such a reconciliation with animals (Lapidge 1989: 80–1; Backhouse 1995: 113). Most famous is St Francis in 'converting' the wolf of Gubbio. These may seem to be odd examples but it should be understood that they represent an extensive tradition that expresses not just reconciliation but holiness characterized by divine power over nature. Whether these stories are believed to be history does not detract from the point that early in Christian thought, there existed the view that the fundamental nature of animals could be redeemed through the redemption of human beings.

The key biblical passage for this belief is Isaiah 11.6–9 which we looked at in Chapter 4. The way this passage is treated by contemporary commentators is instructive. For example, Watts gives no discussion of the animal imagery beyond the messianic theme and its bringing of 'justice to the people and peace to all of God's creation' (Watts 1985: 175). This is typical of most of the commentaries, which engage little with the place of animals either in creation or new creation. Brueggemann honestly comments:

> 'The poet imagines a coming time ... when all relationships of hostility and threat, in the animal world as in the human environment, shall be overcome. ... This lyrical statement is one of the most remarkable assertions in the Bible that there will be 'all things new' in creation when God fully authorises the right human agents. The phrasing is so overwhelming that a commentator (at least this one) is at a loss to know how to interpret adequately its majestic scenario'. (Brueggemann 1998: 102)

Nevertheless he claims that as human violation produces enemies of nature, so the reordering of human society through the reign of the messianic king leads to new scenario for nature. Yet he does not go on to engage with what this 'new scenario for nature' actually means, commenting as we noted previously that 'this poem is about the impossible possibility of the new creation!' (Brueggemann 1998: 103) Brueggemann is wise not to speculate too much on the basis of one passage that is primarily focused on the messianic reign. However, we are left with the question of whether the 'impossible possibility' means a fundamental change to the nature and purpose of animals in the new creation.

Here we encounter again, the way biblical commentators have struggled to represent the combination of continuity and discontinuity in eschatological passages. In order not to fall into the trap of saying that this present creation is of no value, recent commentators and systematic theologians have stressed the continuity between creation and new creation. This is shown in recent interpretations of Isaiah 11.6–9, which see the passage simply as an ecological imperative (Widyapranawa 1990: 70). The reign of the Messiah, which changes human beings, is thus worked out by bringing harmony to nature in the present creation (Rogerson 1998: 13). Oswalt also interprets the passage figuratively. Figures of speech make the overarching point that in the Messiah's reign fears associated with insecurity, danger and evil will be removed for the individual and the world (Oswalt 1988: 283). However, in order to do this he dismisses a more literal interpretation, which says that in new creation the nature of the animal kingdom is changed. His dismissal is on the basis that a 'lion's carnivorousness is fundamental to what a lion is'. This he feels makes it clear that the writer was suggesting that another interpretation is intended.

While it is undeniable that the overarching point is about the consequences of the Messiah's reign, we must question whether the literalistic interpretation is dismissed too quickly. Oswalt's argument depends on 'what is fundamental to what a lion is'. However this will in turn depend on what is fundamental. Does the present biological and physiological reality reflect what is fundamental or is nature in some way fallen? C. S. Lewis stresses that animals should always be seen in community with human beings yet asks what the future for the animal kingdom will be. He suggests each species has a corporate self:

> 'If the earthly lion could read the prophecy of that day when he shall eat hay like an ox, he would regard it as a description not of heaven, but of

hell. And if there is nothing in the lion but carnivorous sentience, then he is unconscious and his "survival" would have no meaning. But if there is a rudimentary Leonine self, to that also God can give a "body" as it pleases Him – a body no longer living by the destruction of the lamb, yet richly Leonine in the sense that it expresses whatever energy and splendor and exulting power dwelled within the visible lion on this earth ... indeed, that we shall then first see that of which the present fangs and claws are a clumsy, and satanically perverted, imitation.' (Lewis 1984: 130–131)

Such a view is very platonic in the sense of 'Lionhood' being more important than the particular entity of a lion. It utilizes a fall of the natural world to separate out the attractive and non-attractive features of the lion. This view is also represented in a few commentaries which take a more literalistic interpretation. For example, Motyer suggests that the renewed creation will be characterised by a reconciliation of old hostilities where predators and prey are reconciled, a change of nature where carnivores become herbivores, and the curse of the fall is removed so that serpent and child can play together (Motyer 1993).

Thus Brueggemann in his 'impossible possibility of the new creation', Lewis in his present biological world being a 'perverted imitation' and Motyer in his change of nature removing the curse of the fall, are all pointing to a discontinuity between new creation and old creation in the biblical traditions as it refers to the animal kingdom. This is far more convincing than the 'ecological' interpretations of Rogerson and others who want to stress continuity. If the context is the experience of a rural village where danger and violence is observed in the animal kingdom, then images of lions eating straw go far beyond our exploitation of the planet. In particular, the images go far beyond human ability to change. So little of the vision is 'humanly possible' that the passage is more about discontinuity than continuity.

This discontinuity is also important to the animal theology and ethics of Andrew Linzey. His theological starting point is Barth's criticism of Schweitzer's ethics based on 'reverence' for the whole of creation (Schweitzer 1923). In turn Linzey criticizes Barth's distinction between the importance of human life over animal life. He makes four points. First, Barth's Christology is inadequate, having no relation to the non-human creation. Second, the patristic principle that what is not assumed in the incarnation is not healed in the redemption does not mean that only human life is healed in redemption. Barth argues that Jesus did not come as angel or animal but man and therefore sees the incarnation as an affirmation of humanity alone (Barth 1936–62: III. 1.16). However, Linzey argues that the incarnation is not an affirmation simply of humanity but of 'God's Yes to creation' as a whole. Third, Barth does not take seriously the themes of the reconciliation of all things in the New Testament (e.g. Col 1.19–20) and in early theologians such as Athanasius and Irenaeus. Fourth, the Old Testament theme of God's covenant with the earth demonstrates God's continued commitment to the non-human creation. On the basis of this Linzey argues for the importance of animal rights in ethics, and indeed the importance of animals in eschatological models.

Linzey is correct in his criticisms of Barth. In fact, his case is strengthened by more exploration of the doctrines of creation and incarnation. If, as argued above, humans and animals form a limited community in creation, then this needs to be taken seriously in ethics and in thinking about redemption. Barth, Brunner and others have stressed that one of the fundamental aspects of the nature of human beings created in the image of God is their diversity and community. This recognition of the nature of creation has in part meant an emphasis on the relational and communal aspects of redemption and new creation. In the same way, the creation account's linking of humans and animals reminds us of its importance in eschatology. In addition, the setting of the incarnation in the context of Jesus as Logos and creator of all creation (Jn 1.1–18; Col 1.15–20; Heb 1.1–4) gives a Christology that includes the whole of creation. It is from that basis that the New Testament speaks of the reconciliation of all things in Christ (Galloway 1951; Murray 1992). Linzey may or may not be convincing in his argument for animal rights (Linzey 1976; Griffiths 1982; Barclay 1992: 49–61; Linzey 1994), but he does show the important place that animals have in creation and new creation.

He then goes on to consider eschatology, asking what is the ultimate end of all creation in the light of the pattern of creation, crucifixion and redemption as disclosed in the person of Jesus Christ? He suggests that human beings, being 'the centre of recreation' through Christ, have to recognise their responsibility for 'the moral liberation of other species' (Linzey 1976: 75). Linzey rightly argues that this eschatological understanding has implications for the way we care for the environment and in particular issues of animal testing, hunting and cruelty. Yet Linzey goes further interpreting Romans 8 as liberation from pain and suffering not just for human beings but for those 'animals sharing a similar capacity for sentiency' (Linzey 1976: 76). Thus animals are liberated from their futility. Hick had earlier objected to the postulate of a new animal creation of millions and millions individual animals as a response to animal suffering (Hick 1968: 352). Linzey argues against this, suggesting that a similar type of argument could be used against a heaven for millions and millions of human beings.

Then in a key statement, Linzey suggests that natural law should not be discovered in the way things are but in the sense of what should be. Armstrong had criticized the Isaianic vision of the lion lying down with the lamb as an attempt 'to get rid of the beasts of prey or change their nature beyond recognition' (Armstrong 1981: 44). However, Linzey sees animals in bondage to violence and the predatory nature of the non-human biological world. The Isaianic vision for Linzey is the situation as God wants it to be, and represents the real nature of animals so that 'God's transforming love is not determined even by what we think we know of elementary biology' (Linzey 1994: 83). Clark makes a similar point in warning of reading God's will from our experience of the natural world, stating, 'If nature is unambiguously God's will, God apparently wants us to be predatory nepotists' (Clark 1998: 123). Yet Linzey is not content with simply a negative statement about not reading God's will from the present reality. He wants to make the future the representation of God's will. It is on this basis that Linzey argues for vegetarianism for Christians. The redeemed human being must act in accordance with the reality of the new creation rather than the nature of the carnivorous and predatory reality of this creation.

Apart from the ethical debate about vegetarianism, this argument raises important questions for systematic theology. It is based on seeing God's purposes in new creation. Yet does this devalue this present creation? Interestingly, Linzey does not make a great deal of Genesis 1.30 where animals may only eat plants, or indeed the number of texts which show the widespread belief in antiquity that humans and the animals were once vegetarian (Westermann 1984: 163–164). Such a position can say that this creation was 'not good' from the start or is somehow fallen. Indeed, Linzey does argue that the Genesis 9.3 permission to eat animals is separated from the vegetarianism of Genesis 1.29–30 by the fall and the flood, showing that carnivorousness is part of the world not intended by God (Linzey 1998: 4). In contrast the 'creation spirituality' of Matthew Fox rejects the fall of creation and therefore accepts eat and be eaten as the God given law of the Universe (Fox 1983). Linzey will not accept that the fundamental nature of the animal kingdom is that of aggression.

Linzey convincingly makes the case for discontinuity between creation and new creation in terms of the animal kingdom, but does he go too far? From the future of the Universe we have seen the importance of discontinuity when eschatology is brought into contact with the scientific world. Yet we have also seen the importance of keeping a tension with continuity. How might this work for the biological world?

8.1.3 Holding together creation and new creation in the animal world

Holding continuity and discontinuity together means that our understanding of the biological world in creation and new creation is more complicated than either Linzey or Fox allow. We see that not least in the handling of the biblical material. For example, Linzey uses Isaiah 11 and Romans 8 to paint a picture of a new reality which reveals God's ideal, but ignores Job 38.39–40 which points to God's will in the provision of prey for the lion. God's will cannot be read from either creation or new creation; it must be read from both.

In addition to this we need to ask whether animal sacrifice, the dietary laws and the example of Jesus further complicate the picture. If animal sacrifice was sanctioned by God was this an affirmation of the predatory and violent nature of the animal world, and God's affirmation of our right to kill animals? However, Rogerson suggests that for some it symbolized 'the failure of humanity as represented by Israel to live in the world as God intended' (Rogerson 1998: 17). He argues that it therefore registers human failure and also the hope of a world to come. This he suggests is shown by the priestly system of animal sacrifice being presented against the backdrop of the Priestly account of the origins of the world that paints a picture of an original creation that was vegetarian (Rogerson 1998: 58). This is interesting but not totally convincing. Rogerson himself acknowledges that this may just be a small strand of the understanding of sacrifice. We see again that the biblical material is not simple to interpret. In terms of dietary laws, Houston argues that these laws of clean and unclean animals 'mediate the contradiction between the ideal of a non violent world and the fact of unrestrained violence against animals' (Houston 1998: 24). In a similar way to

Rogerson he points out that in the Priestly historical work the original creation did not have killing for food. He sees the dietary laws as a mediating solution in a fallen world. But even if they are a 'mediating' solution, on this view they would still be part of God's provision.

However, the biblical picture is even more complex when we examine the life of Jesus. Bauckham points out that Jesus showed concern for animals, which even supersedes the requirement to observe the Sabbath law. Jesus reflects the value of animals and compassionate action towards them. Yet Jesus did send the demons in the Gadarene swine, ate fish and lamb at the Passover, and possibly would have participated in animal sacrifice (Bauckham 1998a: 33–48; 1998b: 49–60). Clearly, although animals have value, humans are more important than animals. The fact that Jesus does not demonstrate vegetarianism undermines in part Linzey's argument that God's will can be seen in biblical passages that support vegetarianism. Indeed, we can add to Bauckham's point by noting that there is no evidence of any Jews or Christians adopting vegetarianism out of a desire to return to the paradisal condition of humanity. In particular, Peter is directed by God to kill and eat on the basis that 'Do not call anything impure that God has made clean' (Acts 10.9–16).

It is therefore difficult to find a consistent and simple picture of the Bible's view of the animal world in creation and new creation. This is a severe problem for Linzey who wants to read God's intention from certain eschatological passages. The biblical authors are struggling to hold together a good creation, a fallen world and a new world to come. Many commentators do not seem to follow the same struggle. For example, Lloyd argues that the predatory nature of the animal world goes against the 'movement of Christ's self offering' (Lloyd 1998: 149). Yet Christ's self offering involves pain and death. It does not of course justify animal suffering but is a reminder that in this creation there may be suffering that serves a higher purpose.

In addition to the complexity of the biblical evidence, a theological understanding of the natural world is also complex. What is the nature of the natural world as creation? Is it as God intended and therefore is it perfect? Or is it ambiguous containing both moral good and natural evil? If it is the latter and indeed our work so far indicates that it is, can it be at the same time as God intended and in process towards some goal? If Linzey stresses too much discontinuity, then others overstress continuity. Pantheism has fuelled the sense of the natural world as perfect. Lovelock's 'Gaia' hypothesis, representing the Earth as a self maintaining, self repairing system, has been interpreted by some to deserve our reverence and by others to deserve our worship (Lovelock 1989). The decline of belief in traditional theism with its 'other worldliness' of life after death means that this world is as good as we get, and human beings rather than being stewards of creation are simply a small part of Mother Nature. Some theologians, guilty at the environmental damage blamed by some historians on the Judaeo-Christian tradition, have followed this line. These theologians:

'All insist that true doctrine rejects any split between Spirit and Nature, the Eternal and the Here and Now ... Jewish or Christian stories and doctrines that seem to imply otherwise must be interpreted "metaphorically" if they are to be acceptable: notions like "Original Sin", "Fallen World", "the World to Come" are suspect'. (Clark 1998: 127)

Clark rejects such pantheism, pointing out that such a view justifies anything. For example, pollution can in fact simply be seen as evolution in action. Instead, he argues for Christian theism, which distinguishes deity and nature and gives human beings a moral framework for caring for the environment.

In addition, the cross shows us that the world is not as God intended and there is something different ahead:

'The Cross of Christ tells us unmistakably that all physical evil, not only pain, suffering, disease, corruption, death and of course cruelty and venom in animal as well as human behaviour, but also "natural" calamities, devastations, and monstrosities, are an outrage against the love of God and a contradiction of good order in his creation. This does not allow us to regard evil and disorder in the universe as in any way intended or as given a direct function by God in the development of His creation, although it does mean that even these enormities can be made to serve His final end for the created order'. (Torrance 1981: 139)

So even if 'cruelty and venom' are a contradiction of good order, they can nevertheless be used by God in achieving his purposes. Indeed, there is a sense that the new creation is only possible because of the cost of this creation. The risen Jesus showing his scars and receiving glory as the 'lamb who was slain' suggests that God's purposes are worked out in a fallen creation. It is too simplistic to identify the eschatological hope of Isaiah 11 with a return to Eden. The predatory nature of the creation at present may be a perversion of God's original intention but it still represents part of God's preparation for new creation. Smith has criticized an instrumentalist view of animal suffering as anthropocentric and leaving God responsible for suffering (Smith 1991: 159–174). Indeed he uses this as argument against the existence of a loving and powerful God. However this only works if God is the source of animal suffering and if the world as we have it is divorced totally from any hope of new creation.

The source of evil is of course a traditional problem for philosophical theology. As we shall see in the next section, it has become popular to stress the freedom inherent in creation either from the insights of chaos and quantum theory or from a theological understanding of God's kenosis. This freedom is viewed either as a gift given by God or an inherent feature of reality to which God is subject. The consequence of this freedom is that the future is open, although this openness is often overstated. Attempts have been made to use process theology to understand animal suffering (Hosinki 1998: 137; McDaniel 1998: 161). They helpfully enable an understanding of animal life as ambiguous containing both good and evil and stress the risk inherent in creation. However, their weakness is that there is no sense of a future reality which is different to this creation and which is achieved by the action of God. Without this they are open to Smith's critique. Creation and new creation as the actions of God must be held together.

The insight of the freedom inherent in creation is important but needs to be held together with the purposes of God working to new creation. The same can be said of those who have attempted to use the fall as a way of understanding the predatory nature of the animal world. Lloyd suggests that the fall is cosmic in scope and not limited to human sin. The consequence of this is that 'if nature is fallen, then there is no straightforward line to be drawn from present reality to the purposes of God' (Lloyd 1996: 370). The predatory nature of creation is due to a cosmic fall, but according to Lloyd this cannot be identified as the human fall, as predation existed in a fossil record before humans.

The question then is what fell? Williams had suggested a 'collective fall of the race-soul of humanity in an indefinitely remote past' (Williams 1927: 513), but this has no support either scientific or biblical. A process view might suggest nature itself fell but this is giving to physical and biological processes an anthropomorphic sense of choice. Lloyd suggests that the fall of the angels is the best candidate for an effect on nature. As Mascall and others have argued (Lewis 1984; von Balthasar 1992: 466–501; Plantinga 1974), if there has been a moral revolt within the spiritual dimension of the created order then this may 'drastically disorder the material world, and that, while its development will not be entirely frustrated, it will be grievously hampered and distorted' (Mascall 1956: 36). Thus in Lloyd's view human beings evolve into a world where they are given the task of healing and subduing a disordered creation (Lloyd 1998: 160).

While this may locate the origin of evil outside of God it is dangerous in going too far in devaluing creation itself. Linzey seems to fall into this trap of gazing to new creation and allowing the fall to blot out the importance of creation. In the process which involves freedom or fall, we must see continuity between creation and redemption as well as discontinuity. Blocher rightly cautions that Paul in Romans 8 has to be held together with the psalms and texts in Job which celebrate the beauty of this creation (Blocher 1984: 487). Gunton also comments on the importance of holding together creation and new creation:

> 'the distinctively Christian contributions to the process are in generating an awareness of the penultimacy of all matters to do with this world of time and space, and yet of the capacity that even this penultimate has to praise the God who made it'. (Gunton 1993: 124)

Linzey while rightly seeing discontinuity in the eschatological vision does not hold together sufficiently creation and new creation. By basing his ethics so much on new creation he ignores the complexity of the fall and the limited nature of the description of new creation. Gunton cautions:

> 'It is not for us to say where the whole Universe or even the whole earth is going. We know in part. There is a "sometimes" because eschatology is never completely realised, except it be in Christ. And even there, all is in one sense not yet complete ... the logic of the resurrection is that Jesus' story awaits completion'. (Gunton 1993: 126)

Thus when we address questions of eschatology to the biological world, especially the animal kingdom, the biblical and theological arguments stress the importance of holding discontinuity between creation and new creation. However, discontinuity may be pushed too far creating too much of a wedge between creation and new creation. The animal theology of Linzey gives an example of this. By using the fall to say that we cannot read God's purposes from our experience of the world as it is now, and by a literal reading of certain eschatological passages from the Bible, Linzey rightly stresses discontinuity but then pushes it too far. His ethical claims particularly in the area of vegetarianism are therefore weakened.

A more convincing picture recognises a transformation of animal nature in new creation. That transformation will represent both continuity and discontinuity. The relationships that animals have with humans and with each other will be changed. Such a picture while not insisting on vegetarianism does however give a strong ethical imperative for Christians to be involved in animal welfare issues where relationships between animals and human express community characteristic both of creation and new creation (Webb 1998; Linzey 2009).

8.2 Openness theology in an accelerating Universe

Providence has traditionally encompassed the doctrine of creation in terms of God's relationship with the Universe but has also included the doctrines of preservation, incarnation, resurrection and miracle (Wilkinson 2004: 142–154). Rarely has it included eschatology. This is especially the case in two specific areas of the discussion of providence. The first is in the way that scientific insights inform a doctrine of providence and second in the current and controversial area of open and relational theologies. Can the scenarios of the end of the Universe sharpen up the question of providence in these two areas?

Bringing scientific insights into dialogue with the doctrine of providence is an important task. The biblical theology movement wanted to stress that at the heart of the Bible was 'a confessional recital of the gracious and redemptive acts of God' (Wright 1952: 120). However, while this affirmed the action of God recorded in the Bible, by continuing to accept that God does not intervene in a world described by the predictability of science, the biblical theologians left the concept of the act of God empty or equivocal (Gilkey 1961: 195; Dilley 1965: 66–80). They called for philosophical theology to address this problem of where is God's action located, yet did not explore themselves the fundamental question of whether the world of modern science actually does deny the concept of God's action (Thomas 1983).

In fact, many of the classic texts on providence in the twentieth century demonstrate a serious ignorance of contemporary science, even though they were all written embarrassingly some 40 years after the discovery of quantum theory (Bultmann 1983; Ogden 1963: 164–187; Cobb 1973: 207–22; Griffin 1975: 342–60; Kaufman 1968: 175–201; Wiles 1971: 1–12). Quantum theory at the very least questioned the classical view of cause, effect and predictability.

Even today many explorations of providence are predicated on this mechanistic world-view stemming out of the predictability of Newtonian systems. But the scientific world has moved on, not just through quantum uncertainty at the atomic level but the uncertainty of chaotic systems at the everyday level. In 1986, the International Union of Theoretical and Applied Mechanics made a public apology:

> 'We collectively wish to apologize for having misled the general educated public by spreading ideas about the determinism of systems satisfying Newton's laws of motion that, after 1960, were proved to be incorrect … Modern theories of dynamical systems have clearly demonstrated the unexpected fact that systems governed by the equations of Newtonian dynamics do not necessarily exhibit the "predictability property."' (Lighthill 1986: 38, 35)

While Gilkey could complain that providence had been demoted to the level of a footnote in twentieth century theology (Gilkey 1963: 171) and Ricoeur spoke of 'the death of the God of providence' (Ricoeur 1974: 455), the last 40 years have seen a growth in interest. This goes beyond the simple use of the language of providence in situations of crisis that continues to have a strong tradition in Christian spirituality. There has been a serious attempt to understand the nature of providence and to bring it into dialogue with insights into the world from science (Russell, Murphy and Isham 1993; Russell, Murphy and Peacocke 1995; Russell, Stoeger and Ayala 1988; Russell et al. 1999). Yet alongside the growth of interest in both providence and eschatology, little has been done to bring them together into a meaningful dialogue.

The results of such a dialogue would be challenging to many models of providence. Bultmann saw God achieving his purposes by 'acting' in the person of faith as they encounter God's word. Leaving aside the problem of how God actually does this, this approach throws the emphasis on human activity as the source of redemption. While this is easy to see in terms of the environmental crisis, it is much more difficult to see in the cosmic context. As we have seen, the eschatologies of Dyson and Tipler do not offer realistic hope. Hope for the physical Universe has to be located in the action of God on a wider canvas than just the human mind. In a similar way, the end of the Universe calls into question the model of Wiles who argues that God is Creator and Sustainer but his action is limited to the single act which caused and keeps the Universe in being (Wiles 1986). His analogy is that of an improvised drama, where the author gives basic characters and the setting. The resulting plot may follow the intention of the author, but the actors have freedom to determine their own outcome.

Wiles can thus offer no hope for the physical Universe and long-term life in the Universe. The author has given the actors freedom to explore their potential in a theatre that is condemned to demolition and the author can do nothing about it. Wiles has no concept of new creation and no concept of the action of God beyond the one creative act.

Panentheism also runs into major problems when confronted with the end of the Universe. It attempts to assimilate God's action in the world to our action in our bodies by using analogies such as the inner action by which the human self constitutes itself (Ogden 1963: 164–187), the world as God's body (Jantzen 1984), or as a foetus in the womb (Peacocke 1979: 158, 370–2). Its strength is that it has a sense of God's transcendence yet intimate involvement in the Universe. In terms of the end of the Universe it is therefore not surprising that there are strengths and weaknesses. Transcendence gives hope beyond the physical processes of the Universe. However the imagining of immanence by means of body makes God vulnerable to the heat death of the Universe. Is God or part of God destined to heat death? At the extreme limit of this, indeed closer to pantheism rather than panentheism, models where God is a superior intelligence totally contained in the Universe, as have been developed by some scientists in a revamped natural theology, become gods who eventually will die (Hoyle 1983; Davies 1983; Dick 2000: 191–208).

Do similar problems present themselves in the field of open and relational theologies? These theologies have become very popular and for many are the natural successors to process theology. Process theology saw each event in the Universe being the selection of a possible outcome followed by actual realization. God works as an agent exercising his power by persuasion rather than coercion (Cobb 1973: 207–22; Cobb and Girffin 1976; Griffin 1975: 342–60; Pailin 1989; Barbour 2000). Objections have long been made on the basis of its metaphysical assumptions and whether the God of process theology is impotent to do anything in the Universe.

Yet since the work of Vanstone and Moltmann (Vanstone 1977; Moltmann 1985), many who reject process theology nevertheless see God's creative love accompanied by vulnerability. In this theology of kenosis God self limits and gives to humans and the Universe, a degree of freedom to explore potentiality. Thus God creates through an evolutionary process that includes chance, to give human beings the possibility of development with the consequent risk of suffering (Ward 1996; Murphy and Ellis 1996: 247; Southgate 2008).

Such a view has resonated with Polkinghorne's view of the openness of the natural world seen in chaotic systems (Polkinghorne 1988). In contrast to the 'clockwork world' deduced from Newtonian mechanics, chaotic systems obey immutable and precise laws that do not act in predictable and regular ways. When the dynamics of a system is chaotic it can only be predicted if the initial conditions are known to infinite precision. This obviously is impossible as even a computer as large as the Universe would not give such precision. This means that for finite beings there is an uncertainty to systems within the everyday world even if the laws of physics are known. It must be stressed that not all systems are chaotic, and even in chaotic systems such as the weather gross features such as global warming can be predicted. Polkinghorne argues that it is in chaotic systems that God has freedom, and that his action is unable to be directly seen. The sensitivity of complex systems to initial circumstance means that they are unpredictable. Polkinghorne then makes a significant step. Viewing science as a critical realist activity, he makes a strong link between epistemology and ontology. On this basis he argues that chaos means that there are systems in the Universe that are inherently open to the future, they are unpredictable and undetermined.

From this crucial step of the intrinsic openness to the future of these systems, three things follow. The first is that here is a genuine justification for human freewill. Second, the future is not implied by the present and thus any kind of Laplacian determinism is ruled out. Third, he argues that God is at work in the flexibility of these open systems as well as being the ground of law. God's particular activity is real but hidden. Polkinghorne extrapolates chaos theory to the limiting case of zero energy, so that God's action is a non-energetic input of information that expresses holistic patterns. God's selection among the envelope of possibilities present in chaotic processes could bring about novel structures and types of order exemplifying systematic higher-level organizing principles (Polkinghorne 1991).

Outside of this dialogue with science, the God who gives openness to the future has provoked major controversy in US evangelical circles. Pinnock and Sanders have argued for it against a bitter backlash from more conservative theologians (Pinnock et al. 1994; Pinnock 2001; Sanders 1998; Long and Kalantzis 2009). This is not only of interest to evangelicals, but the battle has often been presented as between Wesleyan/Arminian views of the providence of God compared to Calvinism (Cross 2000: 30–1).

Pinnock argues that traditional theism championed by Calvinism's view of an all-controlling sovereignty was developed primarily from Greek philosophy and presents God as 'manipulative, futureless, motionless, remote, isolated', and is profoundly unbiblical. In terms of theological method, Pinnock uses the Wesleyan quadrilateral of experience, tradition, reason and scripture, with a primary commitment to scripture. He argues that the Bible uses images of God as a free personal agent who acts in loves, changes his mind, co-operates with his people, and responds to prayer. Thus he concludes:

> 'God's unity will not be viewed as mathematical oneness but as a unity that includes diversity; God's steadfastness will not be seen as a deadening immutability but constancy of character that includes change; God's power will not be seen as raw omnipotence but as the sovereignty of love whose strength is revealed in weakness; and God's omniscience will not be seen as know-it-all but as a wisdom which shapes the future in dialogue with creatures'. (Pinnock 2001: 27)

God creates a world where the future is not yet settled and takes seriously our response. Pinnock speaks of the 'most moved mover' in contrast to the 'unmoved mover' of classical theism and this understanding has practical consequences in the areas of prayer, lifestyle, friendship with God, freedom and guidance.

There are significant similarities here with process theology. However, 'openness theology' would defend significant differences. First, biblical authority is more important than the philosophical system, and second there is a greater stress on God's transcendence. God is not dependent on the Universe, he can intervene in acts of miracle and there will be a definite victory over evil at the end. In process theology God is limited to exercising only by persuasive power and that is in the nature of things rather than freewill choice.

It is claimed that both the process view and the open view share common roots in Wesleyan/Arminian tradition (Stone and Oord 2001). We need to be careful about this. Certainly the affirmation of human freedom is common. However, Wesley and Arminius held to traditional definitions of unchangeability, eternity and omniscience. Both process and openness go beyond this with more radical modifications such as God having a temporal aspect in order to give a more 'coherent' philosophical view.

Such a view has been severely criticized by evangelicals on both sides of the Atlantic from a mishandling of scripture to reducing God's power and agency (Helm 1994; Ware 2000; Picirilli 2000: 259–71; Carson 1996: 215; Geisler 1997: 11–12; Sproul 1997: 143; Bloesch 1995: 254–60; Bray 1998). The debate is fuelled partly by a political struggle within evangelicalism between reformed movements influenced by Calvinist theologies, and the growth of more Arminian Pentecostal and charismatic traditions which would acknowledge a debt in part to Wesley (Cross 2000: 30–1). Fackre sees the strengths of the openness view as connecting with views of God's suffering love, taking seriously the biblical narrative, and giving reality to the experience of daily prayer (Fackre 2002: 319–323). However he also points out Pinnock's aggressive style and the neglect of other positions which may provide a middle way between the above sides (Jewett 1985; Colver 1999).

There is great value in the openness view. It highlights a recurring theme of this book of the control within western systematics of Greek philosophy compared to biblical narrative. Yet we need to note that Pinnock has little to say on the mechanism. However, Polkinghorne does provide a mechanism which gives God freedom to act in the physical world. It is easier to see God's influence acting in chaotic systems rather than at the level of quantum systems. To see God just working in this way may represent continuity between creation and new creation, but does not do justice to discontinuity. To give real hope then God must be capable of working beyond the confines of chaotic systems.

We have developed the theme of new creation in a way which stresses God doing something with the totality of existence. Pinnock characterizes his view of openness as 'God's power will not be seen as raw omnipotence but as the sovereignty of love whose strength is revealed in weakness; and God's omniscience will not be seen as know-it-all but as a wisdom which shapes the future in dialogue with creatures' (Pinnock 2001: 27). This is helpful, in the context of the future of the environment and even in the challenge of asteroid impact and the death of the Sun, to speak of God creating a world where the future is not yet settled and takes seriously our response. However, the futility of the end of the Universe means that we must also emphasize a God who is not dependent on the Universe and a God who is capable of bringing a definite victory over evil at the end.

Second, new creation is a possibility because of the sovereignty of a Creator God. The key questions for open and relational theologies of what God does, chooses not to do, or cannot do as Creator provide the basis for hope for the future. A God who is not free to work in the Universe must watch the slow heat death of his creation.

As we noted earlier, Bauckham is right to attack models of providence that make God dependent on the Universe (Bauckham 1993: 53).

Such models do not allow for new creation. This is an important point. Hope has to be based on a God who is transcendent as well as immanent. A wholly immanent God can never go beyond the possibilities inherent in this creation. Thus new creation needs the transcendent Creator God.

Third, creation and new creation being mutually interdependent is a reminder of something that should be obvious but in practice is often forgotten. Creation needs to be seen in the light of new creation, and new creation needs to be seen in the light of creation. Wood has suggested that providence has been severed from creation (Wood 2002). He rightly sees that providence has been allocated the time 'in between' the world's creation and its consummation and has been drained of any creative significance. Therefore the emphasis in the doctrine has been on preservation, stability, order, and harmony, and that the virtues it inculcates are mainly passive. He then argues that we must recapture the unity of creation and providence in order to see the 'creative character' of the doctrine. Yet we suggest that he could go further to recognize that providence has also been severed from new creation. To recapture the unity of creation, new creation and providence strengthens all, giving providence an encouraging and challenging voice into Christian lifestyle.

A great deal of work in the dialogue of science and religion and in open and relational theologies has concentrated on the doctrine of creation with little reference to the end of the story. Open theologies need to engage with questions of the transformation of this creation into new creation, and the specific acts of God as well as God's action in the process of the world. The scientific picture of the futility of the future of the Universe provides some difficult questions for some open theologies. These may be opportunities more than problems. The need to engage more with themes of new creation, eschatological transformation and resurrection could be very fruitful.

It might drive us to a greater engagement with scripture. Pinnock emphasizes that open theology recognizes the primacy of scripture. Yet, his presentation of scripture is often selective. For example he claims that the parable of the prodigal son (Lk 15.11–32) 'dramatizes the truth of the open view of God' (Pinnock 2001: 4). This is fine as long as you do not complicate the matter by noticing that Luke joins this parable with 2 other parables that 'dramatize' God as taking the initiative seeking a lost sheep and a lost coin (Lk 15.1–10). Here God's sovereignty in salvation is in dramatic tension with the gift of freedom.

This becomes more of a problem for the openness view when it comes to eschatology. Its biblical emphasis wants to reflect eschatological closure in the victory of good over evil but it is difficult to see how this might happen. Further there is virtually no engagement with the major biblical themes of new heaven and new earth. Pinnock does use the analogy of God as the 'master chess player'. He is the consummate guide allowing both freedom to the other person involved in the game and yet able to bring about ultimate victory. But does such an analogy represent genuine openness? The struggle to find an adequate picture shows the limits of the openness view in the light of eschatological closure.

Then as a Wesleyan I want to reflect the importance of prevenient grace. Here is Wesley's understanding of God's free and generous acting in the world, which both gives responsibility to his creatures and characterizes his own responsibility as Creator and Redeemer (Maddox 1994; Cobb 1995: 35–41). In personal salvation, God is active before conversion, during conversion and in the growth to holiness. God is active in both preparing this path and in active help along the way. Therefore, in models of providence, Maddox is right to comment:

'While the longstanding Wesleyan commitment to God's response-ability resonates strongly with the process emphasis on God's temporal, creative, and persuasive nature, it should be no surprise that this same commitment renders many Wesleyans less happy with the apparent restriction of God's role in the ongoing process of the whole of reality to only that of "lure". Is such a God still truly response-able? Where is the basis for eschatological hope within this restriction? Is there not a place for God to engage us more actively than this, without resorting to coercion?' (Maddox 2001: 142)

It is interesting in this context to note a small book by Albert Outler (Outler 1968). Outler observes rightly that quantum theory does not allow us to construct a full model of providence, but cautions us as to the limits of science in predicting the future. For Outler, God is undeniably in charge but also this world is a place where human freedom is real if limited. Grace is seen not only as the giving of freedom to what God has created but also God's active involvement in the world. Thus because of grace 'he is truly free to allow evil as the dark shadow of corrupted good and yet sovereign to veto its final triumph' (Outler 1968: 96).

Outler is interesting in that he resists the tendency within eschatology to over-emphasize continuity or discontinuity in order to attempt to produce a simple or logical philosophical picture. To hold continuity and discontinuity in the same picture is more complex and difficult.

This leads on to a further consideration. While an open future and a God who gives genuine freedom and responsibility to his creation means that our agency can make a significant difference, the goal of new creation gives our agency confidence. Advocates of openness see their position as a motivation to Christian responsibility and action, as our free human agency can make a difference. Boyd links genuine openness of the future to Christian responsibility:

'Knowing that what transpires in the future is not a foregone conclusion but is significantly up to us to decide, we will be more inclined to assume responsibility for the future.' (Boyd 2000: 94)

While this is certainly the case, part of our motivation for Christian witness and action is not just the belief that we can make a difference, but also that the end is assured. Wesley's understanding of new creation gives confidence alongside opportunity. God's plan for new creation, demonstrated in the death and resurrection of Jesus, is about the eventual triumph of good over evil. We can believe that we can make a difference, but also that the end is assured. This gives confidence to Christians alongside opportunity, sustaining sacrificial action.

Finally a fruitful interaction with eschatology and open theologies is the Trinitarian dimension. A welcome move in systematic theology in recent years has been a reaffirmation of the importance of Trinitarian theology. Wood rightly points out that in systematic theology providence has been seen in relation to the Father with the neglect of any Christological or pneumatological considerations (Wood 1999: 138–152). Thus the tendency is to see the providential God as the Supreme Being of philosophical theism and his actions can be determined by natural theology. Such a sterile doctrine of providence is corrected by Trinitarian thinking and indeed open and relational theologies. God is both transcendent and immanent, acting as creator and sustainer, incarnate Christ who dies on the cross, and the power and presence of the Holy Spirit pervading the church and the world. This reminds us once again that the nature of God's providential action is complex and how we perceive it is also complex. The triune pattern is the way God relates to all things but is also the pattern of our knowledge of that relation. To the extent that we can understand how God is related to what goes on, we understand it 'through Jesus Christ' and 'in the Holy Spirit.' Trinitarian thinking has often been neglected in the area of providence in favour of logic or science. It safeguards a specifically Christian understanding while posing creative questions to the doctrine. An example of this can be found in Pannenberg's attempt to describe the work of the Spirit in terms of the force of a field, as an immaterial force causes physical changes. Much can be said against such a suggestion, but it does raise the question about whether some generalized physical theory can serve as meaningful metaphor for God's cosmic presence, and indeed about what are the limits of such a metaphor.

Transformation of this creation is a key understanding in the biblical literature for new creation. This transformation is not just in the matter or space-time but a transformation in context and relationships. The transformative work of the Spirit is at the heart of such a process. A Trinitarian doctrine of providence encourages a sense of the activity and transformative work of God in this creation. Whatever freedom is given to this creation we cannot reach our potential in isolation.

8.3 Acting in hope

How does our consideration of the end of the Universe affect the present? One of Moltmann's strengths has been the way he has seen the importance of the future for the present. Is the heat death of the Universe a few billion years in the future just meaningless speculation or has it anything to contribute in the here and now? The questions it poses for systematic theology in terms of continuity and discontinuity with new creation do have consequences in the following areas of the myth of human progress, ethics and the environment, and the dialogue of science and religion.

8.3.1 *The myth of human progress*

In contrast to the pessimism of the scientific scenarios, popular images of science and technology are often very optimistic. This is the metanarrative of the

177

utopian myth of human progress, that is, the belief that science, technology and education will lead us to a perfect and morally better world. At the turn of the century, the triumph of physics, Darwinian evolution and technological break-throughs encouraged this confidence and optimism.

Bauckham and Hart helpfully suggest that both Marxism and biological evolution gave philosophical models of progress. The linear nature of time from creation to new creation sustained by the actions of God was replaced by human power and responsibility for creating the future. It is often on this basis that continuity becomes dominant in the relationship between this creation and the future. It is fascinating to see the myth of human progress so strongly in the scientific eschatologies of Tipler and Dyson. Yet this dream of progress, in the light of the 20th Century, has become a nightmare (Bauckham and Hart 1999: 8).

Both in science and popular culture we see the myth of human progress quite strongly in some of the responses to the 'cosmic pessimism' of science. There are those who see science and technology not simply as the cause of environmental damage but in fact the way out of such problems. Nuclear technology (and then speculation about cold fusion) was sold as energy that would not use up fossil fuels. In the movie *Armageddon* the world is saved by a combination of technology, human ingenuity and courage. Even within the scientific literature, the end of the Sun is combated by terraforming in other solar systems. Yet at the same time, the *Terminator* and *The Matrix* movies portray science out of control with no hope (Wright 2000). A Christian eschatology that is based on a transcendent and immanent God gives real hope in the midst of this. The Christian hope is not a utopian myth of human progress, nor does it opt of the world. Bauckham and Hart emphasize that it is based on the transcendence of the Creator God, demonstrated in the resurrection.

Yet that hope has to engage with the reality of what experience presents to us. It needs to be earthed or it simply becomes an 'opiate of the people'. The end of the Universe helps us to work this out. It shows decisively that the myth of human progress is extremely limited and cannot give hope in the cosmic sense. I have argued elsewhere that such optimism in future technology and indeed a critique of it is a major feature of recent science fiction (Wilkinson 2000). In particular the *Star Wars* movies of George Lucas suggest that the myth of human progress is inadequate and hope needs to be based on the belief in transcendence. Neither the despair of Weinberg nor the confidence in human progress of Dyson and Tipler give the hope that faith in a transcendent God gives. Tipler is striving for such a thing in his 'Omega Point' theory, but he ultimately fails.

Moltmann argues that 'those who hope in Christ can no longer put up with reality as it is' (Moltmann 1967: 21). Imagining how things can be different, and having the confidence that they can be different, gives energy to action now. The scientific picture of the end of the Universe forces the theologian to take discontinuity and the action of God seriously. The danger of too much continuity in new creation is that the imagination is not stretched enough in terms of difference. This has a debilitating effect on hopeful action. Continuity and discontinuity in new creation gives hope. It also forces trust and confidence away from ourselves, history or technology towards God. Imagination is often stretched through narrative expressing hope. Narrative is an important part of the biblical literature concerning the future of the Universe and it is also a powerful strand in science fiction as it addresses the future (Clark 1995; May 1998; Thacker 2001; Alsford 2000; McGrath 2002: 153–172). Kermode has argued that we deal with the chaos of world by telling a story/narrative and that the end of story is important as it gives meaning to the rest (Kermode 1967). This of course applies to the story of the Universe. So much of recent discussion particularly in the science/religion field has been to find meaning in the beginning of the story with little consideration of the end. Yet the decisive part of the story is God in Jesus redeeming creation from evil. While the story is not yet concluded in terms of the physical Universe, the end point will be accomplished by a transcendent God. If this story is to be our own then these are essential elements. It locates our action within the context of God's action:

'This means that those who live by this story live within it. It gives us our identity, our place in the story, and a part to play in the still-to-be-completed purposes of God for his world. Indeed the story is told precisely so that people may live by it'. (Bauckham and Hart 1999: 36)

Steiner has pointed out that the most creative people in art and poetry make a wager on the world and history having meaning and hope (Steiner 1989: 227). He calls it a wager on the meaningfulness of meaning. The Christian tradition makes a similar wager, but this wager is on the God of the resurrection. The resurrection both disrupts this world's belief that death is the end and that there is no hope, and offers the evidence that God will make things good in the end. Confidence is not placed in human beings or technology but on God. Further, the resurrection reminds us that there is more to hope than just survival.

Bauckham and Hart point this out in a survey of images about the future used in the New Testament. In the future the world will encounter an 'Antichrist', a figure who symbolizes evil and lies. This image is a reminder that the future is not simply progress to a better world. As we have seen the 'Parousia' is an image, which says that sometime in the future Jesus Christ will return in worldwide glory to bring in a new creation and a judgement of evil. These images speak of something God will do. Other images of the future such as creation as a garden city, future life being like Sabbath rest, a marriage feast and the fulfilment of the Kingdom of God, speak of goodness, healing, celebration and the centrality of God. They are images that remind us that the 'myth of human progress' through education, technology and science to Utopia is not the future. The resurrection faith is not faith in the future but in the God of the future:

'In faith we shall see duly, our imagination is engaged, stretched and enabled to accommodate a vision of a meaningful and hopeful future for the world, a meaning which could never be had by extrapolating the circumstances of the tragic drama of history itself'. (Bauckham and Hart 1999: 51)

Houlden sees the resurrection as an invitation to 'an audacious and total hope in the face of life's unintelligible ambiguities of pain and joy' (Houlden 1986:

151–2). Thus in the face of the futility of the end of the Universe or the bleak 'survival' models of Tipler and Dyson, resurrection is the key to hope.

In this it is important to stress that the resurrection needs to be considered in cosmic terms. A basic primer in systematics such as McGrath describes the resurrection in soteriological terms, that is, it demonstrates victory over death and evil. However when describing the eschatological consequences McGrath simply discusses the hope of eternal life without any reference to new creation (McGrath 1998: 384). New creation both in its personal and cosmic setting needs to be part of any discussion of the resurrection in systematic theology.

8.3.2 *Care for the environment in a cosmic setting*

Santmire has pointed out two options in the Christian view of the natural world (Santmire 1985). The 'spiritual motif' sees human beings liberated from this world to a spiritual world in the life to come, but this pushes the discontinuity between creation and new creation too far. In reaction the 'ecological reading of biblical faith' has stressed the importance of creation using themes such as the stewardship of the natural world. The difficulty of this view is that it pushes continuity too far and loses any sense of God's eschatological acts. However Santmire points out that the ethic for care of the environment becomes stronger if it seen in an eschatological perspective. This lays emphasis not only on God's purposes in creation but also in new creation. The original creation is seen as a prototype of new creation. The creation is good but fallen. The new creation is linked to the creation but different. They both need to be held together in ethics.

While the link between ethics and eschatology has been emphasized by a number of writers (Chilton and MacDonald 1987: 129; Braaten 1974: 114), how does this work out in practice? Eschatological ethics need to be in close relationship with creation ethics. Bridger commenting on the relevance of eschatology for ecology rightly comments, 'The coming of the kingdom does not overthrow the natural order but rather vindicates it' (Bridger 1990: 295), and O'Donovan demonstrates the same commitment to holding together creation and new creation in his statement, 'In the resurrection of Christ, creation is restored and the kingdom of God dawns' (O'Donovan 1986b: 15). As we have seen in previous chapters, the resurrection remains the model of the vindication and restoration of creation held together with the dawn of a new creation.

There are ethical questions about the future, which may seem irrelevant to some at this point, but are already being mentioned by scientists and philosophers. It would seem that within the next century, human beings will have the technological and financial ability to live beyond the atmosphere of the Earth. Cities in space or 'terraforming' on planets such as Mars are theoretical possibilities. The ethical questions concerning these possibilities are very real. Terraforming has been considered as a way out of the ecological crisis. As we have seen this reduces worry about global pollution because you can simply move on to another planet. However, it seems likely that the only ones who will 'move on' will be the rich and powerful leaving the rest to the polluted, over populated and exploited planet Earth.

Yet in the light of the end of the Universe, even possibilities of terraforming or cities in space are limited. Does this long-term end of the Universe have any bearing on ethical questions? Bridger argues that our stewardship stems not only from an orientation to the responsibility given in Eden but also from an orientation of what God's purposes for the future will be. It is this combination which encourages ethical obedience (Bridger 1990: 290–301).

In the integration of the scientific and theological pictures, does the holding together of creation and eschatology give a stronger basis for ethics? Hardy has pointed out that in earlier times, moral patterns as well as the physical conditions of the world suggested 'the fundamental shape of the eschata' (Hardy 1996: 155). He suggests that apocalyptic accounts identify the moral issues taken into account in final times, and show how they will be resolved. Does the scientific view of the end of the Universe itself pose a moral question that has to be taken into account in any understanding of how God relates to the last things?

Schweiker sees a connection between morality and the conception of time. He argues that the modern secular world sees time as 'empty', a void waiting to be filled by human choices and the meanings that we make for ourselves. In contrast apocalyptic cosmology presents time as wholly filled with divinely imposed meaning, with the danger of external moral tyranny. However, holding continuity and discontinuity together in a transformed new creation avoids either extreme. Schweiker sees new creation as a 'transvaluation of our values, how we are enabled to respond to the goodness of existence and God's transformations of the patterns of life' (Schweiker 2000: 137). Gregersen makes a complementary point when he comments, 'The futurity of eschatological imagery manifests that judgement is not of our determining' (Gregersen 2000: 172).

This is important in giving a wider ethical basis for Christian concern for an involvement in the environment. With the perspective of the whole Universe we are forced to see the action of God in both continuity and discontinuity. Not only is this creation seen as good it is also seen as the raw material for the new creation. The maintaining of the Earth's environment, its biodiversity and natural resources is not just for present or future generations but part of co-operating with God in the process of transformation (Davis 2007: 256–273). As Steck suggests:

> 'What faith can do, by the power of God in Christ, to preserve the world of creation is to perform untiringly token acts as signs, manifestations of the future salvation in the sphere of the natural world, which testify that God has opened His new world for all created things.' (Steck 1978: 293)

O'Donovan has argued that Christian ethics depends on the resurrection (O'Donovan 1986b). He criticizes those who distinguish 'kingdom ethics' from 'creation ethics' because of the importance of the resurrection. As we have seen, he argues that the resurrection both affirms creation and ushers in the Kingdom that is about God's transforming actions. Thus resurrection becomes the focus of ethics, looking both back and forward, to creation and eschatology. It is the continuity that gives weight to the present ethical imperative. So for example the argument of 1 Corinthians 6.12–20 depends entirely on Paul's belief that what is done with the present body matters precisely because it is to be raised (Thrall 2002: 283–300; Wrighty 2003: 289).

Thielicke argued in a similar way when he stated, 'Ethics has its place therefore precisely in the field of the tension between the old and the new aeons, not in the old alone, nor in the new alone' (Thielicke 1978: 43–4). The tension of continuity and discontinuity in the biblical accounts of resurrection can helpfully form a tension in considering ethics in the future of the Universe. That is, any progress in science either in its impact on the environment or the wider Universe needs to reflect the goodness of creation as gift with the action of God of bringing in new creation.

8.3.3 *The dialogue of science and religion in eschatology*

Barbour has produced a now classic fourfold typology of conflict, independence, dialogue and integration to characterise the relationships between science and religion (Barbour 2000: 113). While others have suggested more complicated models it is instructive to locate our discussion of the end of the Universe within this framework.

The conflict model, used by both scientific atheists and six day creationists (Dawkins 2006; Witham 2005), encounters problems in the end of the Universe. The scientists of the conflict approach see science as the hope for the future:

'Science has never encountered a barrier it has not surmounted or that we can reasonably suppose it has power to surmount ... Religion has failed and its failure should be exposed.' (Atkins 1995: 129, 132)

The trouble is that for all the hope of such statements we have seen that science cannot give hope in the face of the futility of the end of the Universe. For all the achievements of science or the beautiful complexity of evolution, in ultimate terms science needs religion.

At the same time, the creationist case is severely undermined by the futility of the physical Universe. To argue that God created a static perfect creation some 6000 years ago does not do justice to the timescale or future development of the Universe. This creation is not perfect but longs for new creation. Creationism, in neglecting the importance of eschatology for the physical creation, is thus undermined by the scientific data. Of course, creationists will either argue against the scientific data presented in Chapter 2 or argue that the futility is the result simply of a cosmic fall. While we have acknowledged that the doctrine of the fall should not be ignored, it is not strong enough to support such creationist claims. In addition, the increasingly prevalent 'creation evangelism' is shown to be inadequate. The strategy here is to persuade the non-believer that modern science is wrong and creationism is correct on scientific terms. Once that is accepted, then the non-believer will accept the truth of the Bible and become a Christian. This can be critiqued on a whole number of levels, but our work on the end of the

Universe is a strong reminder that the Christian good news is about creation and new creation. An evangelistic strategy which is based on creation to the neglect of new creation is as weak as a strategy based on new creation to the neglect of creation.

The second model that of independence sees science and religion in separate domains, and this has been advocated by theologians in the Barthian tradition, philosophers exploring the nature of language and some scientists (Gould 1999: 207–8). While of course science and religion have different foci in their exploration and description of the world, the end of the Universe challenges such a complete separation. While theology may have neglected eschatology in relationship with the physical Universe, work in this area shows just how fruitful a dialogue can be. It affirms a view of science and theology as critical realist activities, and leads to questions for both science and theology. While some of the insights of Barth have been useful for our argument, we disagree with any position which argues that natural science has little relevance for theology. Consideration of the end of the Universe has exposed anthropocentric constructions of eschatology and God's action in the world. Bringing the biblical images into dialogue with scientific insights has been fruitful to both. A consideration of Romans 8 has enabled us to see the futility of the end of the Universe in the context of a renewed and limited natural theology. At the same time, a consideration of space-time models has enabled us to go beyond certain Greek concepts to take more seriously the temporal nature of new creation narratives. While keeping the concept of revelation central we have been able to say a qualified 'yes' to natural theology. In fact even in the language used by scientists such as Dyson and Tipler we have seen the fallacy of believing that science and religion are non interactive disciplines. We agree with McGrath that the Christian doctrine of creation demands a unitary approach to knowledge (McGrath 2001–3), and indeed would want to extend the basis of the demand to 'the Christian doctrine of creation and new creation'.

Thus the third model of dialogue is much more convincing. We have seen that the end of the physical Universe poses questions to theology in terms of creation, new creation, providence, ethics and hope. In this way scientific claims influence theological thought. Further, science raises questions that it cannot itself answer. We have also seen that concepts from science can be used as analogies for talking about God's relation to the world. The final model of integration takes the concept of dialogue further. It raises the question of whether there is a revised form of natural theology. We have argued that the futility of the physical Universe, while not being a proof in the classical sense of the design argument, may be another pointer in such a revised natural theology. Schloss points out that the impact of thoughtful evolutionary extrapolation is not 'monolithic optimism' but ambivalent longing for something that evolutionary history illuminates the necessity of, but does not assure the attainment of (Schloss 2002: 58). The assurance comes from the revelation of God in Jesus, and in particular the resurrection.

Yet any natural theology and indeed any integration of science with religion must take seriously the complexity, rate of change and ambiguity of the scientific picture. Such integration in the form of process theology may seem attractive in terms of the evolution of structures and life, but does not cope well with the end of the Universe. Therefore we remain cautious of the degree to which integration can be achieved. While we have applauded the attempts of Pannenberg and to an extent Russell to provide integration, we have also pointed out that their optimism in achieving it is still somewhat unfounded, not least in the area of the end of the Universe. The most fruitful and realistic model is that of dialogue between science and religion.

Chapter 9

Conclusion

Einstein once wrote to a child anxious about the fate of the world, 'As for the question of the end of it I advise: Wait and see!' It may be wise advice but sometimes Christian theology may be taking it too literally. We may need to be tentative in our theological speculation about the future. Yet the God of the future who reveals himself in the death and resurrection of Jesus gives us a basis for considering the future now.

Our task has been to respond theologically to the tremendous interest in the future within contemporary culture. From the *Left Behind* novels to political discussions on how to defend the Earth from asteroid impact, we have seen just how important future predictions are within pop culture and science. In particular, the discovery of an accelerating Universe, through observations of distant supernovae and the microwave background, has in the last five years questioned the purpose of the Universe and the place of human beings within its future. The theological questions are clear. The astronomer and theologian Thomas Wright of Durham speculated in 1750 that even the total destruction of our world may be 'no more to the great Author of Nature, than the most common Accident in Life with us'. While Wright was correct in pushing us to a bigger vision of the Universe, he underestimated the way human life is linked to the Universe and the importance of the doctrines of creation and new creation.

The pessimism of contemporary science concerning the future needs to be seen as a challenge for Christian theology, to recapture a bigger view of eschatology, even if the timescales are huge. Rees comments:

'What happens in far-future aeons may seem blazingly irrelevant to the practicalities of our lives. But I don't think the cosmic context is entirely irrelevant to the way we perceive our Earth and the fate of humans'. (Rees 2003: 182)

Certainly, the cosmic context has not been neglected by science. Dyson and Tipler respond to the futility of the end of the Universe through schemes which would maintain intelligent life for as long as possible. In this they attempt to provide a scientific and technological hope. They are unsuccessful, but the fact that the attempt is made shows just how disturbing the end of the Universe can be. Dyson admits the speculative nature of his investigation but argues that it is intellectually worthwhile to explore the consequences of known physical laws 'as far as we can reach into the past or the future', because such extrapolations of known laws into new territory can lead to the asking of important questions (Dyson 1979: 449–50).

We have tried to interact theologically with some of those important questions. Much of this work is speculative but worth pursuing. Polkinghorne is right to say, 'Ultimately the issue is whether we live in a world that makes sense not just now, but totally and for ever' (Polkinghorne 2002b: xiii). However, we have seen that systematic theology even with its resurgence of interest in eschatology has been largely silent about the end of the Universe. Theologians such as Moltmann and Pannenberg have claimed eschatological models which take science seriously but do not deliver when it comes to the end of the physical Universe. This is in part due to their ignorance of contemporary science and in part due to a basic anthropocentricity in eschatology. However, their insights into the centrality of the resurrection for Christian eschatology are to be welcomed. This has also been central to the work of Polkinghorne and Russell who have been among the few who have taken the end seriously.

In the light of these limitations, we have taken a particular way into systematics following the approach of Wesley. Our concern has been to look at the biblical material seriously and in detail and allow it to be in dialogue with the current scientific picture. This has generated some important questions and insights for systematic theology. We can summarise them as follows.

First, if Christian theology is to be in dialogue with the scientific picture of the future of the Universe then it must take seriously the relationship between creation and new creation. Too often the theme of new creation has been neglected. In particular this relationship must be represented by a tension between continuity and discontinuity, a tension that is inherent in the biblical material. An over emphasis on continuity, while attractive if the only context is the Earth's environment, in the light of the future of the Universe means that there is no hope. A belief in the myth of human progress does not deliver and the eschatologies of Dyson and Tipler are inadequate. Yet an over emphasis on discontinuity means that new creation simply becomes a 'second story' with no connection to God's original creative work. Thus the theology behind the popular *Left Behind* series is not biblical and has serious consequences for Christian involvement and discipleship in this world, with a devaluing of the body, the environment and socio-political change.

Second, this tension can be held using the resurrection as a model of the relationship. We see in the resurrection narratives and Pauline thought both continuity and discontinuity between Jesus before the cross and the risen Jesus. This becomes a very helpful model to speak about life after death for the individual and God's purposes in new creation. We have defended strongly the empty tomb and bodily resurrection, the importance of which is that it indicates God's purposes in transforming matter and space-time.

Third, the movement between creation and new creation is transformation of the present creation rather than complete destruction of the old creation. Thus new creation becomes the perspective from which creation should be seen, and creation becomes the perspective from which new creation is seen. God's work in creation is fulfilled in new creation and his work in bringing about new creation is based in his role as Creator. Indeed, in exploring any doctrine of God such as providence, kenosis or incarnation, creation and new creation need to be held together. We have shown that this is often not the case, particularly in the area of providence. We have also suggested that the role of the Holy Spirit needs to be seen in relationship to both creation and new creation. In this way, the Spirit can be seen as mediator between creation and new creation and the ascended yet present Jesus. More work could be fruitfully done on this aspect.

Fourth, we should therefore expect pointers within this creation not just to a Creator God but also to a coming new creation. We do not agree with Russell and others who say that predictions of science are in conflict with the hope of Christian eschatology (Russell 2002a: 6). Christian theology together with contemporary science can accept the ultimate finitude of this Universe. Eschatological hope does not hope to escape death but can accept finitude as an integral part of creation, as hope is based in God's purposes which are beyond this Universe. Therefore the futility of the Universe does not falsify eschatological hope, a point made independently by Conradie (Conradie 2002: 290). In fact, we have argued that the very futility expressed by the scientific predictions of the end of the Universe may itself be a pointer to new creation, part of the groaning of eager expectation of this creation as Paul would describe it in Romans 8. Thus, the futility of the scientific future may provide a pointer to transcendence within a revised and limited natural theology

Fifth, the action of God and the faithfulness of God must be held together in both creation and new creation. As evidenced by the resurrection and the images of the Parousia, God's transformative work will be both in event and in process, in the initiative of grace and in the co-operative work of grace with his new community. We differ in emphasis here with Polkinghorne who stresses the faithfulness of God. While there is much agreement between us, we want to stress a little more the specific activity of God in creation and new creation. This reflects more the biblical material and gives a stronger basis for hope.

Sixth, we have tried to work out what the tension of continuity and discontinuity means in terms of space-time and the nature of matter in creation and new creation. We argue that space and time are real in both creation and new creation, thus opposing any view that eternity will be atemporal. A multi-dimensional model of God's relationship with time is proposed which proves fruitful in reflecting the biblical images and current scientific thinking. We tentatively suggest on the basis of this that any quantum theory of gravity would involve higher dimensions of space-time and would also explain the observed arrow of time. While the flow of time is coupled with the experience of both growth and decay in this creation, we suggest that in new creation that the flow of time is characterized only by growth and that space-time is real but not limiting in the same way as in this creation. Further, we argue that matter cannot be divorced from space-time or its relational context, and that transformation affects the whole of this complex reality rather than being focused simply on the constituent atoms of matter. We therefore disagree with a revival of the language of soul in order to maintain continuity in the transformation. Both scientifically and theologically this is not a helpful avenue. Continuity and discontinuity will characterise the transformation of information bearing pattern, relationships and the form and composition of matter itself.

We have then attempted to apply these insights to other areas of contemporary interest outside of the context of the future of the physical Universe. Holding

continuity and discontinuity in creation and new creation has important consequences for thinking about Christian eschatology as it relates to the biological
world. In particular, we see that the animal theology of Linzey goes too far in
stressing discontinuity. In contemporary models of providence we see that the
models of Wiles, process theology and to an extent panentheism face serious
challenges in terms of the future of the Universe. We argue that there is both
predictability and openness to the future of the Universe, reflecting God's
freedom to act and his self limiting in creation, in terms of his sustaining of the
physical process and his working toward new creation. However, we conclude
that many models of providence are far too simplistic to reflect theological and
scientific richness, but we do set out from a Methodist theological perspective
how that richness might be explored. Finally we make a plea for creation and
new creation to be held together in Christian environmental concern and the
ongoing dialogue between science and the Christian faith.

This work was started independently of the significant work in this area
carried out by Polkinghorne. Our strategies and theological perspectives have
been different. In particular this work has interacted at a more detailed level with
contemporary cosmology, systematic theology and with the biblical material. It
has also been characterized by a Methodist approach to theology. It is therefore
interesting that while differences remain between us in terms of the action of
God, the nature of the soul, and whether the new creation represents a panentheistic context, in broad outline we come to similar conclusions. This is due to our
shared commitment to critical realism in science and theology and the central
importance of the resurrection.

Many questions remain in such a work. Among them are how should the
doctrine of the fall be worked into the relationship of creation and new creation
and how do we characterise the nature and place of the risen body of Jesus in this
transition between creation and new creation? More work by biblical scholars
and systematic theologians would be helpful on these issues.

Nevertheless, in spite of these qualifications and uncertainties, it is clear that
Christian theology has something important to both learn and say in its dialogue
with contemporary science and culture. In particular, it is a prophetic voice to
the cosmic pessimism of science. In the face of those who view the futility of
the future of the Universe with great despair, the resurrection is in the words of
Moltmann not only 'a consolation in a life ... doomed to die, but it is God's
contradiction of suffering and death' (Moltmann 1967: 21).

Appendix

A Note on Millennium Theology

The term millennium refers to the period of 1000 years mentioned in Revelation 20.2–7 of the reign of Christ and the saints over the Earth. Maddox points out that the notion of the millennium emerged in pre-Christian Judaism as a way of handling the alternative models of the future hope offered in Isaiah (long life in this world) and Daniel (eternal life in a reconstituted world). To reconcile these two models, Isaiah was seen as describing a yet future thousand-year golden age in this world, while Daniel was describing the final state after this age. For Christians there was also the influence of Hellenistic culture which portrayed earthly existence as inherently defective and the ultimate human hope as release at the moment of death from this earthly setting into the realm of purely spiritual reality (Maddox 2002).

Various millennial views then emerged (Gundry 1977: 45–55; Daley 1991; Hill 2002; Bauckham 1988: 428–430). Irenaeus saw the millennium as a time where God's rule was fulfilled in the present creation and to provide time for the additional spiritual growth that most believers needed before they would be ready to enter God's glorious presence. This intermediate state needed the presence of the glorified Christ on the Earth to initiate the millennium, so this general model became known as premillennialism. Christ would come, the resurrected saints would enjoy 1000 years rule on the Earth before eternal life in heaven. Later 19th Century premillennialism also saw the return of Christ and the bodily resurrection of the saints preceding the millennium, but in the dispensationalist theology of J. N. Darby and others saw a secret rapture of believers preceding the coming of Christ (Wilkinson 2007).

Augustine objected to this, and amillennialism saw believers enter directly into paradise at death, where they participate consciously in God's eternal rule (Riddlebarger 2003: 246). This became the dominant view in the West after the belief in a millennial kingdom was condemned at the Council of Ephesus (431 CE). In this view the millennial reign of Christ is the age of the church, from Christ's resurrection to the Parousia. Maddox argues that on this view the role of a future resurrection and a new creation fades from view if believers go straight to be with the Lord. Further the earthly expression of the God's present rule became closely correlated with existing structures and reality, and so the status quo is underwritten. The Lutheran, Reformed, and Anglican traditions ultimately reaffirmed the model, at least wherever they achieved status as the established church, now giving appropriate expression to God's present rule.

However, some Reformed communities, such as the Puritans in early seventeenth-century England, did not have political power. They argued that the final period of this present earthly age (which they discerned as imminent) would witness the incursion of the full reign of God through the power of the Spirit and the correlated faithful efforts of believers (Toon 1970: 23–41). This became known as postmillennialism, which looked forward to a fuller expression of God's Rule, but did not assume that it must be preceded by the return of Christ and the resurrection of the saints.

Bibliography

Abbott, E. A. 1999, *Flatland*, London: Penguin Books.

Achtner, W., S. Kunz and T. Walter 2002, *Dimensions of Time: The Structures of the Time of Humans, of the World, and of God*, Grand Rapids: Eerdmans.

Adams, F. C. and G. Laughlin 1997, A Dying Universe: The Long Term Fate and Evolution of Astrophysical Objects, *Reviews of Modern Physics* 69.337–72.

Allison, D. C. 1987, *The End of the Ages Has Come*, Philadelphia: Fortress.

Allison, D. C. 1998, *Jesus of Nazareth: Millenarian Prophet*, Philadelphia: Fortress.

Allmen, D. von. 1966, L'apocalyptique juive et le retard de la parousie en II Pierre 3.1–13, *RTP* 16. 262.

Alsford, M. 2000, *What If? Religious Themes in Science Fiction*, London: DLT.

Aristotle, 1985, *The Politics, rev. TJ Saunders*, Translated by T. A. Sinclair, Harmondsworth: Penguin.

Armstrong, J. 1981, *The Idea of Holiness and the Humane Response: A Study in the Concept of Holiness and its Social Consequences*, London: Allen and Unwin.

Ashbrook, J. B. and C. R. Albright 1997, *The Humanizing Brain: Where Religion and Neuroscience Meet*, Cleveland: Pilgrim.

Asher, J. R. 2001, SPEIRETAI: Paul's Anthropogenic Metaphor in 1 Corinthians 15.42–44, *JBL* 120. 103.

Asimov, I. 1955, *The End of Eternity*, London: Abelard.

Atkins, P. 1986, Time and Dispersal: The Second Law, in *The Nature of Time*, edited by R. Flood and M. Lockwood, Oxford: Basil Blackwell 80–98.

Atkins, P. 1995, The Limitless Power of Science, in *Nature's Imagination*, edited by J. Cornwall, Oxford: Oxford University Press 122–32.

Augustine, 1946, *St. Augustine's Confessions*, Cambridge, Mass: Harvard University Press.

Augustine, 1993, *The City of God – De Civitate Dei*, New York: Modern Library.

Aune, D. E. 1998, *Revelation 17–22 Word Biblical Commentary*, Waco, Texas: Word.

Backhouse, J. 1995, 'Outward and Visible Signs': The Lindisfarne Gospels, in *The Sense of the Sacramental: Movement and Measure in Art and Music, Place and Time*, edited by D. Brown and A. Loades, London: SPCK 103–21.

Bailey, M. E., D. A. Wilkinson and A. W. Wolfendale 1987, Can Episodic Comet Showers Explain the 30 Myr Cyclicity in the Terrestrial Record, *Mon. Not. R. astr. Soc.* 227. 863–85.

Baillie, D. 1958, *The Theology of the Church and Other Papers*, London: Faber and Faber.

Barbour, I. 2000, *When Science Meets Religion Enemies, Strangers or Partners?* London: SPCK.

Barbour, I. 2003, *Nature, Human Nature and God*, London: SPCK.

Barclay, J. M. G. 1996, The Resurrection in Contemporary New Testamant Scholarship, in *Resurrection Reconsidered*, edited by G. D'Costa, Oxford: Oneworld 13–30.

Barclay, O. 1992, Animal Rights: A Critique, *Science and Christian Belief* 4 (10). 49–61.

Barnes-Svarney, P. 1996, *Asteroid Earth Destroyer or New Frontier?* New York: Pelnum Press.

Barr, J. 1992, *The Garden of Eden and the Hope of Immortality*, London: SCM.

Barrett, C. K. 1957, *A Commentary on the Epistle to the Romans, Blacks New Testament Commentaries*, London: A & C Black.

Barrett, C. K. 1994, *The First Epistle to the Corinthians*, London: A & C Black.

Barrett, C. K. 1978, *The Gospel According to St John*, London: SPCK.

Barrow, J. D. 1983a, Natural Units before Planck, *QJRAS* 24. 24.

Barrow, J. D. 1983b, Dimensionality, *Phil Trans R Soc A* 310. 337.

Barrow, J. D. 1988, *The World Within the World*, Oxford: Clarendon.

Barrow, J. D. 1993, *The Observer*, 7th May.

Barrow, J. D. 2002a, The Far, Far Future, in *The Far Future Universe: Eschatology from a Cosmic Perspective*, edited by G. F. R. Ellis, Radnor: Templeton Foundation Press 23–40.

Barrow, J. D. 2002b, *The Constants of Nature: from alpha to omega*, London: Jonathan Cape.

Barrow, J. D. 2002c, Cosmology: A matter of all and nothing, *Astronomy and Geophysics* 43 (4). 4.8.

Barrow, J. D. and M. Dabrowski 1995, Oscillating Universes, *Mon. Not. R. astr. Soc.* 275. 850–62.

Barrow, J. D., J. Magueijo and H. Sandvik 2002a, Is it e or is it c? Experimental Tests of Varying Alpha. *Phys. Lett.* B549. 284–89.

Barrow, J. D., J. Magueijo and H. Sandvik 2002b, A Cosmological Tale of Two Varying Constants, *Phys. Lett.* B541. 201–10.

Barrow, J. D., J. Magueijo and H. Sandvik 2002c, Variations of Alpha in Space and Time, *Phys. Rev. D.* 66. 043515.

Barrow, J. D., and F. J. Tipler 1986, *The Anthropic Cosmological Principle*, Oxford: OUP.

Barth, K. 1933, *The Epistle to the Romans*, Oxford: OUP.

Barth, K. 1936–62, Church Dogmatics, edited by G. W. Bromiley and T. F. Torrance, Edinburgh: T&T Clark.

Barth, K. 1959, *A Shorter Commentary on Romans*, London: SCM.

Barth, K. 1963, *Evangelical Theology: An Introduction*, London: Weidenfeld & Nicolson.

Bauckham, R. 1980, The Delay of the ParousiaTyndale Bulletin, *Tyn B* 31. 3–36.

Bauckham, R. 1983, *Jude 2 Peter, Word Biblical Commentary*, Waco, Texas: Word.

Bauckham, R. 1986, First Steps to a Theology of Nature, *Evangelical Quarterly* 58.3. 239.

Bauckham, R. 1988, Millennium, in *The New Dictionary of Theology*, edited by S. B. Ferguson and D. F. Wright, Leicester: IVP 428–30.

Bauckham, R. 1989, *The Bible in Politics: How to Read the Bible Politically*, Louisville: Westminster/John Knox.

Bauckham, R. 1993, *The Theology of the Book of Revelation*, Cambridge: CUP.

Bauckham, R. 1994, Jesus and the Wild Animals (Mark 1.13): A Christological Image for an Ecological Age, in *Jesus of Nazareth: Lord and Christ: Essays on the Historical Jesus and New Testament Christology, Festschrift for I. Howard Marshall*, edited by J. B. Green and M. Turner, Grand Rapids: Eerdmans 3–21.

Bauckham, R. 1997, Must Christian Eschatology be Millenarian? A Response to Jürgen Moltmann, in *Eschatology in Bible and Theology*, edited by K. E. Brower and M. W. Elliott, Downers Grove, IL: InterVarsity Press 263–77.

Bauckham, R. 1998, The Future of Jesus Christ, *Scottish Bulletin of Evangelical Theology* 16.97–110.

Bauckham, R. 1998a, Jesus and Animals I: What did he teach? In *Animals on the Agenda*, edited by A. Linzey and D. Yamamoto, London: SCM 33–48.

Bauckham, R. 1998b, Jesus and Animals II: What did he practice? In *Animals on the Agenda*, edited by A. Linzey and D. Yamamoto, London: SCM 49–60.

Bauckham, R. 1998c, Life, Death and the Afterlife in Second Temple Judaism, in *Life in the Face of Death: The Resurrection Message of the New Testament*, edited by R. N. Longenecker, Grand Rapids: Eerdmans 80–95.

Bauckham, R. 2002, *Gospel Women: Studies of the Named Women in the Gospels*, Grand Rapids: Eerdmans.

Bauckham, R. ed. 1999, *God Will Be All in All: The Eschatology of Jürgen Moltmann*, Edinburgh: T&T Clark.

Bauckham, R. and T. Hart. 1999, *Hope Against Hope Christian Eschatology in Contemporary Context*, London: DLT.

Beale, G. K. 1997, The Eschatological Conception of New Testament Theology, in *Eschatology In Bible and Theology*, edited by K. E. Brower and M. W. Elliott, Downers Grove, IL: InterVarsity Press 11–52.

Beale, G. K. 1999, *The Book of Revelation NIGTC*, Grand Rapids: Eerdmans.

Beasley-Murray, G. R. 1974, *The Book of Revelation*, London: Oliphants.

Beasley Murray, G. R. 1999, *John, Word Biblical Commentary*, Waco, Texas: Word.

Belton, M. J. S., ed. 2003, *Report of the Workshop on Scientific Requirements for Mitigation of Hazardous Comets and Asteroids*: National Optical Astronomy Observatory.

Bence, C. 1979, Processive Eschatology: A Wesleyan Alternative, *Wesleyan Theological Journal* 14.1.45–59.

Bence, C. 1981, John Wesley's Teleological Hermeneutic, Ph.D., Emory University, Atlanta.

Benjamin, M. 1998, *Living at the End of the World*, London: Picador.

Benz, A. 2000, *The Future of the Universe*, London: Continuum.

Berger, K. 2003, *Identity and Experience in the New Testament*, Minneapolis: Fortress.

Berkson, W. 1974, *Fields of Force The Development of a World View from Faraday to Einstein*, New York: John Wiley and Sons.

Berlin, A. 1994, *Zephaniah Anchor Bible 25A*, New York: Doubleday.

Berry, R. J. 1994, In *Pastoral Ethics*, edited by D. Atkinson, Oxford: Lynx.

Berry, R. J. 1995, Creation and Environment, *Science and Christian Belief* 7 (1). 39.

Berry, R. J., ed. 2000, *The Care of Creation*, Leicester: IVP.

Berry, R. J. 2003, *God's Book of Works: The Nature and Theology of Nature*, London: Continuum.

Best, E. 1987, *Second Corinthians, Interpretation*, Louisville: John Knox Press.

Bietenhard, H. 1976, Heaven, in *The New International New Testament Dictionary of Theology*, edited by C. Brown, Exeter: Paternoster 189.

Billoski, T. V. 1987, Triceratops extinction linked to asteroid collision, *Science* 79 (7). 75–76.

Birch, C. and L. Vischer 1997, *Living With the Animals: The Community of God's Creatures*, WCC Publications: Geneva.

Black, M. 1976, The New Creation in 1 Enoch, in *Creation, Christ and Culture. FS T. R. Torrance*, edited by R. McKinney, Edinburgh: T&T Clark 13–21.

Blake, C. 2008, The WiggleZ Dark Energy Survey, *A&G* 49 (5). 19–24.

Bloch, E. 1986, *The Principle of Hope*, 3 vols. Oxford: Blackwell.

Blocher, H. 1984, *In the Beginning*, Leicester: IVP.

Bloesch, D. G. 1995, *God the Almighty*, Downers Grove: IVP.

Boden, M. A. 1999, Is Metabolism Necessary? *Brit. J. Phil. Sci.* 50. 231–48.

Boden, M. A. 2000, Autopoiesis and Life, *Cog. Sci. Q.* 1.115–43.

Boden, M. A. 2002, Artificial Intelligence and the Far Future, in *The Far Future Universe: Eschatology from a Cosmic Perspective*, edited by G. F. R. Ellis, Radnor: Templeton Foundation Press 207–24.

Boismard, M-E. 1999, *Our Victory Over Death: Resurrection?* Collegeville: Liturgical Press.

Booth, D. 1998, Human Nature: Unitary or Fragmented? Biblical Language and Scientific Understanding, *Science and Christian Belief* 10. 145–62.

Bordo, S. 1993, *Unbearable Weight: Feminism, Western Culture and the Body*, Berkeley: University of California Press.

Borg, M. J. 1994, *Jesus in Contemporary Scholarship*, Valley Forge: Trinity Press International.

Borg, M. J. 1999, The Irrelevancy of the Empty Tomb, in *Will the Real Jesus Please Stand Up: A Debate Between William Lane Craig and John Dominic Crossan*, edited by P. Copan, Grand Rapids: Baker 117–28.

Boring, M. E. 1989, *Revelation*, Louisville: John Knox.

Bostrom, N. 2002, *Anthropic Bias: Observation Selection Effects in Science and Philosophy*, New York: Routledge.

Boyd, G. A. 2000, *God of the Possible: A Biblical Introduction to the Open View of God*, Grand Rapids: Baker.

Braaten, C. E. 1974, *Eschatology and Ethics*, Minnesota: Augsburg.

Braaten, C. E. and P. Clayton 1988, Preface, in *The Theology of Wolfhart Pannenberg: Twelve American critiques, with an autobiographical essay and response*, edited by C. E. Braaten and P. Clayton, Minneapolis: Augsburg.

Braine, D. 1994, God, Time and Eternity, *Evangelical Quarterly* 66. 340.

Bray, G. 1998, *The Personal God: Is the Classical Understanding of God Tenable?* Carlisle: Paternoster.

Bridger, F. 1990, Ecology and Eschatology: A Neglected Dimension, *Tyndale Bulletin* 41.2. 290–301.

Brooks, R. A. 1991, Intelligence Without Representation, *Art. Intell.* 47. 139–59.

Broom, N. 2001, *How Blind is the Watchmaker?* Leicester: IVP.

Brown, D. 1999, *Tradition and Imagination: Revelation and Change*, Oxford: OUP.

Brown, D. and A. Loades 1995, Introduction: the Dance of Grace, in *The Sense of the Sacramental: Movement and Measure in Art and Music, Place and Time*, edited by D. Brown and A. Loades, London: SPCK 2–3.

Brown, P. 1993, *The Body and Society: Men, Women and Sexual Renunciation in the Early Church*, New York: Columbia University Press.

Brown, R. E. 1983, *The Gospel According to John*, New York: Doubleday.

Brown, R. E. 1993, *The Virginal Conception and Bodily Resurrection of Jesus*, London: Geoffrey Chapman.

Brueggemann, W. 1997, *The Theology of the Old Testament: Testimony, Dispute, Advocacy*, Minneapolis: Fortress.

Brueggemann, W. 1998, *Isaiah 1–39*, Louisville: Westminster John Knox Press.

Brunner, E. 1951, The Christian Understanding of Time, *Scottish Journal of Theology* 4. 1–12.

Bultmann, R. 1968, *The History of the Synoptic Tradition*, Oxford: Blackwell.

Bultmann, R. 1983, The Meaning of God as Acting, in *God's Activity in the World: The Contemporary Problem*, edited by O. C. Thomas, Chico, California: Scholars Press 61–76.

Burnet, T. 1684–90, *The Theory of the Earth*, Vol. 2 vols., London: Walter Kettilby.

Burney, C. F. 1925–6, Christ as the Arche of Creation, *JTS* 27. 160–77.

Butler, A. 1946, *Lives of the Saints, Revised by H. Thurston and D. Attwater*, New York: P. J. Kennedy and Sons.

Bynum, C. W. 1995, *The Resurrection of the Body in Western Christianity*, New York: Columbia University Press.

Byrne, B. 1986, *Reckoning with Romans*, Wilmington: Glazier.

Caird, G. B. 1966, *A Commentary on the Revelation of St John the Divine, Harpers/Blacks New Testament Commentaries*, New York: Harper and Row.

Caird, G. B. 1997, *The Language and Imagery of the Bible*, Grand Rapids: Eerdmans.

Calder, L. and O. Lahav 2008, *Dark Energy: back to Newton? A&G* 49 (1). 13.

Calvin, J. 1965, *A Commentary on Genesis*, London: The Banner of Truth Trust.

Calvin, J. 1996, *The First Epistle of Paul The Apostle to the Corinthians*, edited by D. W. Torrance and T. F. Torrance, *Calvin's Commentaries*, Grand Rapids: Eerdmans.

Carnley, P. 1987, *The Structure of Resurrection Belief*, Oxford: OUP.

Carson, D. A. 1991, *The Gospel According to John*, Leicester: IVP.

Carson, D. A. 1996, *The Gagging of God: Christianity Confronts Pluralism*, Grand Rapids: Zondervan.

Carter, B. 1983, The anthropic principle and its implications for biological evolution, *Phil. Trans. R.Soc. A* 310. 347.

Cassidy, R. 1971, Paul's Attitude to Death in II Corinthians 5.1–10, *Evangelical Quarterly* 43. 210–217.

Chaitin, G. J. 1990, *Algorithmic Information Theory*, Cambridge: CUP.

Chalmers, D. 1996, *The Conscious Mind*, Oxford: OUP.

Chamberlain, J. K. 1993, Psychology, in *Dictionary of Paul and His Letters*, edited by G. H. Hawthorne et al., Downers Grove: IVP 765–74.

Chester, A. 2001, Resurrection and Transformation, in *Aufersehung-Resurrection*, edited by F. Avemarie and H. Lichtenberger, Tübingen: Mohr-Siebeck 65–67.

Chester, A. and R. P. Martin 1994, *The Theology of the Letters of James, Peter and Jude*, Cambridge: CUP.

Childs, B. 1992, *Biblical Theology of the Old and New Testaments*, Minneapolis: Fortress.

Chilton, B. and J. I. MacDonald 1987, *Jesus and the Ethics of the Kingdom*, London: SPCK.

Clark, A. J. 1997, *Being There: Putting Brain, Body, and World Together Again*, Cambridge: MIT Press.

Clark, S. R. L. 1995, *How to Live Forever: Science Fiction and Philosophy*, London: Routledge.

Clark, S. R. L. 1998, Is Nature God's Will? In *Animals on the Agenda*, edited by A. Linzey and D. Yamamoto, London: SCM 123–26.

Clark, S. R. L. 2002, Deep Time, in *The Far Future Universe: Eschatology from a Cosmic Perspective*, edited by G. F. R. Ellis, Radnor: Templeton Foundation Press 177–95.

Clifford, Anne M. 1995, When Being Human Becomes Truly Earthly, in *In the Embrace of God: Feminist Approaches to Theological Anthropology*, edited by A. O'Hara Graff, New York: Orbis Books 173–189.

Cobb, J. B. 1973, Natural Causality and Divine Action, *Idealistic Studies* 3. 207–22.

Cobb, J. B. 1995, *Grace and Responsibility: A Wesleyan Theology for Today*, Nashville: Abingdon.

Cobb, J. B. and D. R. Griffin 1976, *Process Theology: An Introductory Exposition*, Philadelphia: Westminster Press.

Collins, R. F. 1999, *First Corinthians*, Collegeville: Glazier/Liturgical Press.

Colver, E. M., ed. 1999, *Evangelical Theology in Transition: Theologians in Dialogue with Donald Bloesch*, Downers Grove: IVP.

Conradie, E. M. 2000, *Hope for the Earth*, Bellville: University of the Western Cape Publications.

Conradie, E. M. 2002, Resurrection, Finitude and Ecology, in *Resurrection: Theological and Scientific Assessments*, edited by T. Peters, R. J. Russell and M. Welker, Grand Rapids: Eerdmans 277–96.

Conway Morris, S. 2002, Does Biology Have An eschatology, and If So Does it Have Cosmological Implications? In *The Far Future Universe: Eschatology from a Cosmic Perspective*, edited by G. F. R. Ellis, Radnor: Templeton Foundation Press 158–74.

Cooey, P., S. Farmer and M. E. Ross, eds. 1987, *Embodied Love: Sensuality and Relationship as Feminist Values*, San Francisco: Harper and Row.

Cooke, B. 1983, *Sacraments and Sacramentality*, Mystic, CT: Twenty-Third Publications.

Cooper, J. W. 1989, *Body, Soul and Life Everlasting: Biblical Anthropology and the Monism-Dualism Debate*, Grand Rapids: Eerdmans.

Cooper, J. W. 2001, Biblical Anthropology and the Body-Soul Problem, in *Soul, Body and Survival*, edited by K. Corcoran, Ithaca: Cornell University Press 218–22.

Coulson, C. A. 1953, *Christianity in an Age of Science*, Oxford: OUP.

Coulson, C. A. 1955, *Science and Christian Belief*, Oxford: OUP.

Coveney, P. and R. Highfield 1991, *The Arrow of Time*, London: Flamingo.

Craig, W. L. and Q. Smith 1995, *Theism, Atheism and Big Bang Cosmology*, Oxford: OUP.

Craig, W. L. 1991, *Divine Foreknowledge and Human Freedom: The Coherence of Theism-Omniscience*, Leiden: E. J. Brill.

Cranfield, C. E. B. 1959, *The Gospel According to Mark*, Cambridge: CUP.

Cranfield, C. E. B. 1975, *The Epistle to the Romans*, Vol. 1, *International Critical Commentary*, Edinburgh: T&T Clark.

Cranfield, C. E. B. 1974, Some observations on Romans 8.19–21, in *Reconciliation and Hope: Essays on Atonement and Eschatology*, edited by R. Banks, Grand Rapids: Eerdmans 224–30.

Crevier, D. 1993, *AI: The Tumultuous History of the Search for Artificial Intelligence*, New York: Basic Books.

Crites, S. 1971, The Narrative Quality of Experience, *Journal of the American Academy of Religion* 39. 291–309.

Cross, T. L. 2000, The Rich Feast of Theology: Can Pentecostals Bring the Main Course or Only the Relish? *Journal of Pentecostal Theology* 16. 30–1.

Crossan, J. D. 1998, *The Birth of Christianity: Discovering What Happened in the Years Immediately After the Execution of Jesus*, San Francisco: HarperSanFrancisco.

Crüsemann, F. 2002, Scripture and Resurrection, in *Resurrection: Theological and Scientific Assessments*, edited by T. Peters, R. J. Russell and M.Welker, Grand Rapids: Eerdmans 89–102.

Crutchfield, J., et al. 1986, Chaos, *Scientific American* 255 (6). 38.

Crutchfield, L. V. 1992, *The Origins of Dispensationalism: The Darby Factor*, Lanham: University Press of America.

Cullmann, O. 1951, *Christ and Time*, London: SCM.

Cunningham, D. S. 1988, *These Three Are One*, Oxford: Blackwell.

Dabney, L. 2001, 'Justified by the Spirit': Soteriological Reflections on the Resurrection, *International Journal of Systematic Theology* 3. 61–62.

Dahl, N. A. 1964, Christ, Creation and the Church, in *The Background of the New Testament and Its Eschatology*, edited by W. D. Davies and D. Daube, Cambridge: CUP 422–43.

Daley, B. E. 1991, *The Hope of the Early Church*, Cambridge: CUP.

Daley, B. E. 2002, A Hope for Worms: Early Christian Hope, in *Resurrection: Theological and Scientific Assessments*, edited by T. Peters, R. J. Russell and M. Welker, Grand Rapids: Eerdmans 136–64.

Davies, J. 1999, *Death, Burial and Rebirth in the Religions of Antiquity*, London: Routledge.

Davies, P. 1983, *God and the New Physics*, Harmondsworth: Pelican.

Davies, P. 1995, *About Time*, London: Penguin.

Davies, P. 1998, *The Fifth Miracle: The Search for the Origin of Life*, London: Allen Lane.

Davies, P. 2002, Eternity: Who Needs It? In *The Far Future Universe: Eschatology from a Cosmic Perspective*, edited by G. F. R. Ellis, Radnor: Templeton Foundation Press 41–52.

Davis, J. J. 1999, Cosmic Endgame: Theological Reflections on Recent Scientific Speculations on the Ultimate Fate of the Universe, *Science and Christian Belief* 11. 15–27.

Davis, J. J. 2007, Will There be New Work in the New Creation? *Evangelical Review of Theology* 31 (3). 256–273.

Davis, S. T. 1983, *Logic and the Nature of God*, Grand Rapids: Eerdmans.

Davis, S. T. 1993, *Risen Indeed: Making Sense of the Resurrection*, London: SPCK.

Dawkins, R. 1989, *The Selfish Gene*, Oxford: Oxford University Press.

Dawkins, R. 1995, *River Out of Eden*, New York: Basic Books.

Dawkins, R. 2003, *A Devil's Chaplain*, London: Weidenfeld & Nicholson.

Dawkins, R. 2006, *The God Delusion*, London: Bantam Press.

De Boer, M. C. 1988, *The Defeat of Death: Apocalyptic Eschatology in 1 Cor 15 and Rom 5*, Sheffield: JSOT Press.

de Duve, C. 1995, *Vital Dust: Life as a Cosmic Imperative*, New York: Basic Books.

de Jonge, M. 1998, *God's Final Envoy: Early Christology and Jesus Own View of His Mission*, Grand Rapids: Eerdmans.

Deane-Drummond, C. E. and D. Clough, eds. 2009, *Creaturely Theology: God, Humans and other animals*, London: SCM Press.

Delumeau, J. 1995, *History of Paradise: the Garden of Eden in myth and tradition*, New York: Continuum.

DeMar, G. 2001, *End Times Fiction*, Nashville: Thomas Nelson.

Dembski, W. A. 2002a, *Intelligent Design: The Bridge Between Science & Theology*, Downers Grove: IVP.

Dembski, W. A. 2002b, *No Free Lunch: Why Specified Complexity Cannot Be Purchased Without Intelligence*, Lanham: Rowman & Littlefield Publishers.

Dennett, D. C. 1993, *Consciousness Explained*, Harmondsworth: Penguin.

Dennett, D. C. 1996, *Kinds of Mind: Towards an Understanding of Consciousness*, London: Weidenfeld and Nicolson.

Denton, D. R. 1982, Apokaradokia, *Zeitschrift für die neutestamentliche Wissenschaft* 73. 138–40.

Dick, S. J. 2000, Cosmotheology: Theological Implications of the New Universe, in *Many Worlds: The New Universe, Extraterrestrial Life and the Theological Implications*, edited by S. J. Dick, Radnor: Templeton Foundation Press 191–208.

Dilley, F. B. 1965, Does The 'God Who Acts' Really Act, *The Anglican Theological Review* 47. 66–80.

Dodd, C. H. 1951, *The Coming of Christ*, Cambridge: CUP.

Downey, M. and R. Fragomeni, eds. 1992, *A Promise of Presence: Studies in Honour of David N. Power, OMI*, Washington: The Pastoral Press.

Doyle, R. C. 2000, *Eschatology and the Shape of Christian Belief*, Carlisle: Paternoster Press.

Drees, W. 1997, Contingency, Time and the Theological Ambiguity of Science, in *Beginning with the End: God, Science and Wolfhart Pannenberg*, edited by C. R. Albright and J. Haugen, Chicago, Illinois: Open Court 217–48.

Duffy, R. 1982, *Real Presence: Worship, Sacraments and Commitment*, San Francisco: Harper and Row.

Dunn, J. D. G. 1977, *Unity and Diversity in the New Testament*, London: SCM.

Dunn, J. D. G. 1985, *The Evidence for Jesus*, London: SCM.

Dunn, J. D. G. 1988, *Commentary on Romans 1–8, Word Biblical Commentary*, Waco, Texas: Word.

Dunn, J. D. G. 1996, *The Epistles to the Colossians and to Philemon*, Carlisle: Paternoster.

Dunn, J. D. G. 1997, He will come again, *Interpretation* 51. 42–56.

Durant, J., ed. 1985, *Darwinism and Divinity*, Oxford: Blackwell.

Dyson, F. J. 1979, Time without end: Physics and Biology in an Open Universe, *Reviews of Modern Physics* 51. 3. 449–50.

Dyson, F. J. 1988, *Infinite in All Directions*, New York: Harper & Row.

Dyson, F. J. 2002, Life in the Universe: Is Life Digital or Analogue? In *The Far Future Universe: Eschatology from a Cosmic Perspective*, edited by G. F. R. Ellis, Radnor: Templeton Foundation Press 140–157.

Eaves, L. 1989, Spirit, Method and Content in Science and Religion: The Theological Perspective of a Geneticist, *Zygon: Journal of Religion and Science* 24. 185–215.

Eckstein, H. J. 2002, Bodily Resurrection in Luke, in *Resurrection: Theological and Scientific Assessments*, edited by T. Peters, R. J. Russell and M. Welker, Grand Rapids: Eerdmans 115–23.

Edgar, B. 2000, Paul and the Person, *Science and Christian Belief* 12. 151–64.

Edwards, T. C. 1885, *A Commentary on the First Epistle to the Corinthians*, London: Hodder and Stoughton.

Ehrman, B. 1999, *Jesus: Apocalyptic Prophet of the New Millennium*, Oxford: OUP.

Einstein, A. 1905, Zur Elektrodynamik bewegter Korper, *Ann. Physik* 17. 891.

Einstein, A. 1916, Die Grundlage der allgemeinen Relativitätstheorie, *Ann. Physik* 49. 771.

Einstein, A. 1920, *Relativity: The Special and General Theory*, New York: Henry Holt and Company.

Eliade, M. 1969, *The Quest: History and Meaning in Religion*, Chicago: University of Chicago Press.

Ellis, G. F. R. 2002, Natures of Existence (Temporal and Eternal), in *The Far Future Universe: Eschatology from a Cosmic Perspective*, edited by G. F. R. Ellis, Radnor: Templeton Foundation Press 316–51.

Ellis, G. F. R., ed. 2002, *The Far Future Universe: Eschatology from a Cosmic Perspective*, Radnor: Templeton Foundation Press.

Ellis, G. F. R. and D. H. Coule 1994, Life at the End of the Universe, *General Relativity and Gravitation* 26. 7. 738.

Elphinstone, A. 1976, *Freedom, Suffering and Love*, London: SCM.

Elsdon, R. 2000, Eschatology and Hope, in *The Care of Creation*, edited by R. J. Berry, Leicester: IVP 161–66.

Evans, C. F. 1970, *Resurrection and the New Testament*, London: SCM.

Everett III, H. 1957, Relative State Formulation of Quantum Mechanics, *Reviews of Modern Physics* 29. 3. 454–62.

Fackre, G. 1993, *Interpretation*, 47. 304–6.

Fackre, G. 2002, Review, *Theology Today* 59 (2). 319–323.

Fahri, A. and A. H. Guth 1987, An Obstacle to Creating a Universe in a Laboratory, *Phys. Lett. B* 183. 149.

Farrer, A. 1962, *Love Almighty and Ills Unlimited*, London: Collins.

Farrer, A. 1964, *The Revelation of St John the Divine*, Oxford: Clarendon.

Farrow, D. 1999, *Ascension and Ecclesia*, Grand Rapids: Eerdmans.

Farrow, D. 2000, Eucharist, Eschatology and Ethics, in *The Future as God's Gift*, edited by D. Fergusson and M. Sarot, Edinburgh: T&T Clark 199–215.

Fee, G. D. 1987, *The First Epistle to the Corinthians*, *NICNT*, Grand Rapids: Eerdmans.

Feinberg, T. E. 2001, *Altered Egos: How the Brain Creates the Self*, Oxford: OUP.

Fergusson, D. 2000, Introduction, in *The Future as God's Gift*, edited by D. Fergusson and M. Sarot, Edinburgh: T&T Clark 1–7.

Feuerbach, L. 1957, *The Essence of Christianity*, New York: Harper & Row.

Feynman, R. 1964, *The Feynman Lectures on Physics*, Vol. 2, Reading Massachusetts: Addison-Wesley.

Findlay, G. G. 1961, *St Paul's First Epistle to the Corinthians*, in *The Expositors Greek Testament*, edited by W. R. Nicoll, Grand Rapids: Eerdmans. Original edition, 1900.

Fitzmyer, J. A. 1993, *Romans*. London: Doubleday.

Fletcher-Louis, C. 1997, *Luke-Acts: Angels, Christology and Soteriology*, *Wissenschaftliche Untersuchungen zum Neuen Testament 2. 94*, Tübingen: Mohr Siebeck.

Foerst, A. 1997, Christian Theology in an Age of Computers, *Science and Spirit* 8 (4). 6.

Fowl, S. E. 1998, *Engaging Scripture: A Model for Theological Interpretation*, Oxford: Blackwell.

Fox, M. 1983, *Original Blessing: A Primer in Creation Spirituality*, Santa Fe: Bear and Company.

Frautschi, S. 1982, Entropy in an Expanding Universe, *Science* 217 (4560). 599.

Frykholm, A. J. 2004, *Rapture culture: left behind in Evangelical America*, Oxford, England; New York: Oxford University Press.

Fuchs, E. 1949, *Die Freiheit des Glaubens Römer 5–8 ausgelegt*, Munich: Kaiser.

Fukuyama, F. 1992, *The End of History and the Last Man*, Toronto: The Free Press.

Fuller, R. 1980, *The Formation of the Resurrection Narratives*, Philadelphia: Fortress Press.

Funk R. W., et al. 1997, *The Five Gospels: What Did Jesus Really Say?* New York: Harper Collins.

Fürst, J. 1867, *Hebrew and Chaldee Lexicon 3rd edition tr. S. Davison*, London: Williams and Norgate.

Gaard, G., ed. 1993, *Ecofeminism, Women, Animals, Nature*, Philadelphia: Temple University Press.

Gager, J. G. 1970, Functional Diversity in Paul's Use of End Time Language, *JBL* 89. 329.

Gale, R. M. 1991, *On the Nature and Existence of God*, Cambridge: Cambridge University Press.

Galloway, A. D. 1951, *The Cosmic Christ*, London: Nisbet and Co.

Garriga, J. and A. Vilenkin 2001, Many Worlds in One, *Phys. Rev. D.* 64. 043511.

Garrigou-Lagrange, R. 1934, *God: His Existence and Nature*, St. Louis: B. Herder.

Geisler, N. L. 1997, *Creating God in the Image of Man? The New 'Open' View of God – Neotheism's Dangerous Drift*, Minneapolis: Bethany House.

Geraci, R. M. 2010, *Apocalyptic AI : visions of heaven in robotics, artificial intelligence, and virtual reality*, Oxford, New York: Oxford University Press.

Gibbons, G. W., E. P. S. Shellard and S. J. Rankin, eds. 2003, *The Future of Physics and Cosmology: Celebrating Stephen Hawking's 60th Birthday*, Cambridge: CUP.

Gilkey, L. B. 1961, Cosmology, Ontology and the Travail of Biblical Language, *Journal of Religion* 41. 203.

Gilkey, L. B. 1963, The Concept of Providence in Contemporary Theology, *The Journal of Religion* 43. 171.

Gilkey, L. B. 1973, Pannenberg's Basic Questions in Theology: A Review Article, *Perspective* 14. 53.

Gillman, J. 1982, Transformation in 1 Cor 15.50–53, *ETL* 58. 327.

Gingerich, O. 1988, *Nature*, 336. 288.

Gingerich, O. 2006, *God's Universe*, Camb, Mass: Belknap Press.

Gleick, J. 1993, *Chaos: Making a New Science*, London: Abacus.

Gödel, K. 1949, An Example of a New Type of Cosmological Solutions of Einstein's Field Equations of Gravitation, *Reviews of Modern Physics* 21. 447–50.

Goldingay, J. 2000, Biblical Narrative and Systematic Theology, in *Between Two Horizons: Spanning New Testament Studies and Systematic Theology*, edited by J. B. Green and M. Turner, Grand Rapids: Eerdmans 123–42.

Goldstein, M. and I. F. Goldstein 1993, *The Refrigerator and the Universe*, Cambridge: Harvard University Press.

Gooch, P. W. 1987, *Partial Knowledge: Philosophical Studies in Paul*, Notre Dame: University of Notre Dame Press.

Gore, C. 1902, *St Paul's Epistle to the Romans*. 2 vols. Vol. 1, London: John Murray.

Gott, J. R. 1993, Implications of the Copernican Principle for our Future Prospects, *Nature* 363. 315–319.

Gould, S. J. 1999, *Rocks of Ages Science and Religion and the Fullness of Life*, New York: Ballantine.

Goulder, M. D. 1996, The Baseless Fabric of a Vision, in *Resurrection Reconsidered*, edited by G. D'Costa, Oneworld: Oxford 48–61.

Grayston, K. 1990, *The Gospel of John*, *Epworth Commentaries*, London: Epworth.

Green, G. 2000, Imagining the Future, in *The Future as God's Gift*, edited by D. Fergusson and M. Sarot, Edinburgh: T&T Clark 73–88.

Green, J. B. 1998, Bodies – that is human lives: a re-examination of human nature in the Bible, in *Whatever Happened to the Soul? Scientific and Theological Portraits of Human Nature*, edited by W. Brown, N. Murphy and H. N. Maloney, Minneapolis: Fortress 149–73.

Green, J. B. 1999a, Restoring the Human Person: New Testament Voices for a Wholistic and Social Anthropology, in *Neuroscience and the Person: Scientific Perspectives on Divine Action*, edited by R. J. Russell, N. Murphy, T. C. Meyering and M. A. Arbib, Notre Dame: Vatican Observatory/University of Notre Dame Press 3–22.

Green, J. B. 1999b, Scripture and the Human Person: Further Reflections, *Science and Christian Belief* 11. 51–64.

Green, J. B. 2000, Scripture and Theology: Uniting the Two So Long Divided, in *Between Two Horizons: Spanning New Testament Studies and Systematic Theology*, edited by J. B. Green and M. Turner, Grand Rapids: Eerdmans 23–43.

Green, J. B. 2002a, Eschatology and the Nature of Humans: A Reconsideration of Pertinent Biblical Evidence, *Science and Christian Belief* 14. 33–50.

Green, J. B. 2002b, Private Communication.

Green, J. B. 2004a, Resurrection of the Body: New Testament Voices Concerning Personal Continuity and the Afterlife, in *What About the Soul? Neuroscience and Christian Anthropology*, edited by J. B. Green, Nashville: Abingdon 85–100.

Green, J. B., ed. 2004b, *What About the Soul? Neuroscience and Christian Anthropology*, Nashville: Abingdon.

Gregersen, N. H. 2000, The Final Crucible, in *The Future as God's Gift*, edited by D. Fergusson and M. Sarot, Edinburgh: T&T Clark 169–80.

Gregersen, N. H. 2003, *From complexity to life : on the emergence of life and meaning*, Oxford: Oxford University Press.

Gregersen, N. H, W. B. Drees and U. Görman, (eds.) 2000, *The Human Person in Science and Theology*, Edinburgh: T&T Clark.

Grenz, S. J. 1990, *Reason for hope: The systematic theology of Wolfhart Pannenberg*, New York: Oxford University Press.

Grenz, S. J. 1991, Pannenberg and Evangelical Theology: Sympathy and Caution, *Christian Scholar's Review* 20 (3). 272–85.

Grenz, S. J. 1992, *The Millennial Maze*, Downers Grove, IL: InterVarsity.

Griffin, D. R. 1975, Relativism, Divine Causation and Biblical Theology, *Encounter* 36. 342–60.

Griffiths, R. 1982, *The Human Use of Animals*, Cambridge: Grove Books.

Grundmann, W. 1964–76, *Theological Dictionary of the New Testament*, Vol. II. Grand Rapids: Eerdmans.

Guastello, S. J., M. Koopmans and D. Pincus 2009, *Chaos and complexity in psychology: the theory of nonlinear dynamical systems*, Cambridge; New York: Cambridge University Press.

Gudorf, C. E. 1994, *Body, Sex and Pleasure: Reconstructing Christian Sexual Ethics*, Cleveland: Pilgrim Press.

Gundry, R. H. 1976, *SOMA in Biblical Theology*, Vol. 29, *SNTSMS*. Cambridge: CUP.

Gundry, R. H. 1994, The Essential Physicality of Jesus' Resurrection according to the New Testament, in *Jesus of Nazareth: Lord and Christ: Essays on the Historical Jesus and New Testament Christology*, edited by J. B. Green and M. Turner, Grand Rapids: Eerdmans 204–19.

Gundry, S. 1977, Hermeneutics or Zeitgeist as the Determining Factor in the History of Eschatologies, *Journal of the Evangelical Theological Society* 20. 45–55.

Gunter, W. S. et. al. 1997, *Wesley and the quadrilateral: renewing the conversation*, Nashville: Abingdon Press.

Gunton, C. E. 1991, *The Promise of Trinitarian Theology*, Edinburgh: T&T Clark.

Gunton, C. E. 1993, *Christ and Creation*, Carlisle: Paternoster.

Gutenson, C. E. 2004, Time, Eternity and Personal Identity: The Implications of Trinitarian Theology, in *What About the Soul? Neuroscience and Christian Anthropology*, edited by J. B. Green, Nashville: Abingdon 117–32.

Guyatt, N. 2007, *Have a nice doomsday: why millions of Americans are looking forward to the end of the world*, New York: Harper Perennial.

Habgood, J. 1995, *The Sacramentality of the Natural World*, in *The Sense of the Sacramental: Movement and Measure in Art and Music, Place and Time*, edited by D. Brown and A. Loades, London: SPCK 19–30.

Hamilton, N. Q. 1957, *The Holy Spirit and Eschatology in Paul, SJT Occasional Papers*, Edinburgh: Oliver and Boyd.

Handyside, J. 1929, *Kant's Inaugural Dissertation and Early Writings on Space*, Chicago: University of Chicago Press.

Harbeck, H., H. G. Link and C. Brown 1976, 'New', in *The New International Dictionary of New Testament Theology*, edited by C. Brown, Exeter: Paternoster 669–74.

Hardy, D. W. 1996, *God's Ways with the World*, Edinburgh: T&T Clark.

Hardy, D. W. 1997, Creation and Eschatology, in *The Doctrine of Creation*, edited by C. Gunton, Edinburgh: T&T Clark 105–34.

Harris, M. J. 1983, *Raised Immortal: Resurrection and Immortality in the New Testament*, Grand Rapids: Eerdmans.

Harrisville, R. A. 1960, *The Concept of Newness in the New Testament*, Minneapolis: Augsburg.

Hart, T. 1995, *Faith Thinking: The Dynamics of Christian Theology*, London: SPCK.

Hart, T. 2000, Tradition, Authority and a Christian Approach to the Bible as Scripture, in *Between Two Horizons: Spanning New Testament Studies and Systematic Theology*, edited by J. B. Green and M. Turner, Grand Rapids: Eerdmans 183–204.

Hartley, T. 1764, *Paradise Restored; or, A Testimony to the Doctrine of the Blessed Millennium ... To which is added, A Short Defense of the Mystical Writers against a late work entitled, The Doctrine of Grace, or, The Office and Operations of the Holy Spirit vindicated*, London: Richardson.

Harvey, A. E. 1994, They Discussed Among Themselves What This 'Rising from the Dead' Could Mean, in *Resurrection: Essays in Honour of Leslie Houlden*, edited by S. Barton and C. Stanton, London: SPCK 69–78.

Hasker, W. 1989, *God, Time and Knowledge*, Ithaca, N.Y: Cornell University Press.

Hasker, W. 1999, *The Emergent Self*, Ithaca/London: Cornell University Press.

Haught, J. F. 1995, *Science and Religion: From Conflict to Conversation*, Mahweh NJ: Paulist Press.

Haught, J. F. 1999, *God After Darwin*, Boulder: Westview.

Hawking, S. W. 1968, The Existence of Cosmic Time Functions, *Proc. Roy. Soc. London* A 308. 433–35.

Hawking, S. W. 1988, *A Brief History of Time*, London: Bantam.

Hawking, S. W. 1993, *Black Holes and Baby Universes*, London: Bantam.

Hawking, S. W. 2001, *The Universe in a Nutshell*, London: Bantam.

Hawthorne, G. T. 1983, *Philippians, Word Biblical Commentary*, Waco, Texas: Word.

Hay, D. M. 2000, *Colossians, Abingdon New Testament Commentaries*, Nashville: Abingdon.

Hays, R. B. 1997, *First Corinthians, IBC*, Nashville: Abingdon.

Hays, R. B. 1999, The Conversion of the Imagination: Scripture and Eschatology in 1 Corinthians, *NTS* 45. 391–412.

Hays, R. B. 2001, Why Do You Stand Looking Up Toward Heaven? New Testament Eschatology at the Turn of the Millennium, in *Theology and Eschatology At The Turn of the Millennium*, edited by J. Buckley and L. G. Jones, Oxford: Blackwell 113–31.

Hebblethwaite, B. 1984, *The Christian Hope*, Grand Rapids: Eerdmans.

Hefner, P. 1989, The Role of Science in Pannenberg's Theological Thinking, *Zygon: Journal of Religion and Science* 24. 135–51.

Heller, M, and W. Sasin 1998, Emergence of Time, *Phys. Lett.* A 250. 48–54.

Helm, P. 1994, *The Providence of God*, Downers Grove: IVP.

Hengel, M. 1987, The Interpretation of the Wine Miracle at Cana: John 2. 1–11, in *The Glory of Christ in the New Testament Fs. G.B. Caird*, edited by L. D. Hurst and N. T. Wright, Oxford: Clarendon 83–112.

Herzfeld, N.L. 2002a, Cybernetic Immortality versus Christian Resurrection, in *Resurrection: Theological and Scientific Assessments*, edited by T. Peters, R. J. Russell and M. Welker, Grand Rapids: Eerdmans 192–201.

Herzfield, N. L. 2002b, *In Our Image: Artificial Intelligence and the Human Spirit*, Minneapolis: Fortress.

Hick, J. 1968, *Evil and the God of Love*, London: Fontana.

Hick, J. 1976, *Death and Eternal Life*, New York: Harper and Row.

Hill, C. C. 2002a, *In God's Time: The Bible and the Future*, Grand Rapids: Eerdmans.

Hill, C. E. 2002b, *Regnum Caelorum: Patterns of Future Hope in Early Christianity*, Oxford: Clarendon.

Hillyer, N. 1992, *1 and 2 Peter, Jude, New International Biblical Commentary*, Carlisle: Paternoster.

Hitchcock, M. 2004, *The Four Horsemen of the Apocalypse: End Times Answers, Book Seven*, Sisters: Multnomah Publishers.

Hoekema, A. A. 1979, *The Bible and the Future*, Grand Rapids: Eerdmans.

Holleman, J. 1996, *Resurrection and Parousia: A Traditio-Historical Study of Paul's Eschatology in 1 Cor 15*, Vol. 84, *NovTSup*. Leiden: Brill.

Hormann, K. 1961, *An Introduction to Moral Theology*, London: Burns and Oates.

Horrell, D. G. 2010, *The Bible and the environment: towards a critical ecological biblical theology, Biblical challenges in the contemporary world*, London; Oakville, CT: Equinox Pub. Ltd.

Horsley, R. A. 1976, Pneumatikos vs. Psychikos, Distinctions of Spiritual Status among the Corinthians. *HTR* 69. 269–88.

Hosinki, T. 1998, How does God's Providential Care Extend to Animals? In *Animals on the Agenda*, edited by A. Linzey and D. Yamamoto, London: SCM 137–43.

Houghton, J. T. 1989, New Ideas of Chaos in Physics, *Science and Christian Belief* l. 41–51.

Houghton, J. T. 1995, *The Search for God: Can science help?* Oxford: Lion.

Houghton, J. T., ed. 2001, *Climate Change 2001: The Scientific Basis, The Intergovernmental Panel on Climate Change*, Cambridge: CUP.

Houghton, J. T. 2004, *Global warming the complete briefing*, Cambridge, UK; New York: CUP.

Houlden, J. L. 1986, *Connections: The Integration of Theology and Faith*, London: SCM.

Houston, W. 1998, What was the Meaning of Classifying Animals as Clean or Unclean? In *Animals on the Agenda*, edited by A. Linzey and D. Yamamoto, London: SCM 18–24.

Hoyle, F. 1983, *The Intelligent Universe*, London: Michael Joseph.

Hoyle, F., G. Burbidge and J. V. Narlikar 2000, *A Different Approach to Cosmology: From a Static Universe Through Big Bang Towards Reality*, Cambridge: CUP.

Hughes, P. E. 1990, *The Book of Revelation*, Grand Rapids: Eerdmans.

Inge, W. 1934, *God and the Astronomers*, London: Longmans Green.

Irenaeus, 1992, *Against the heresies*, translated by D. J. Unger and J. J. Dillon, New York: Paulist Press.

Islam, J. N. 1983, *The Ultimate Fate of the Universe*, Cambridge: CUP.

Jackelén, A. 2002, *Time and Eternity: The Question of Time in Church, Natural Science and Theology*, Neukirchen Vluyn: Neukirchener.

Jaki, S. L. 1977, The History of Science and the Idea of an Oscillating Universe, in *Cosmology, History and Theology*, edited by W. Yourgrau and A. D. Beck, New York: Plenum p 233–51.

Jaki, S. L. 1980, *Cosmos and Creator*, Edinburgh: Scottish Academic Press.

Jammer, M. 1957, *Concept of Force*, Cambridge Massachusetts: Harvard University Press.

Jammer, M. 1971–84, in *Historisches Wörterbuch der Philosophie*, edited by J. Ritter, Basil: J. Ritter.

Jammer, M. 1999, *Einstein and Religion*, Princeton: Princeton University Press.

Jantzen, G. 1984, *God's World, God's Body*, London: DLT.

Jarvis, P. 1995, *Adult and Continuing Education*, London and NY: Routledge.

Jeeves, M. 1997, *Human Nature at the Millennium: Reflections on the Integration of Psychology and Christianity*, Downers Grove: IVP.

Jeeves, M. 2002, Changing Portraits of Human Nature, *Science and Christian Belief* 14. 3–32.

Jeeves, M. 2004, Mind Reading and Soul Searching in the Twenty-first Century: The Scientific Evidence, in *What About the Soul? Neuroscience and Christian Anthropology*, edited by J. B. Green, Nashville: Abingdon. 13–30

Jeeves, M. A. and R. J. Berry 1998, *Science, Life and Christian Belief*, Leicester: Apollos.

Jeremias, J. 1956, Flesh and Blood Cannot Inherit the Kingdom of God, *NTS* 2. 151–59.

Jeremias, J. 1972, *The Parables of Jesus*, London: SCM.

Jewett, P. K. 1985, *Election and Predestination*, Grand Rapids: Eerdmans.

Jewett, R. 1984, Coming to Terms with the Doom Boom, *Quarterly Review* 4 (3). 9–22.

Johnson, A. 1996, Firstfruits and Death's Defeat: Metaphor in Paul's Rhetorical Strategy in 1 Cor 15.20–28, *Word and World* 16. 461.

Johnson, A. 2003, Turning the World Upside Down in 1 Corinthians 15: Apocalyptic Epistemology, the Resurrected Body, and the New Creation *Evangelical Quarterley* 75.4, 291–309.

Johnson, E. A. 1993, *Women, Earth and Creator Spirit*, New York: Paulist Press.

Johnson, L. T. 2001, *The First and Second Letters to Timothy*, *The Anchor Bible*, New York: Doubleday.

Johnston, P. S. 2002, *Shades of Sheol: Death and Afterlife in the Old Testament*, Downers Grove: IVP.

Jones, B. F. 2007, *Marks of his wounds: gender politics and bodily resurrection*, Oxford: Oxford University Press.

Jones, D. G. 2004, A Neurobiological Portrait of the Human Person: Finding a Context for Approaching the Brain, in *What About the Soul? Neuroscience and Christian Anthropology*, edited by J. B. Green, Nashville: Abingdon 31–46.

Jones, F. S. 1987, *'Freiheit' in den Briefen des Apostels Paulus*, Göttingen: Vandenhoek & Ruprecht.

Jones, G. 1996, The Resurrection in Contemporary Systematic Theology, in *Resurrection Reconsidered*, edited by G. D'Costa, Oxford: Oneworld 31–47.

Käsemann, E. 1960, *Exegetische Versuche und Besinnungen*, Vol. II, Göttingen: Vandenhoeck and Ruprecht.

Käsemann, E. 1969, *New Testament Questions of Today*, Philadelphia: Fortress.

Käsemann, E. 1980, *Commentary on Romans*, Grand Rapids: Eerdmans.

Kauffman, S. 1995, *At Home in the Universe*, Oxford: OUP.

Kaufman, G. D. 1968, On the meaning of 'Act of God', *Harvard Theological Review* 61. 175–201.

Kendall, R. E. 2001, The Distinction Between Mental and Physical Illness, *Brit. J. Psychiatry* 178. 490–493.

Kennedy, H. A. A. 1904, *St. Paul's Conception of the Last Things*, London: Hodder and Stoughton.

Kermode, F. 1967, *Sense of an Ending*, London: OUP.

Kidner, D. 1967, *Genesis*, London: Tyndale.

Kim, J. H. and J. Stringer, eds. 1992, *Applied Chaos*, New York: John Wiley & Sons.

Kirshner, R. P. 2004, *The extravagant universe: exploding stars, dark energy, and the accelerating cosmos*, Princeton, N.J.; Woodstock: Princeton University Press.

Kittel, G. and G. Friedrich, eds. 1964–76, *Theological Dictionary of the New Testament*, Vol. 6, Grand Rapids: Eerdmans.

Kloos, C. 1986, *Yhwh's Combat with the Sea: A Canaanite Tradition in the Religion of Ancient Israel*, Leiden Brill Amsterdam: G. A van Oorschot.

Kneale, W. C. 1960–1, Time and Eternity in Theology, *Proceedings of the Aristotelian Society*, 87–108.

Knight, J. 1736, *A Discourse on the Conflagration and Renovation of the World*, London: J. Cox.

Knop, R. A. et. al. 2003, New Constraints on Ω_M, Ω_A, and w from an Independent Set of Eleven High-Redshift Supernovae Observed with HST, *Astrophys. J.* 598. 102–37.

Koester, H. 1992, Jesus the Victim, *Journal of Biblical Literature* 111. 14.

Koyré, A. 1957, *From the closed world to the infinite Universe*, Baltimore: John Hopkins University Press.

Kragh, H. 1996, *Cosmology and Controversy: The Historical Development of New Theories of the Universe*, Princeton: Princeton University Press.

Krauss, L. *The Physics of Star Trek*, London: Flamingo.

Krauss, L. and G. Starkman 1999, The Fate of Life in the Universe, *Sci. Amer.* 281. 58–65.

Krauss, L. and G. Starkman 2000, Life, the Universe and Nothing: Life and Death in an Ever Expanding Universe, *Astrophysics Journal* 531. 22–31.

Kümmel, W. G. 1974, *The Theology of the New Testament*, London: SCM.

Künneth, W. 1965, *The Theology of the Resurrection*, London: SCM.

Küppers, B.-0. 1985, *Molecular Theory of Evolution*, New York: Springer-Verlag.

Küppers, B.-0. 1990, *Information and the Origin of Life*, Cambridge: MIT Press.

Küppers, B.-0. 1995, The Context-Dependence of Biological Information, *Ludus Vitalis*, *3* (5). 5–17.

Kurzweil, R. 1999, *The Age of Spiritual Machines: When Computers Exceed Human Intelligence*, New York: Penguin.

Kvanvig, J. L. 1986, *The Possibility of an All-Knowing God*, London: Macmillan.

Kyle, R. 1998, *The Last Days Are Here Again: A History of the End Times*, Grand Rapids: Baker.

Ladd, G. E. 1974, *The Presence of the Future: The Eschatology of Biblical Realism*, Grand Rapids: Eerdmans.

LaHaye, T. 1999, *Revelation Unveiled*, Grand Rapids: Zondervan.

LaHaye, T. and J. Jenkins 1995, *Left Behind*, Illinois: Tyndale.

LaHaye, T. and J. Jenkins 1999, *Are We Living in the End Times?* Illinois: Tyndale.

Lampe, P. 2002, Paul's Concept of a Spiritual Body, in *Resurrection: Theological and Scientific Assessments*, edited by T. Peters, R. J. Russell and M. Welker, Grand Rapids: Eerdmans 103–14.

Lapidge, M. 1989, Bede's Metrical Vita S. Cuthberti, in *St. Cuthbert, His Cult and Community*, edited by G. Bonner, D. Rollason and C. Stancliffe, Woodbridge: Boydell.

Leenhardt, F. J. 1961, *The Epistle to the Romans*, London: Lutterworth.

LeRon Schults, F. 1999, *The Postfoundationalist Task of Theology: Wolfhart Pannenberg and the New Theological Rationality*, Grand Rapids: Eerdmans.

Leslie, J. 1998, *The End of the World*, London: Routledge.

Leslie, J. 2000, Intelligent Life in our Universe, in *Many Worlds: The New Universe, Extraterrestrial Life and the Theological Implications*, edited by S. J. Dick, Radnor: Templeton Foundation Press 119–34.

Lewis, C. S. 1967, *Miracles: a preliminary study*, London: Fontana Books.

Lewis, C. S. 1984, *The Problem of Pain*, London: Fount.

Lichtenberg, A. J. and M. A. Lieberman 1983, *Regular and Stochastic Motion*, New York: Springer Verlag.

Lietzmann, H. 1949, *An die Korinther*, edited by W. G. Kümmel, Tübingen: Mohr/Siebeck.

Lighthill, J. 1986, The Recently Recognized Failure of Predictability in Newtonian Dynamics, *Proceedings of the Royal Society of London* A407. 38, 35.

Lincoln, A. T. 1981, *Paradise Now and Not Yet*, Vol. 43, *SNTSMS*. Cambridge: CUP.

Lindars, B. 1983, The Resurrection and the Empty Tomb, in *The Resurrection of Jesus Christ*, edited by P. Avis, London: DLT 116–35.

Lindars, B. 1987, *The Gospel of John, The New Century Bible Commentary*, Grand Rapids: Eerdmans.

Linde, A. 1994, The Self Reproducing Inflationary Universe, *Scientific American* 32 (5). 32–39.

Lindemann, A. 2000, *Der Erste Korintherbrief*, Tübingen: Mohr.

Lindsay, H. 1970, *The Late Great Planet Earth*, New York: Bantam.

Linzey, A. 1976, *Animal Rights: A Christian Assessment of Man's Treatment of Animals*, London: SCM.

Linzey, A. 1994, *Animal Theology*, London: SCM.

Linzey, A. and D.C. Sherbok, eds. 1997, *After Noah: Animals and the Liberation of Theology*, London: Mowbray.

Linzey, A. 1998, Introduction, in *Animals on the Agenda*, edited by A. Linzey and D. Yamamoto, London: SCM 3–7.

Linzey, A. 1998, Is Christianity Irredeemably Speciesist? In *Animals on the Agenda*, edited by A. Linzey and D. Yamamoto, London: SCM xi–xx.

Linzey, A. 2009, *Why Animal Suffering Matters: Philosophy, Theology, and Practical Ethics*, New York: OUP.

Lissauer, J. J. 1999, How Common Are Habitable Planets? *Nature* 402. C11–C14.

Lloyd, M. 1996, The Fall, in *Dictionary of Ethics, Theology and Society*, edited by P. B. Clarke and A. Linzey, London: Routledge 370.

Lloyd, M. 1998, Are Animals Fallen? In *Animals on the Agenda*, edited by A. Linzey and D. Yamamoto, London: SCM 147–60.

Loewenstein, W. 1998, *The Touchstone of Life*, New York: Oxford University Press.

Long, D. S. and G. Kalantzis 2009, *The sovereignty of God debate*, Eugene, Or.: Cascade Books.

Lorenz, E. N. 1963, Deterministic Nonperiodic Flow, *Journal of the Atmospheric Sciences* 20. 130–41.

Lovelock, J. 1989, *The Ages of Gaia*, Oxford: OUP.

Lucas, J. R. 1973, *A Treatise on Time and Space*, London: Meuthuen & Co.

Lüdemann, G. 1994, *The Resurrection of Jesus*, London: SCM.

Macquarrie, J. 1977, *Principles of Christian Theology*, London: SCM Press.

Maddox, R. 1994, *Responsible Grace: John Wesley's Practical Theology*, Nashville: Kingswood Books.

Maddox, R. 2001, Seeking a Response-able God: The Wesleyan Tradition and Process Theology? In *In Thy Nature and Thy Name is Love: Process and Wesleyan Theologies in Dialogue*, edited by B. Stone and T. Oord, Nashville: Kingswood Books 111–42.

Maddox, R. 2004, Nurturing The New Creation: Reflections On A Wesleyan Trajectory, in *Wesleyan Perspectives on the New Creation*, edited by M. D. Meeks, Kingswood Books 21–52.

Manson, T. W. 1962, 'Romans', in *Peake's Commentary on the Bible*, edited by M. Black and H. H. Rowley, London: Thomas Nelson 940–53.

Marshall, I. H. 1978, *The Gospel of Luke: A Commentary on the Greek Text, NIGTC*, Exeter: Paternoster.

Martin, D. B. 1995, *The Corinthian Body*, New Haven: Yale University Press.

Martin, R. P. 1984, *The Spirit and the Congregation: Studies in 1 Cor 12–15*, Grand Rapids: Eerdmans.

Martin, R. P. 1986, *2 Corinthians, Word Biblical Commentary*, Waco, Texas: Word.

Martos, J. 1991, *Doors to the Sacred*, Tarrytown: Triumph Books.

Martyn, J. L. 1997, Epistemology at the Turn of the Ages, in *Theological Issues in the Letters of Paul*, Nashville: Abingdon 89–110.

Marxsen, W. 1970, *The Resurrection of Jesus of Nazareth*, Philadelphia: Fortress Press.

Mascall, E. L. 1943, *He Who Is: A Study in Traditional Theism*, London: Longmans, Green and Co.

Mascall, E. L. 1956, *Christian Theology and Natural Science*, London: Longmans Green and Co.

Mascall, E. L. 1966, *The Christian Universe*, London: DLT.

Mason, R. 2000, Life Before and After Death in the Old Testament, in *Called to One Hope*, edited by J. Coldwell, Carlisle: Paternoster 67–82.

May, S. 1998, *Stardust and Ashes: Science Fiction in Christian Perspective*, London: SPCK.

Mayor, M. and P.-Y. Frei 2003, *New Worlds in the Cosmos: The Discovery of Exoplanets*, Cambridge: Cambridge University Press.

McClendon Jr., J. W. 1994, *Doctrine: Systematic Theology*, Vol. 2, Nashville: Abingdon.

McDaniel, J. 1998, Can Animal Suffering be Reconciled with Belief in an All-Loving God? In *Animals on the Agenda*, edited by A. Linzey and D. Yamamoto, London: SCM 161–70.

McDannell, C. and B. Lang 1988, *Heaven: A History*, New Haven: Yale University Press.

McFague, S. 1993, *The Body of God: An Ecological Theology*, Minneapolis: Fortress Press.

McFague, S. 2008, *A new climate for theology: God, the world, and global warming*, Philadelphia: Fortress.

McGowan, A. T. B. 2006, *Always reforming: explorations in systematic theology*, Leicester: Apollos.

McGrath, A. 1990, *The Genesis of Doctrine: A Study in the Foundation of Doctrinal Criticism*, Grand Rapids: Eerdmans.

McGrath, A. 1998, *Christian Theology: An Introduction*, Oxford: Blackwell.

McGrath, A. 2001–3, *A Scientific Theology*, Vol. 1 Nature, Grand Rapids: Eerdmans.

McGrath, J. 2002, Religion, But Not as We Know It: Spirituality and Sci-Fi, in *Religion in Entertainment*, edited by C. K. Robertson, New York: Peter Lang 153–72.

McKay, C. P. 2000, Astrobiology: The Search for Life Beyond the Earth, in *Many Worlds: The New Universe, Extraterrestrial Life and the Theological Implications*, edited by S. J. Dick, Radnor: Templeton Foundation Press 45–58.

McMullin, E. 1981, How Shall Cosmology Relate to Theology? In *The Sciences and Theology in the Twentieth Century*, edited by A. R. Peacocke, Notre Dame: University of Notre Dame Press 50–2.

McMullin, E. 2000, Biology and the Theology of Human Nature, in *Controlling Our Destinies: Historical, Philosophical and Ethical Perspectives on the Human Genome Project*, edited by P. Sloan, Notre Dame: University of Notre Dame Press 367–93.

McMullin, E. 2000, Life and Intelligence Far From Earth: Formulating Theological Issues, in *Many Worlds: The New Universe, Extraterrestrial Life and the Theological Implications*, edited by S. J. Dick, Radnor: Templeton Foundation Press 151–76.

McTaggart, J. M. E. 1927, *The Nature of Existence*, Cambridge: The University Press.

Mealy, J. W. 1992, *After the Thousand Years JSNT Supplement Series 70*, Sheffield: JSOT.

Melling, P. 1999, *Fundamentalism in America*, Edinburgh: Edinburgh University Press.

Meyer, H. A. W. 1884, *Critical and Exegetical Handbook to the Epistles to the Corinthians*. 2 vols., Vol. 2, Edinburgh: T&T. Clark.

Middleton, E. 2002, *The New Flatlanders: A Seeker's Guide to the Theory of Everything*, Godalming: Highland.

Milburn, G. 1998, *The Feynman Processor*, Sydney: Allen & Unwin.

Miller, P. D. 1994, Whatever happened to the soul, *Theology Today* 50. 507–19.

Miller, P. D. 2004, What is a Human Being? The Anthropology of Scripture, in *What About the Soul? Neuroscience and Christian Anthropology*, edited by J. B. Green, Nashville: Abingdon. 63–74

Milne, E. A. 1952, *Modern Cosmology and the Christian Idea of God*, London: OUP.

Mitchell, M. M. 1992, *Paul and the Rhetoric of Reconciliation: An exegetical investigation of the language and composition of 1 Corinthians*, Louisville: Westminster/Knox.

Moffatt, J. 1938, *The First Epistle of Paul to the Corinthians*, *Moffatt New Testament Commentary*, London: Hodder and Stoughton.

Molnar, P. 1995, Some Problems with Pannenberg's Solution to Barth's 'Faith Subjectivism', *Scottish Journal of Theology* 48. 330.

Moltmann, J. 1967, *Theology of Hope: On the Grounds and Implications of a Christian Eschatology*, London: SCM Press.

Moltmann, J. 1981, *The Trinity and the Kingdom of God*, London: SCM.

Moltmann, J. 1985, *God in Creation: An Ecological Doctrine of Creation*. London: SCM.

Moltmann, J. 1990, *The Way of Jesus Christ*, London: SCM.

Moltmann, J. 1996a, *The Coming of God: Christian Eschatology*, London: SCM Press.

Moltmann, J. 1996b, The Resurrection of Christ: Hope for the World, in *Resurrection Reconsidered*, edited by G. D'Costa, Oxford: Oneworld 73–86.

Moltmann, J. 2000a, *Experiences in Theology: Ways of Forms of Christian Theology, Part I, 6: Natural Theology*, London: SCM.

Moltmann, J. 2000b, Is the World Coming to an End or Has Its Future Already Begun? In *The Future as God's Gift*, edited by D. Fergusson and M. Sarot, Edinburgh: T&T Clark 129–38.

Moltmann, J. 2000c, Is There Life After Death? In *The End of the World and the Ends of God: Science and Theology on Eschatology*, edited by J. C. Polkinghorne and M. Welker, Harrisburg, PA: Trinity Press International 238–55.

Moltmann, J. 2002, Cosmos and Theosis: Eschatological Perspectives on the Future of the Universe, in *The Far Future Universe: Eschatology from a Cosmic Perspective*, edited by G. F. R. Ellis, Radnor: Templeton Foundation Press 249–65.

Monbiot, G. 2006, *Heat: how to stop the planet burning*, London: Allen Lane.

Moravec, H. 1988, *Mind Children: The Future of Robot and Human Intelligence*, Cambridge: Harvard University Press.

Moreland, J. P. and S. B. Rae 2000, *Body and Soul: Human Nature and the Crisis in Ethics*, Downers Grove: IVP.

Morgan, R. 1994, Flesh is Precious: The Significance of Luke 24.36–43, in *Resurrection: Essays in Honour of Leslie Holden*, edited by S. Barton and G. Stanton, London: SPCK 8–20.

Morris, L. 1971, *The Gospel According to John*, London: Marshall, Morgan and Scott.

Morris, L. 1982, *Paul's Apocalyptic Gospel*, Philadelphia.

Morris, L. 1985, *1 Corinthians*, *Tyndale New Testament Commentaries*, Leicester: IVP.

Morris, L. 1988, *The Epistle to the Romans*, Grand Rapids: Eerdmans.

Motyer, A. N. 1993, *The Prophecy of Isaiah*, Leicester: IVP.

Moulaison, J. B. 2007, 'Our bodies, our selves?' The body as source in feminist theology, *Scottish Journal of Theology*, 60 341–59.

Mullholland, M. R. 1990, *Revelation*, Grand Rapids: Eerdmans.

Murphy, N. 2000, Science and Society, in *Systematic Theology, Vol 3: Witness*, edited by J. W. McClendon and N. Murphy, Nashville: Abingdon 99–131.

Murphy, N. 2002, The Resurrection Body and Personal Identity: Possibilities and Limits of Eschatological Knowledge, in *Resurrection: Theological and Scientific Assessments*, edited by T. Peters, R. J. Russell and M. Welker, Grand Rapids: Eerdmans 202–18.

Murphy, N. and G Ellis 1996, *On the Moral Nature of the Universe: Theology, Cosmology and Ethics*, Minneapolis: Fortress Press.

Murray, R. 1992, *The Cosmic Covenant, Biblical Themes of Justice Peace and the Integrity of Creation*, London: Sheed and Ward.

Myers, D. G. and M. A. Jeeves 2002, *Psychology Through the Eyes of Faith*, San Francisco: Harper.

Newton, I. 1952, *Optiks*, 4th ed, New York: Dover. Original edition, 1730.

Norden, E. 1923, *Agnostos Theos: Untersuchungen zur Formengeschichte Religiöser Rede*, Darmstadt: Wissenschaftliche Buchgesellschaft.

North, R. 1974, in *Theological Dictionary of the Old Testament*, edited by G. J. Botterwick and H. Ringgren, Grand Rapids: Eerdmans 225–44.

Northcott, M. S. 2007, *A moral climate: the ethics of global warming*, London: Darton Longman & Todd.

O'Brien, P. T. 1982, *Colossians, Philemon, Word Biblical Commentary*, Waco, Texas: Word.

O'Collins, G. 1978, *What are they saying about the Resurrection*, New York: Paulist Press.

O'Collins, G. 1987, *Jesus Risen*, New York: Paulist Press.

O'Collins, G. and D. Kendall 1997, *The Bible for Theology: Ten Principles for the Theological Use of Scripture*, New York: Paulist.

O'Donovan, O. 1986a, The Political Thought of the Book of Revelation, *Tyndale Bulletin* 37. 90.

O'Donovan, O. 1986b, *Resurrection and Moral Order*, Leicester: IVP.

Oberdorfer, B. 2002, Schleiermacher on Eschatology and Resurrection, in *Resurrection: Theological and Scientific Assessments*, edited by T. Peters, R. J. Russell and M. Welker, Grand Rapids: Eerdmans 165–82.

Ogden, S. M. 1963, What Sense Does It Make To Say 'God Acts in History'? In *The Reality of God and Other Essays*, New York: Harper and Row 164–87.

Ostriker, J. P. and P. J. Steinhardt 2001, The Quintessential Universe, *Sci. Am.*, January: 46–63.

Oswalt, J. N. 1988, *The Book of Isaiah Chapters 1–39*, Grand Rapids: Eerdmans.

Outler, A. 1968, *Who Trusts in God: Musings on the Meaning of Providence*, New York: Oxford University Press.

Owen, H. P. 1984, *Christian Theism: A Study in Its Basic Principles*, Edinburgh: T&T Clark.

Padgett, A. G. 1992, *God, Eternity and the Nature of Time*, New York: St Martins.

Padgett, A. G. 2002a, The Body in Resurrection: Science and Scripture on the Spiritual Body (1 Cor 15.35–58), *Word and World* 22 (2). 155ff.

Padgett, A. G. 2002b, Private Communication.

Page, R. 1985, *Ambiguity and the Presence of God*, London: SCM.

Page, R. 1996, *God and the Web of Creation*, London: SCM.

Pailin, D. 1989, *God and the Processes of Reality: Foundations of a Credible Theism*, London: Routledge.

Paley, W. 1825, Natural Theology (1802), in *The Works of William Paley*, edited by R. Lyman, London.

Pannenberg, W. 1968, *Jesus: God and Man*, London: SCM.

Pannenberg, W. 1970, Kotingenz und Naturgestz, in *Erwängungen zu einer Theologie der Natur*, edited by A. M. K. Müller and W. Pannenberg, Gütersloh: Verslagshaus Gerd Mohn.

Pannenberg, W. 1970, *What is Man?* Philadelphia: Fortress Press.

Pannenberg, W. 1971, The God of Hope, in *Basic Questions in Theology*, Philadelphia: Fortress Press 2.237.

Pannenberg, W. 1972, *The Apostles' Creed in the Light of Today's Questions*, London: SCM.

Pannenberg, W. 1981, Theological Questions to Scientists, *Zygon* 16. 65–77.

Pannenberg, W. 1984, Constructive and Critical Functions of Christian Eschatology, *Harvard Theological Review* 72. 119–39.

Pannenberg, W. 1985, *Anthropology in Theological Perspective*, Edinburgh: T&T Clark.

Pannenberg, W. 1988, A Response to My American Friends, in *The Theology of Wolfhart Pannenberg: Twelve American critiques, with an autobiographical essay and response*, edited by C. E. Braaten and P. Clayton, Minneapolis: Augsburg 313–36.

Pannenberg, W. 1988, Theology of Nature, *Zygon* 23. 1. 21.

Pannenberg, W. 1989, Theological Appropriation of Scientific Understandings: Response to Hefner, Wicken, Eaves and Tipler, *Zygon: Journal of Religion and Science* 24. 255–71.

Pannenberg, W. 1991–98, *Systematic Theology*, 3 vols., Grand Rapids: Eerdmans.

Pannenberg, W. 1993, *Towards a Theology of Nature: Essays on Science and Faith*, edited by T. Peters, Louisville, Kentucky: Westminster/John Knox Press.

Pannenberg, W. 1995, Breaking a Taboo: Frank Tipler's The Physics of Immortality, *Zygon* 30. 309–14.

Pannenberg, W. 1996, History and the Reality of the Resurrection, in *Resurrection Reconsidered*, edited by G. D'Costa, Oxford: Oneworld 62–72.

Pannenberg, W. and L. Ford 1977, A Dialog about Process Philosophy, *Encounter* 38. 319–20.

Parsons, S. F. 1996, *Feminism and Christian Ethics*, Cambridge: CUP.

Patterson, S. J. 1998, *The God of Jesus: The Historical Jesus and the Search for Meaning*, Harrisburg: TPI.

Patzia, A. G. 1995, *Ephesians, Colossians, Philemon, New International Bible Commentary*, Carlisle: Paternoster.

Peacock, R. E. 1989, *A Brief History of Eternity*, Tunbridge Wells: Monarch.

Peacocke, A. 1979, *Creation and the World of Science*, Oxford: Clarendon.

Peacocke, A. 1990, *Theology for a Scientific Age*, London: SCM.

Peacocke, A. 1995, God's Interaction with the World, in *Chaos and Complexity: Scientific Perspectives on Divine Action*, edited by R. J. Russell, N. Murphy and A. R. Peacocke, Notre Dame: Vatican Observatory/University of Notre Dame Press 263–88.

Peacocke, A. 1998, Welcoming the disguised friend – a positive theological appraisal of biological evolution, in *Evolutionary and Molecular Biology:*

Scientific Perspectives on Divine Action, edited by R. J. Russell, F. J. Ayala and W. R. Stoeger, Notre Dame, Indiana: Vatican Observatory and the Center for Theology and the Natural Sciences/University of Notre Dame Press 357–76.

Peacocke, A. 2001, *Paths From Science Towards God: The End of all our Exploring*, Oxford: Oneworld.

Pearson, B. A. 1973, *The Pneumatikos-Psychikos Terminology in 1 Corinthians: A Study in the Theology of the Corinthian Opponents of Paul and Its Relation to Gnosticism*, Missoula: Scholars Press.

Peiris, H. V. et. al., 2003, First Year Wilkinson Microwave Anisotropy Probe (WMAP) Observations: Implications for Inflation, *Astrophys.J.Suppl.* 148. 213.

Penrose, R. 1989, *The Emperor's New Mind: Concerning Computers, Minds and the Laws of Physics*, Oxford: OUP.

Perkins, P. 1984. *Resurrection: New Testament Witness and Contemporary Reflection.* Garden City: NY.

Perlmutter, S. 2003. Supernovae, Dark Energy, and the Accelerating Universe. *Physics Today* April 2003. 53–60.

Peters, T. 1993, *God as Trinity: Relationality and Temporality in the Divine Life*, Louisville: Westminster/John Knox Press.

Peters, T. 2002, Introduction, in *Resurrection: Theological and Scientific Assessments*, edited by T. Peters, R. J. Russell and M.Welker, Grand Rapids: Eerdmans viii–xvii.

Phan, P. C. 1995, Woman and the Last Things, in *In the Embrace of God: Feminist Approaches to Theological Anthropology*, edited by A. O'Hara Graff, New York: Orbis Books 206–28.

Picirilli, R. E. 2000, Foreknowledge, Freedom and the Future, *Journal of the Evangelical Theological Society* 43. 259–71.

Pike, N. 1970, *God and Timelessness*, London: Routledge & Kegan Paul.

Pinnock, C. H. 1996, *Flame of Love: A Theology of the Holy Spirit*, Downers Grove: IVP.

Pinnock, C. H. 2001, *Most Moved Mover: A Theology of God's Openness*, Grand Rapids: Baker.

Pinnock, C. H., R. Rice, J. Sanders, W. Hasker and D. Basinger 1994, *The Openness of God: A Biblical Challenge to the Traditional Understanding of God*, Downers Grove: IVP.

Pittenger, W. N. 1959, *The Word Incarnate*, London: Nisbet.

Placher, W. 1992, Revealed to Reason: Theology as 'Normal Science', *The Christian Century* 109. 195.

Plantinga, A. 1974, *God, Freedom and Evil*, New York: Harper and Row.

Plantinga, A. 1987, On Ockham's Way Out, in *The Concept of God*, edited by T. V. Morris, Oxford: Oxford University Press 171–200.

Polk, D. P. 1988, The All-Determining God and The Peril of Determinism, in *The Theology of Wolfhart Pannenberg: Twelve American critiques, with an autobiographical essay and response*, edited by C. E. Braaten and P. Clayton, Minneapolis: Augsburg 152–68.

Polkinghorne, J. C. 1988, *Science and Providence*, London: SPCK.

Polkinghorne, J. C. 1991, *Reason and Reality*, London: SPCK.

Polkinghorne, J. C. 1994a, *Science and Christian Belief*, London: SPCK.

Polkinghorne, J. C. 1994b, *The Faith of a Physicist*, Princeton: Princeton University Press.

Polkinghorne, J. C. 1996a, *Beyond Science*, Cambridge: CUP.

Polkinghorne, J. C. 1996b, *Scientists as Theologians*, London: SPCK.

Polkinghorne, J. C. 1998, *Science and Theology*, London: SPCK.

Polkinghorne, J. C. 2000, Eschatology, in *The End of the World and the Ends of God: Science and Theology on Eschatology*, edited by J. C. Polkinghorne and M. Welker, Harrisburg, PA: Trinity Press International 29–41.

Polkinghorne, J. C. 2002a, Eschatological Credibility: Emergent and Teleological Processes, in *Resurrection: Theological and Scientific Assessments*, edited by T. Peters, R. J. Russell and M. Welker, Grand Rapids: Eerdmans 43–55.

Polkinghorne, J. C. 2002b, *The God of Hope and the End of the World*, London: SPCK.

Polkinghorne, J. C. ed. 2001, *The Work of Love*, London: SPCK.

Polkinghorne, J. C. and M. Welker, eds. 2000, *The End of the World and the Ends of God: Science and Theology on Eschatology*, Harrisburg, PA: Trinity Press International.

Porter, S. E. 1999, Resurrection, the Greeks and the New Testament, in *Resurrection*, edited by S. E. Porter, M. A. Hayes and D. Tombs, Sheffield: Sheffield Academic Press 52–81.

Prance, G. 1996, *The Earth Under Threat: A Christian Perspective*, Iona: Wild Goose Publications.

Price, R. M. 2007, *The paperback apocalypse: how the Christian church was left behind*, Amherst, N.Y.: Prometheus Books.

Prigogine, I. 1997, *The End of Certainty: Time, Chaos, and the New Laws of Nature*, New York: Free Press.

Prokes, M. T. 1996, *Toward a Theology of the Body*, Edinburgh: T&T Clark.

Quinton, A. 1973, *The Nature of Things*, London: Routledge and Kegan Paul.

Race, A. 1994, Global Threats and Global Hope in Multi-religious Perspective, in *Resurrection: Essays in Honour of Leslie Holden*, edited by S. Barton and G. Stanton, London: SPCK 177–87.

Radford Ruether, R. 1983, *Sexism and God-Talk: Towards a Feminist Theology*, London: SCM.

Radford Ruether, R. 1990, Eschatology and Feminism, in *Lift Every Voice: Constructing Christian Theologies from the Underside*, edited by S. Brooks Thistlewaite and M. Potter Engel, San Francisco: Harper.

Radford Ruether, R. 1992, *Gaia and God: An Ecofeminist Theology of Earth Healing*, San Francisco: Harper.

Rahner, K. 1963, *The Church and the Sacraments*, New York: Sheed and Ward.

Rahner, K. 1966, *Theological Investigations Vol. 4*, translated by K. Smyth, London: DLT.

Rahner, K. 1974, The Hermeneutics of Eschatological Assertions, in *Theological Investigations Vol. 4*, London: DLT 323–46.

Randall, L. and R. Sundrum 1999, An Alternative to Compactification, *Phys. Lett.* 83. 4690.

Rees, M. 2000, *Just Six Numbers: The Deep Forces that Shape the Universe*, London: Weidenfeld and Nicholson.

Rees, M. 2002, Living in a Multiverse, in *The Far Future Universe: Eschatology from a Cosmic Perspective*, edited by G. F. R. Ellis, Radnor: Templeton Foundation Press 65–88.

Rees, M. 2003, *Our Final Hour*, New York: Basic Books.

Reicke, B., quoted in M. Green 1983, *2 Peter and Jude*, Leicester: IVP.

Ricoeur, P. 1974, Religion, Atheism, and Faith, in *The Conflict of Interpretations: Essays in Hermeneutics*, edited by D. Ihde, Evanston, IL: Northwestern University Press 455–67.

Ricoeur, P. 1984, *Time and Narrative*, Chicago: University of Chicago Press.

Riddlebarger, K. 2003, *A case for amillennialism: understanding the end times*, Leicester, England; Grand Rapids, Michigan: Baker Books, Inter-Varsity Press.

Riess, A. et.al., 1998, Observational Evidence from Supernovae for an Accelerating Universe and a Cosmological Constant, *Astron. J.* 116. 1009.

Riess, A. et. al., 2001, The Farthest Known Supernova: Support for an Accelerating Universe and a Glimpse of the Epoch of Deceleration, *Astrophys. J.* 560. 49–71.

Riley, G. 1995, *Resurrection Reconsidered: Thomas and John in Controversy*, Minneapolis: Fortress.

Robertson, A. and A. Plummer 1916, *A Critical and Exegetical Commentary on the First Epistle of St. Paul to the Corinthians*, *ICC*, New York: Scribner's.

Robertson, D. S., M. C. McKenna, O. B. Toon, S. Hope and J. A. Lillegraven 2004, Survival in the first hours of the Cenozoic, *Geological Society of America Bulletin* 116 (5). 760–68.

Robinson, J. A. T. 1950, *In the End, God ... A Study of the Christian Doctrine of the Last Things*, London: James Clarke.

Robinson, J. A. T. 1957, *Jesus and His Coming: The Emergence of a Doctrine*, London: SCM.

Robinson, J. A. T. 1979, *Wrestling with Romans*, London: SCM.

Robinson, J. M. 1957, A Formal Analysis of Colossians 1.15–20, *JBL* 76. 270–87.

Robinson, J. M. 1982, Jesus from Easter to Valentinus (or to the Apostles Creed), *Journal of Biblical Literature* 101. 5–37.

Rogerson, J. W. 1998, What was the Meaning of Animal Sacrifice? In *Animals on the Agenda*, edited by A. Linzey and D. Yamamoto, London: SCM 8–17.

Ross, H. 1999, *Beyond the Cosmos*, Colorado Springs: Navpress.

Ross, S. A. 1993, Body, in *New Dictionary of Catholic Spirituality*, edited by M. Downey, Collegeville: Liturgical Press 93–100.

Ross, S. A. 1998, *Extravagant Affections: A Feminist Sacramental Theology*, London: Continuum.

Rowland, C. C. 1982, *The Open Heaven: A Study of Apocalyptic in Judaism and Early Christianity*, SCM Press: London.

Rowland, C. C. 1985, *Christian Origins: From Messianic Movement to Christian Religion*, London: SPCK.

Rudrum, A. 1989, Henry Vaughn, The Liberation of Creatures, and Seventeenth-Century English Calvinism, *Seventeenth Century* 4. 34–54.

Runyon, T. H. 1998, *The New Creation: John Wesley's Theology Today*, Nashville: Abingdon.

Russell, B. 1957, *Why I am not a Christian*, New York: George Allen and Unwin.

Russell, R. J. 1988, Contingency in Physics and Cosmology: A Critique of the Theology of Wolfhart Pannenberg, *Zygon: Journal of Religion and Science* 23. 23–43.

Russell, R. J. 2000, Time in Eternity: Special Relativity and Eschatology, *Dialog* 39 (1). 46–55.

Russell, R. J. 2002a, Bodily Resurrection, Eschatology and Scientific Cosmology, in *Resurrection: Theological and Scientific Assessments*, edited by T. Peters, R. J. Russell and M. Welker, Grand Rapids: Eerdmans 3–30.

Russell, R. J. 2002b, Eschatology and Physical Cosmology: A Preliminary Reflection, in *The Far Future Universe: Eschatology from a Cosmic Perspective*, edited by G. F. R. Ellis, Radnor: Templeton Foundation Press. 266–315

Russell, R. J. 2008, *Cosmology: from alpha to omega: the creative mutual interaction of theology and science*, Minneapolis: Fortress Press.

Russell, R. J., N. Murphy and C. J. Isham, eds. 1993, *Quantum Cosmology and the Laws of Nature: Scientific Perspectives on Divine Action*, Notre Dame: Vatican Observatory/University of Notre Dame Press.

Russell, R. J., N. Murphy, T. C. Meyering and M. A. Arbib, eds. 1999, *Neuroscience and the Person: Scientific Perspectives on Divine Action*, Notre Dame: Vatican Observatory/University of Notre Dame Press.

Russell, R. J., N. Murphy and A. R. Peacocke, eds., 1995, *Chaos and Complexity: Scientific Perspectives on Divine Action*, Notre Dame: Vatican Observatory/University of Notre Dame Press.

Russell, R. J., W. R. Stoeger and F. J. Ayala, eds., 1998, *Evolutionary and Molecular Biology: Scientific Perspectives on Divine Action*, Notre Dame: Vatican Observatory/University of Notre Dame Press.

S. Cyril, Archbishop of Alexandria. 1874–1885, *Commentary on the Gospel according to S. John*, Oxford: J. Parker.

Sagan, C. 1997, *Billions and Billions: Thoughts on Life and Death at the Brink of the Millennium*, New York: Random House.

Sanday, W. and A. C. Headlam 1902, *A Critical and Exegetical Commentary on the Epistle to the Romans, International Critical Commentary*, Edinburgh: T&T Clark.

Sanders, E. P. 1977, *Paul and Palestinian Judaism*, London: SCM.

Sanders, E. P. 1985, *Jesus and Judaism*, London: SCM.

Sanders, E. P. 1993, *The Historical Figure of Jesus*, London: Allen Lane.

Sanders, J. 1998, *The God Who Risks: A Theology of Providence*, Downers Grove: IVP.

Santmire, H. P. 1985, *The Travail of Nature*, Philadelphia: Fortress Press.

Santmire, H. P. 1996, Review of Toward a Theology of Nature, *Interpretation* 50. 88–90.

Sauter, G. 1988, The Concept and Task of Eschatology: Theological and Philosophical Reflections, *SJT* 41. 499.

Schillebeeckx, E. 1963, *Christ the Sacrament of the Encounter with God*, New York: Sheed and Ward.

Schillebeeckx, E. 1979, *Jesus: An Experiment in Christology*, New York: Seabury.

Schillebeeckx, E. 1980, *Christ: The Experience of Jesus as Lord*, New York: Seabury.

Schlatter, A. 1959, *Gottes Gerechtigkeit ein Kommentar zum Römer-brief*, Stuttgart: Calwer.

Schloss, J. P. 2002, From Evolution to Eschatology, in *Resurrection: Theological and Scientific Assessments*, edited by T. Peters, R. J. Russell and M.Welker, Grand Rapids: Eerdmans 56–85.

Schmemann, A. 1965, *The World as Sacrament*, London: DLT.

Schmithals, W. 1971, *Gnosticism in Corinth: An Investigation of the Letters to the Corinthians*, Nashville: Abingdon.

Schüssler Fiorenza, F. 1993, Review Essay: Wolfhart Pannenberg's Systematic Theology Volume 1, *Pro Ecclesia* 2. 239.

Schwarz, H. 2000, *Eschatology*, Grand Rapids: Eerdmans.

Schweickart, R. L., E. T. Lu, P. Hut and C. R. Chapman 2003, The Asteroid Tugboat, *Sci. Amer.* 289 (5). 34–41.

Schweiker, W. 2000, Time as a Moral Space: Moral Cosmologies, Creation and Last Judgement, in *The End of the World and the Ends of God: Science and Theology on Eschatology*, edited by J. C. Polkinghorne and M. Welker, Harrisburg, PA: Trinity Press International 124–40.

Schweitzer, A. 1923, *Civilisation and Ethics*, London: A. & C. Black.

Schwöbel, C. 2000, Last Things first? The Century of Eschatology in Retrospect, in *The Future as God's Gift*, edited by D. Fergusson and M. Sarot, Edinburgh: T&T Clark 217–41.

Seay, C. and G. Garrett 2003, *The Gospel Reloaded*, Colorado Springs: Pinon.

Sellin, G. 1986, *Der Streit um Auferstehung der Toten: Ein religionsgeschichtliche und exegetische Untersuchung von 1 Korinther 15*, Göttingen: Vandenhoeck and Ruprecht.

Senge, P. 1992, *The Fifth Discipline*, New York: Doubleday.

Setzer, C. 2001, Resurrection of the Dead as Symbol and Strategy, *Journal of the American Academy of Religion* 69. 1. 96.

Shankland, R. S. 1961, *Atomic and Nuclear Physics*, New York: Macmillan.

Shults, F. LeRon 2003, *Reforming Theological Anthropology: After the Philosophical Turn to Relationality*, Grand Rapids: Eerdmans.

Sider, R. J. 1977, St Paul's Understanding of the Nature and Significance of the Resurrection in 1 Cor 15.1–19, *NovT* 19.

Slovan, G. 1988, *John, Interpretation*, Atlanta: John Knox Press.

Smith, Q. 1991, An Atheological Argument from Evil Natural Laws, *International Journal for Philosophy of Religion* 29/3. 159–174.

Smolin, L. 1997, *The Life of the Cosmos*, Oxford: OUP.

Southgate, C. 2008, *The groaning of creation: God, evolution, and the problem of evil*, Louisville: Westminster John Knox Press.

Sponheim, P. 1997, To Expand and Deepen the Provisional, in *Beginning with the End: God, Science and Wolfhart Pannenberg*, edited by C. R. Albright and J. Haugen, Chicago, Illinois: Open Court 390–4.

Sproul, R. C. 1997, *Willing to Believe: The Controversy Over Freewill*, Grand Rapids: Baker.

St. Chrysostom 1989, *Homilies on First and Second Corinthians, The Nicene and Post Nicene Fathers Vol. XII*, Grand Rapids: Eerdmans.

St. Maximus Confessor 1862, Ambiguorum Liber, VI, 31, in *Patrologiae cursus completus*, edited by J. P. Migne. Series Graeca: Paris.

Stannard, R. 1989, *The Grounds of Reasonable Belief,* Edinburgh: Scottish Academic Press.

Steck, O. 1978, *World and Environment*, Nashville: Abingdon.

Steiner, G. 1989, *Real Presences Is there anything in what we say?* London: Faber.

Stendahl, K. 1984, *Meanings. The Bible as Document and Guide*, Philadelphia: Fortress.

Stenger, N. 1991, Mind is a Leaking Rainbow, in *Cyberspace: First Steps*, edited by M. Benedikt, Cambridge: MIT 49–58.

Stewart, I. 1989, *Does God Play Dice? The Mathematics of Chaos*. Oxford: Basil Blackwell.

Stewart, J. A. 2000, *Reconstructing Science and Theology in Postmodernity: Pannenberg, ethics and the human sciences*, Aldershot: Ashgate.

Stoeger, W. R. and G. F. R. Ellis 1995, A response to Tipler's omega-point theory, *Science and Christian Belief* 7 (2). 163.

Stone, B. P. and T. J. Oord 2001, *Thy Nature and Thy Name is Love: Wesleyan and Process Theologies in Dialogue*, Nashville: Kingswood.

Stonier, T. 1992, *Beyond Information: The Natural History of Intelligence*, London: Springer.

Strack, H. and P. Billerbeck 1926, *Kommentar zum Neuen Testament*, Munich: Beck'she.

Stuart, E. 2000, Disruptive Bodies: Disability, Embodiment and Sexuality, in *The Good News of the Body – Sexual Theology and Feminism*, edited by L. Isherwood, Sheffield: Sheffield Academic Press 166–85.

Stump, E. and N. Kretzmann 1987, Eternity, in *The Concept of God*, edited by T. V. Morris, Oxford: Oxford University Press 219–52.

Sweet, J. P. M. 1979, *Revelation*, London: SCM.

Swinburne, R. 1981, *Space and Time*, London: Macmillan.

Swinburne, R. 1986, *The Evolution of the Soul*, Oxford: OUP.

Taliaferro, C. 1994, *Consciousness and the Mind of God*, Cambridge: CUP.

Tanner, K. 2000, Eschatology Without a Future, in *The End of the World and the Ends of God: Science and Theology on Eschatology*, edited by J. C. Polkinghorne and M. Welker, Harrisburg, PA: Trinity Press International 222–37.

Tegmark, M. 1998, Is 'the theory of everything' merely the ultimate ensemble theory? *Ann. Phys, (NY)* 270. 1.

Temple, W. 1934, *Nature, Man and God*, London: Macmillan.

Thacker, A. 2001, *A Closer Look at Science Fiction*, Eastbourne: Kingsway.

Thielicke, H. 1978, *Theological Ethics*, 3 vols., Vol. 1, Grand Rapids: Eerdmans.

Thiselton, A. C. 1964, *Eschatology and the Holy Spirit in Paul With Special Reference to 1 Cor*, M.Th., London.

Thiselton, A. C. 1978, Realized Eschatology at Corinth, *NTS* 24. 510–26.

Thiselton, A. C. 1992, *New Horizons in Hermeneutics: The Theory and Practice of Transforming Biblical Reading*, London: HarperCollins.

Thiselton, A. C. 2000a, Signs of the Times: Towards a Theology for the Year 2000 as a Grammar of Grace, Truth and Eschatology in Contexts of So-Called Postmodernity, in *The Future as God's Gift*, edited by D. Fergusson and M. Sarot, Edinburgh: T&T Clark 9–39.

Thiselton, A. C. 2000b, *The First Epistle to the Corinthians*, Grand Rapids: Eerdmans.

Thomas, G. 2002, Resurrection to New Life: Pneumatological Implications of the Eschatological Transition, in *Resurrection: Theological and Scientific Assessments*, edited by T. Peters, R. J. Russell and M. Welker, Grand Rapids: Eerdmans 255–76.

Thomas, O. C. 1983, Introduction, in *God's Activity in the World: The Contemporary Problem*, edited by O. C. Thomas, Chico, California: Scholars Press 1–14.

Thomson, W. 1852, On a Universal Tendency in Nature to the Dissipation of Mechanical Energy, *Philosophical Magazine* 4.4. 304–6.

Thrall, M. E. 2002, Paul's understanding of Continuity Between the Present Life and the Life of the Resurrection, in *Resurrection in the New Testament (FS J. Lambrecht)*, edited by R. Bieringer, V. Koperski and B. Lataire, Leuven: Peeters 283–300.

Tillich, P. 1951, *Systematic Theology*, Chicago: University of Chicago.

Tipler, F. J. 1988, *Times Higher Education Supplement*, 832. 23.

Tipler, F. J. 1989, The Omega Point as Eschaton: Answers to Pannenberg's Questions For Scientists, *Zygon: Journal of Religion and Science* 24. 217–253.

Tipler, F. J. 1994, *The Physics of Immortality*, London: Weidenfeld & Nicolson.

Toon, P. 1970, The Latter Day Glory, in *Puritan Eschatology*, edited by P. Toon, London: James Clarke 23–41.

Torrance, T. F. 1969, *Space, Time and Incarnation*, London: OUP.

Torrance, T. F. 1974, The Relation of the Incarnation to Space in Nicene Theology, in *The Ecumenical World of Orthodox Civilisation, Russia and Orthodoxy, Vol III, Essays in Honor of Georges Flovousky*, edited by A. Blane and T. E. Bird, The Hague: Mouton 43–70.

Torrance, T. F. 1976, *Space, Time and Resurrection*, Edinburgh: Handsel Press.

Torrance, T. F. 1981, *Divine and Contingent Order*, Oxford: OUP.

Tracey, D. 1982, *The Analogical Imagination: Christian Theology and the Culture of Pluralism*, New York: Crossroad.

Travis, S. H. 1980, *Christian Hope and the Future*, Downers Grove: IVP.

Turner, M. 2000, Historical Criticism and Theological Hermeneutics of the New Testament, in *Between Two Horizons: Spanning New Testament Studies and Systematic Theology*, edited by J. B. Green and M. Turner, Grand Rapids: Eerdmans 44–70.

Vaillancourt, R. 1979, *Toward a Renewal of Sacramental Theology*, Collegeville: The Liturgical Press.

van den Brom, L. J. 1993, *Divine Presence in the World: A Critical Analysis of the Notion of Divine Omnipresence*, Kampen: Kok Pharos.

van den Brom, L. J. 2000, Eschatology and Time, in *The Future as God's Gift*, edited by D. Fergusson and M. Sarot, Edinburgh: T&T Clark 159–67.

van der Horst, P. W. and J. Mansfield 1974, *An Alexandrian Platonist against Dualism Alexander of Lycopolis' Treatise 'Critique of the Doctrines of Manichaeus'*, Leiden: Brill.

van Unnik, W. C. 1976, *Het godspredikaat 'Het begin en het einde' bij Flavius Josephus en in de openbaring van Johannes*, Amsterdam: Noord-Hollandsche Uitgevers Maatschappij.

Vanhoozer, K. 1998, *Is There a Meaning In This Text? The Bible, the Reader, and the Morality of Literary Knowledge*, Grand Rapids: Eerdmans.

Vanstone, W. H. 1977, *Love's Endeavour, Love's Expense*, London: DLT.

Vermes, G. 1975, *The Dead Sea Scrolls in English*, Harmondsworth: Penguin.

Vögtle, A. 1985, 'Dann sah ich einen neuen Himmel und eine neue Erde …'(Apk 21,1), in *Glaube und Eschatologie FS W. G. Kümmel*, edited by E. Grässser and O. Merk, Tübingen: Mohr-Siebeck 301–33.

Volf, M. 1996, *Exclusion and Embrace: A Theological Exploration of Identity, Otherness and Reconciliation*, Nashville: Abingdon.

Volf, M. 1999, After Moltmann: Reflections on the Future of Eschatology, in *God Will Be All in All: The Eschatology of Jürgen Moltmann*, edited by R. Bauckham, Edinburgh: T&T Clark 232–57.

Volf, M. 2000, Enter into Joy! Sin, Death and the Life of the World to Come, in *The End of the World and the Ends of God: Science and Theology on Eschatology*, edited by J. C. Polkinghorne and M. Welker, Harrisburg, PA: Trinity Press International 256–78.

von Arnim, J. 1921–24, *Stoicorum Veterum Fragmenta*, Leipzig: BG Teubner.

von Balthasar, H. U. 1960, Umrisse der Eschatologie, in *Verbum Caro*, Einsiedeln: Johannes Verlag.

von Balthasar, H. U. 1988, *The Last Act*, translated by G. Harrison, Vol. 5, *Theo-Drama*, San Francisco: Ignatius Press.

von Balthasar, H. U. 1992, *Dramatis Personae*, Vol. 3, *Theo-Drama*, San Francisco: Ignatius Press.

von Helmholtz, H. 1961, On the Interaction of the Natural Forces, Reprinted in *Popular Scientific Lectures*, edited by M. Kline, Dover: New York.

von Weizsäcker, C. F. 1949, *The History of Nature*, Chicago: University of Chicago Press.

Waddell, H. 1934, *Beasts and Saints*, Constable.

Wainwright, G. 1971, *Eucharist and Eschatology*, London: Epworth Press.

Wall, R. W. 1995, Toward a Wesleyan Hermeneutic of Scripture, *Wesleyan Theological Journal* 30. 50–67.

Walliss, J., and K. G. C. Newport 2009, *The end all around us: apocalyptic texts and popular culture, Millennialism and society*, London; Oakville, CT: Equinox Pub.

Walls, J. L. 2008, *The Oxford handbook of eschatology, Oxford handbooks*, Oxford; New York: Oxford University Press.

Walsh, B. 1992, Introduction to Pannenberg's Systematic Theology, Vol 1: A Symposium, *Calvin Theological Journal* 27. 306.

Walvoord, J. F. 1964, *The Rapture Question*, Grand Rapids: Dunham.

Ward, K. 1995, Review of Toward a Theology of Nature, *Zygon* 30. 343.

Ward, K. 1996, *God, Chance and Necessity*, Oxford: One World Publications.

Ward, K. 1998, *Religion and Human Nature*, Oxford: Clarendon.

Ward, K. 2002, Cosmology and Religious Ideas About the End of the World, in *The Far Future Universe: Eschatology from a Cosmic Perspective*, edited by G. F. R. Ellis, Radnor: Templeton Foundation Press 236–48.

Ward, P. and D. Brownlee 2004, *The Life and Death of Planet Earth: How the New Science of Astrobiology Charts the Ultimate Fate of our World*, New York: Owl Books.

Ware, B. A. 2000, *God's Lesser Glory: The Diminished God of Open Theism*, Wheaton: Crossway Books.

Watts, J. D. W. 1985, *Isaiah 1–33, Word Biblical Commentary*, Waco, Texas: Word.

Watts, J. D. W. 1987, *Isaiah 34–66 Word Biblical Commentary*, Waco, Texas: Word.

Webb, J. K. et. al., 2001, Possible Evidence for a Variable Fine Structure Constant from QSO Absorption Lines – I. Motivations, Analysis and Results, *Mon. Not. R. astr. Soc.* 327. 1208.

Webb, S. H. 1998, *On God and dogs: a Christian theology of compassion for animals*, New York, Oxford: Oxford University Press.

Wedderburn, A. J. M. 1999, *Beyond Resurrection*, London: SCM.

Weder, H. 2000, Hope and Creation, in *The End of the World and the Ends of God: Science and Theology on Eschatology*, edited by J. C. Polkinghorne and M. Welker, Harrisburg, PA: Trinity Press International 184–204.

Weinberg, S. 1977, *The First Three Minutes*, New York: Basic Books.

Weinberg, S. 1992, *Dreams of a Final Theory*, New York: Pantheon.

Weiss, J. 1910, *Der erste Korintherbrief*, Göttingen: Vandenhoeck & Ruprecht.

Welker, M. 1998, God's Eternity, God's Temporality and Trinitarian Theology, *Theology Today* 55. 317–28.

Welker, M. 2002, Theological Realism and Eschatological Symbol Systems, in *Resurrection: Theological and Scientific Assessments*, edited by T. Peters, R. J. Russell and M. Welker, Grand Rapids: Eerdmans 31–42.

Wenham, D. 1987, Being 'Found' On the Last Day: New Light on 2 Peter 3.10 and 2 Corinthians 5.3, *New Testament Studies* 33. 477–9.

Wenham, J. W. 1984, *Easter Enigma*, Exeter: Paternoster.

Wesley, J. 1931, *The Letters of the Rev. John Wesley*, edited by J. Telford, London: Epworth.

Wesley, J. 1978, *The Works of Rev. John Wesley*, edited by T. Jackson, Grand Rapids: Baker Book House.

Wesley, J. 1988, *The Works of John Wesley*, edited by A. C. Outler, Nashville: Abingdon.

Wesley, J. 1993, *The Works of John Wesley*, edited by W. R. Ward and R. P. Heitzenrater, Nashville: Abingdon.

Westermann, C. 1969, *Isaiah 40–66*, London: SCM.

Westermann, C. 1984, *Genesis 1–11*. Vol. 1, London: SPCK.

Weston, F. 1920, *The Revelation of Eternal Love*, London: Mowbray.

White, L. 1967, The Historical Roots of our Ecological Crisis, *Science* 155. 1203.

Whitrow, G. 1955, *Why physical space has three dimensions*. Brit. J. Phil. *Sci.*, 6. 13.

Whitrow, G. 1959, *The Structure and Evolution of the Universe*, London: Hutchinson.

Wicken, J. S. 1988, Theology and Science in an Evolving Cosmos: A Need for Dialogue, *Zygon: Journal of Religion and Science* 23. 45–55.

Widyapranawa, S. H. 1990, *The Lord is Savior: Faith in National Crisis Isaiah 1–39*, Grand Rapids: Eerdmans.

Wilder, A. N. 1959, *Eschatology and Ethics in the Teaching of Jesus*, New York: Harper.

Wiles, M. 1971, Religious Authority and Divine Action, *Religious Studies* 7. 1–12.

Wiles, M. 1986, *God's Action in the World*, London: SCM.

Wilkinson, D. 1997, *Alone in the Universe? The X-Files, Aliens and God*, Crowborough: Monarch.

Wilkinson, D. 2000, *The Power of the Force: The Spirituality of the Star Wars Films*, Oxford: Lion.

Wilkinson, D. 2001, *God, Time and Stephen Hawking*, Crowborough: Monarch.

Wilkinson, D. 2002, *Creation, The Bible Speaks Today Bible Themes*, Leicester: IVP.

Wilkinson, D. 2004, The Activity of God: A Methodist Perspective, in *In Unmasking Methodist Theology*, edited by C. Marsh, B. Beck, A. Shier-Jones and H. Wareing, London: Continuum 142–54.

Wilkinson, D. and R. Frost 2000, *Thinking Clearly About God and Science*, Crowborough: Monarch.

Wilkinson, D. A. 1990, The Revival of Natural Theology in Contemporary Cosmology, *Science and Christian Belief* 2 (2). 95–116.

Wilkinson, P. R. 2007, *For Zion's sake: Christian zionism and the role of John Nelson Darby, Studies in evangelical history and thought*, Milton Keynes: Paternoster.

Williams, N. P. 1927, *The Ideas of the Fall and of Original Sin*, London: Longmans Green and Co.

Williams, R. 1996, Between the Cherubim: The Empty Tomb and the Empty Throne, in *Resurrection Reconsidered*, edited by G. D'Costa, Oxford: Oneworld 87–101.

Williams, R. 2000, *On Christian Theology*, Oxford: Blackwell.

Wilson, W. E., 1920, *Exp Tim*, 32. 44–45.

Wiltshire, D. 2007, Exact solution to the averaging problem in cosmology *Physics Rev. Lett.*, 99. 251101.

Witham, L. 2005, *Where Darwin meets the Bible: creationists and evolutionists in America*, Oxford; New York: Oxford University Press.

Witherington, B. 1992, *Jesus, Paul and the End of the World*, Carlisle: Paternoster.

Witherington, B. 1995, *Conflict & Community in Corinth: A Socio-Rhetorical Commentary on 1 and 2 Corinthians*, Grand Rapids: Eerdmans.

Witherington, B. 2002, Living in the Reign: The Dominion of God in the Wesleyan Tradition, in *The Wesleyan Tradition: A Paradigm for Renewal*, edited by P. Chilcote, Nashville: Abingdon 52–65.

Wojcik, D. 1997, *The End of the World As We Know It: Faith, Fatalism and Apocalypse in America*, New York: New York University Press.

Wolfendale, A. W. and D. A. Wilkinson 1989, Periodic Mass Extinctions, in *Catastrophes & Evolution*, edited by S. V. M. Clube, Cambridge: CUP 231–9.

Wolters, A. 1987, Worldview and Textual Criticism in 2 Peter 3. 10, *Westminster Theological Journal* 49. 405–13.

Wolterstorff, N. 1975, God Everlasting, in *God and the Good: Essays in Honour of Henry Stob*, edited by C. Orlebeke and L. Smedes, Grand Rapids: Eerdmans 181–203.

Wolterstorff, N. 2000, God and Time, *Philosophia Christi* 2. 5–10.

Wood, C. M. 1999, How Does God Act? *International Journal of Systematic Theology* 1. 138–152.

Wood, C. M. *Providence and a New Creation* [http://www.oxford-institute.org/pdfs/WorkingGroup4/Pap4Wood7-15-02.pdf] 2002.

Worgul, G. S. 1980, *From Magic to Metaphor: A Validation of the Christian Sacraments*, New York: Paulist.

Wright, G. E. 1952, *God Who Acts: Biblical Theology as Recital*, London: SCM.

Wright, N. T. 1986, *Colossians and Philemon*, Grand Rapids: Eerdmans.

Wright, N. T. 1991, *The New Testament and the People of God*, Minneapolis: Fortress.

Wright, N. T. 1996, *Jesus and the Victory of God*, Minneapolis: Fortress Press.

Wright, N. T. 2000, The Letter to the Galatians: Exegesis and Theology, in *Between Two Horizons: Spanning New Testament Studies and Systematic Theology*, edited by J. B. Green and M. Turner, Grand Rapids: Eerdmans 205–36.

Wright, N. T. 2000, New Heavens, New Earth, in *Called to One Hope*, edited by J. Coldwell, Carlisle: Paternoster 31–51.

Wright, N. T. 2003, *The Resurrection of the Son of God*, London: SPCK.

Wright, N. T. 2007, *Surprised by Hope*, London: SPCK.

Wright, R. 2000, The Matrix Rules, *Film-Philosophy* 4(3).

Yamamoto, D. 1998, Aquinas and Animals: Patrolling the Boundaries, in *Animals on the Agenda*, edited by A. Linzey and D. Yamamoto, London: SCM. 80–9

Yang, Ang, and Yin Shan, 2008, *Applications of complex adaptive systems*, Hershey, PA: IGI Pub.

Yndurain, F. 1991, Disappearance of Matter Due to Causality and Probability Violations in Theories with Extra Timelike Dimensions, *Physics Letters B* 256. 15.

Yockey, H. 1992, *Information Theory and Molecular Biology*, Cambridge: Cambridge University Press.

Zeisler, J. 1989, *Paul's Letter to the Romans*, London: SCM.

Zubrin, R. and R. Wagner 1997, *The Case for Mars*, New York: The Free Press.

Index of Biblical References

Modern Author Index

Subject Index